Microsoft 365 Certified Fundamentals MS-900 Exam Guide

Second Edition

Understand the Microsoft 365 platform from concept to execution and pass the MS-900 exam with confidence

Aaron Guilmette

Yura Lee

Marcos Zanre

BIRMINGHAM—MUMBAI

Microsoft 365 Certified Fundamentals MS-900 Exam Guide

Second Edition

Group Product Manager: Vijin Boricha

Publishing Product Manager: Prachi Sawant

Senior Editor: Shazeen Iqbal

Content Development Editor: Romy Dias

Technical Editor: Arjun Varma

Copy Editor: Safis Editing

Project Coordinator: Shagun Saini

Proofreader: Safis Editing

Indexer: Manju Arasan

Production Designer: Shyam Sundar Korumilli

First published: February 2020

Second edition: November 2021

Production reference: 1181121

Published by Packt Publishing Ltd.
Livery Place
35 Livery Street
Birmingham
B3 2PB, UK.

ISBN 978-1-80323-116-7

www.packt.com

To the doctors, nurses, public health officials, and first responders who are protecting us from COVID-19.

Contributors

About the authors

Aaron Guilmette is a senior program manager at Microsoft, providing architectural guidance as well as taking specifications from customers and giving them to engineers. He primarily focuses on collaborative and automation technologies, including Microsoft Exchange and Teams, Power Automate, and scripting solutions.

He has been involved with technology since 1998, working with customers that span the government, education, and commercial sectors. Aaron has also worked on certification exams and instructional design.

Aaron lives in Detroit, Michigan, with his five kids. When he's not busy solving technical problems, writing, or running his kids to events, he's trying to decide whether to make pizza or tacos.

I'd like to thank my girlfriend, Christine, who has now suffered through my authoring of eight books. She's ready for a vacation. I'd also like to thank my children because they'd be upset if I didn't.

I wish to thank the team at Packt for another great opportunity to help the Microsoft technical community.

Finally, I want to thank Microsoft for continuing to develop products that empower all of us to do more, even if it means occasionally taking tests.

Yura Lee is a technical specialist at Microsoft, focusing on all things associated with the modern workplace. She has a Microsoft 365 and Azure consulting background. Today, she focuses on helping state and local governments realize the potential of Microsoft 365 from a collaboration, productivity, and security perspective, while practicing growth and challenging mindset skills.

Yura lives in New Jersey with her husband.

I want to thank my wonderful husband, Chris, for giving me the space and support I've needed to write this book, even while the COVID-19 global pandemic was raging around us. I'd also like to thank Aaron, Marcos, and the team at Packt for granting me the opportunity and time to complete this journey. The whole Packt editing team has helped this first-time book author immensely, but I'd like to give special thanks to Romy Dias, who edited most of my work.

Marcos Zanre is a senior program manager at Microsoft, working with Brazilian customers on how to improve Microsoft Teams features and services and enable, along with partners, business transformational scenarios through Teams as a platform and Azure services. Marcos has more than 10 years of IT experience and an extensive background in Microsoft 365 and Office 365 services.

Marcos lives in São Paulo, Brazil, with his wife.

I wish to thank my wonderful wife, Carolina, for giving me the space and support I've needed to write this book, even while the COVID-19 global pandemic was raging around us. I'd also like to thank Aaron and Yura for another opportunity to work and learn together, and the whole Packt editing team, which has helped this first-time book author immensely, but I'd like to give special thanks to Romy Dias, who edited most of my work.

About the reviewers

Sara Jardim Barbosa is a Microsoft 365 evangelist and MCSE, MCP, and MVP Reconnect certified. She is currently working as a service engineer at Microsoft and has over 7 years of Microsoft 365 experience. In 2012, she was awarded the title of Microsoft MVP for her contributions to the Brazilian community for BPOS, Office 365, and SharePoint, and now she is MVP Reconnect certified. Her Twitter handle is @SaraBarbosa.

Mark Deakin started at Microsoft in 2001, shortly after the launch of Windows XP, when "the cloud" was in the sky and not a hyperscale data center. He has undertaken several roles at Microsoft, including support, consulting, evangelism, and product marketing, to name but a few. He has a genuine interest in technology and, at various times, has felt very blessed for being paid to indulge his hobby.

I would like to thank my wife, Ilona, for her love and patience over the last decade, and my kids for the next 50 years. I don't come with an "exam guide," unfortunately, but I consider you all to be certified to "expert" level in putting up with my highs and lows. I am eternally grateful.

Table of Contents

Section 2: Microsoft 365 Core Services and Concepts

3

Core Microsoft 365 Components

4

Comparing Core Services in Microsoft 365

5

Understanding the Concepts of Modern Management

6

Deploying Microsoft 365 Apps

7

Understanding Collaboration and Mobility with Microsoft 365

8

Microsoft 365 Analytics

Section 3: Understanding Security, Compliance, Privacy, and Trust in Microsoft 365

9

Understanding Security and Compliance Concepts with Microsoft 365

10
Understanding Identity Protection and Management

11
Endpoint and Security Management

12
Exploring the Service Trust Portal, Compliance Manager, and the Microsoft 365 Security Center

Section 4: Understanding Microsoft 365 Pricing and Support

13

Licensing in Microsoft 365

14

Planning, Predicting, and Comparing Pricing

15

Support Offerings for Microsoft 365 Services

16
Service Life Cycle in Microsoft 365

Section 5: Practice Exams

17
Mock Exam

18
Assessments

Other Books You May Enjoy

Index

Preface

Microsoft 365 is the premier collaboration and business productivity platform. It is made of up dozens of integrated **Software-as-a-Service (SaaS)** applications, including Exchange Online, SharePoint Online, and Microsoft Teams. Microsoft also offers a full range of cloud data center and development products, made available on the Azure platform. Together, the Microsoft 365 and Azure platforms are used by millions of users and businesses every day to enhance communications, build relationships, connect communities, and create new products.

This book, *Microsoft 365 Certified Fundamentals: Exam MS-900 Guide – Second Edition*, is designed to help you understand key cloud computing concepts and how those concepts are represented across the Microsoft 365 platform.

This book will focus on the following key areas:

- Cloud computing concepts
- Windows 10 services
- Messaging, collaboration, and communication services available in Microsoft 365
- Licensing
- Security, compliance, and governance
- Service-level agreement concepts

The MS-900 exam focuses on the basic concepts and interdependencies between these services. This book will help you understand the basics of identity and authentication in Azure Active Directory as well as ways to secure the identity platform. This book will also help you enumerate the core services of the Microsoft 365 platform and the competitive advantages and features over the on-premises counterparts of these products.

By the end of this book, you'll not only be equipped to pass the exam but also to confidently articulate the features that make the Microsoft 365 platform compelling for business collaboration.

Who this book is for

Microsoft 365 Certified Fundamentals: Exam MS-900 Guide – Second Edition, is targeted at Microsoft 365 service administrators and cloud technologists who want to prove their knowledge by passing the MS-900 certification exam. The qualified exam candidate should be able to demonstrate foundational knowledge of cloud concepts and the Microsoft 365 suite. Mastering the concepts tested in this exam provides a solid stepping stone to other more advanced Microsoft certifications. You can learn more about this exam at `https://docs.microsoft.com/en-us/learn/certifications/exams/ms-900`.

What this book covers

Chapter 1, Introduction to Cloud Computing, begins by explaining the foundational cloud computing concepts and the benefits that customers can expect to take advantage of.

Chapter 2, Cloud Deployment Models and Services, expands the reader's knowledge into areas such as public versus private clouds and the differences between software-as-a-service and infrastructure-as-a-service.

Chapter 3, Core Microsoft 365 Components, explains the basics of what makes up the Microsoft 365 suite.

Chapter 4, Comparing Core Services in Microsoft 365, compares the cloud SaaS components against their on-premises counterparts.

Chapter 5, Understanding the Concepts of Modern Management, provides an introduction to deployment and management options for Windows 10.

Chapter 6, Deploying Microsoft 365 Apps, introduces the Click-to-Run software deployment and servicing method for the Office application suite.

Chapter 7, Understanding Collaboration and Mobility with Microsoft 365, dives into how some of the Office 365 services work together as well as how the Enterprise Mobility + Security suite can be used to protect an organization's assets.

Chapter 8, Microsoft 365 Analytics, discusses analytics and usage reporting across the Microsoft 365 suite, including MyAnalytics, Workplace Analytics, and Viva Insights.

Chapter 9, Understanding Security and Compliance Concepts with Microsoft 365, introduces core security concepts such as users, groups, attributes, permissions, roles, and auditing capabilities inside the Microsoft 365 suite, along with a look at Microsoft Secure Score.

Chapter 10, Understanding Identity Protection and Management, explores key features of the Enterprise Mobility + Security suite and how they can be used to manage and review access to Microsoft 365 resources.

Chapter 11, Endpoint and Security Management, provides an overview of security features that can be used across Active Directory and Azure Active Directory plans, and how they can be used to enable bring-your-own-device scenarios.

Chapter 12, Exploring the Service Trust Portal, Compliance Manager, and the Microsoft 365 Security Center, discusses the tools Microsoft provides for helping customers track and organize compliance activities as well as for gathering supporting documentation.

Chapter 13, Licensing in Microsoft 365, introduces the licensing and acquisition process for Microsoft 365, as well as key selling points of the platform.

Chapter 14, Planning, Predicting, and Comparing Pricing, gives the reader tips on conducting a cost-benefit analysis of Microsoft 365 services versus traditional on-premises services.

Chapter 15, Support Offerings for Microsoft 365 Services, provides guidance on how to obtain support as well as the service-level agreements for Microsoft 365 services.

Chapter 16, Service Life Cycle in Microsoft 365, discusses the various release stages of products in the Microsoft 365 service and how they relate to Microsoft support policies.

Chapter 17, Mock Exam, helps you to gauge the knowledge you've learned throughout the book.

To get the most out of this book

The Microsoft 365 platform is best experienced with either a laptop or desktop computer running a modern operating system, such as Windows 10 or macOS 10.12 or later. Additionally, modern browsers such as Microsoft Internet Explorer 11, Microsoft Edge, or a recent version of Chrome, Safari, or Firefox are necessary for the Office 365 portal user interface to render properly. Older versions of Microsoft Internet Explorer may not work correctly.

An Office 365 tenant will also be required to follow along with some of the configuration examples. You can sign up for a trial tenant (no credit card required) at `https://www.microsoft.com/en-us/microsoft-365/business/compare-more-office-365-for-business-plans`. Some configuration options will require an Azure AD Premium subscription, which you can obtain as part of a Microsoft 365 trial or by activating an Azure AD Premium trial within the Azure portal (`https://portal.azure.com`) once you have obtained a trial Office 365 tenant.

Some examples may require various tools, such as the SharePoint Online Management Shell (`https://www.microsoft.com/en-us/download/details.aspx?id=35588`), the Microsoft Teams module (`https://www.powershellgallery.com/packages/MicrosoftTeams/`), or the Office Deployment Tool (`https://www.microsoft.com/en-us/download/details.aspx?id=49117`).

Download the color images

We also provide a PDF file that has color images of the screenshots and diagrams used in this book. You can download it here: `https://static.packt-cdn.com/downloads/9781803231167_ColorImages.pdf`

Conventions used

There are a number of text conventions used throughout this book.

`Code in text`: Indicates code words in text, database table names, folder names, filenames, file extensions, pathnames, dummy URLs, user input, and Twitter handles. Here is an example: "The `ImmutableID` value in Azure AD is a base64 conversion of an object's on-premises Active Directory object GUID."

Bold: Indicates a new term, an important word, or words that you see onscreen. For instance, words in menus or dialog boxes appear in **bold**. Here is an example: "To export a list of audit log entries, an administrator can open the audited data and click on **Export results**."

> **Tips or important notes**
> Appear like this.

Get in touch

Feedback from our readers is always welcome.

General feedback: If you have questions about any aspect of this book, email us at customercare@packtpub.com and mention the book title in the subject of your message.

Errata: Although we have taken every care to ensure the accuracy of our content, mistakes do happen. If you have found a mistake in this book, we would be grateful if you would report this to us. Please visit www.packtpub.com/support/errata and fill in the form.

Piracy: If you come across any illegal copies of our works in any form on the internet, we would be grateful if you would provide us with the location address or website name. Please contact us at copyright@packt.com with a link to the material.

If you are interested in becoming an author: If there is a topic that you have expertise in and you are interested in either writing or contributing to a book, please visit authors.packtpub.com.

Share Your Thoughts

Once you've read *Microsoft 365 Certified Fundamentals MS-900 Exam Guide - Second Edition*, we'd love to hear your thoughts! Scan the QR code below to go straight to the Amazon review page for this book and share your feedback.

https://packt.link/r/1803231165

Your review is important to us and the tech community and will help us make sure we're delivering excellent quality content.

Section 1: Understanding Cloud Concepts

In this section, you'll discover the three types of clouds and learn about the different types of cloud computing services that are available.

This section comprises the following chapters:

1

Introduction to Cloud Computing

Microsoft 365 Certified Fundamentals: Exam MS-900 Guide, Second Edition is for individuals looking to prove their foundational knowledge of the considerations and benefits of cloud services and cloud models. This exam, revised in April 2021, primarily goes into the details of Microsoft 365 as a **Software-as-a-Service (SaaS)** model, its implementation options, and its benefits. It also covers some fundamentals of cloud services.

To cover all the topics of the MS-900 exam, this book will start by discussing cloud computing concepts. It is critical to understand that cloud computing is not only prevalent in everyday use but also has potential impacts at the enterprise level. The shift to cloud computing changes how technology is acquired, deployed, secured, and managed.

This foundation will also set you up for success in further certifications, should you choose to take more related technology exams. After going through this book, you will be well positioned to not only pass this exam but also, more importantly, demonstrate basic knowledge of the Microsoft 365 platform.

First, we will start with cloud computing by looking at how cloud computing is already part of your daily personal use. Then, we will expand to enterprise scenarios.

In this chapter, we will cover the following topics:

- What is cloud computing?
- Benefits of cloud computing
- Uses of cloud computing

On to the basics!

What is cloud computing?

Cloud computing is everywhere. You use it daily for personal use – we can explore this a little bit, but we will also discuss cloud computing at an enterprise level. By the end of this chapter, you'll be able to clearly explain the benefits of cloud computing and provide some real-life examples. Microsoft 365 is an example of cloud computing. But before we discuss all that, we should explain what cloud computing is first.

The concept of cloud computing has been evolving over decades to help everyone, from daily, personal use cases to those of businesses.

Originally, you could think of cloud computing as the shared computer infrastructure on college campuses. Students and faculty would use dumb terminals to connect to a mainframe or minicomputer, and each user would share the resources of a large system. In today's terms, though, cloud computing refers to using internet-connected devices to consume services provided elsewhere, typically in some sort of shared environment.

A few years ago, you might have used portable USB devices or an external hard drive to store or back up your documents, pictures, or music files. That way, you had your files with you if you were carrying that physical device. Devices with large storage capacities or small physical devices generally cost significant amounts of money, but they have fallen in price over the years.

Now, you may use a cloud storage space such as a OneDrive account for documents, images, and other files. You may be using a certain amount of storage at no cost, and perhaps you can purchase more at a small price. Cloud capabilities allow you to eliminate the need for physical storage items such as hard drives. So long as you are connected to the internet, you can access your data.

Let's switch gears to the enterprise level and see how cloud computing fits there. Cloud computing allows users to access applications and data quickly and efficiently using a service provider's data storage space and computing power. When a service provider builds out a network of computing devices, storage, or applications, a customer can pay to use these resources instead of having to build an infrastructure of their own. You could say that it is like the customer renting these resources from the service provider. Microsoft Azure is an example of **Infrastructure as a Service (IaaS)**, where customers can build entire computing environments using the service provider's hardware, software, network, and storage resources.

Once built, a user can access these resources from anywhere, using any supported internet-connected device. Cloud computing allows organizations to outsource operational tasks such as updating servers and maintaining storage to service providers.

Now that you have a solid idea of cloud computing, we'll explore its benefits in the next section. Understanding the benefits of cloud computing will strengthen your core concepts for the exam and will help you answer any MS-900 exam questions that may come up.

Benefits of cloud computing

You already know how cloud computing can help reduce costs in maintaining your files and data, while also making them easier to access. Now, imagine that at the enterprise level, where an **Information Technology (IT)** department has to support thousands of users and their data. IT departments have a lot more to worry about than just cost and accessibility. Companies use a lot of applications and data as integral parts of their operations.

Important data assets such as **Personally Identifiable Information (PII)** in healthcare companies or **Intellectual Property (IP)** can make up a lot of an organization's data. Therefore, all of the business requirements must be met. Cloud service providers build infrastructure to address these important needs and considerations.

Cloud computing provides a lot of benefits to an organization, including any of the following:

- Cost-effective
- Scalable
- Quick
- Reliable
- Secure
- Current

Let's take a look at each benefit in more detail.

Cost-effective

In many cases, cloud services can help save a lot of operating IT costs. Usually, businesses allocate a budget on a yearly or fiscal basis. This may or may not work out, depending on market changes or large unplanned increases or decreases in business volume. Since Microsoft is a subscription-based service, it is easy to predict how your business expenditure may increase or decrease based on the number of users you need to purchase licenses for.

Business expenditures typically fall into two categories: **Capital Expenditure** or **Capital Expense (CapEx)** and **Operational Expenditure** or **Operational Expense (OpEx)**. CapEx is an upfront cost, such as purchasing a server, a desktop computer, or a network switch. CapEx is frequently for physical items. Additionally, CapEx is frequently amortized over an ownership period.

OpEx, by contrast, is ongoing or recurring costs, such as maintenance or subscription fees, or other operating costs, such as electricity. MS-900 will contain questions about both types of expenditure, so make sure you are familiar with this vocabulary. Microsoft's cloud offerings fall into the OpEx category.

In terms of cloud services' cost-effectiveness, consider this: on-premises infrastructure requires purchasing and maintaining CapEx such as hardware, building space, security systems, and a host of other items. To that, add other OpEx, such as engineers, consultants, and project managers, that are necessary to support the infrastructure. Organizations frequently have trouble determining how much equipment to purchase, especially if their business model has large activity swings. An organization might have to purchase an incredibly expensive and powerful system to ensure they can meet a peak demand or load situation that might only occur once a month or once a quarter, resulting in a system that will likely sit underutilized much of the time.

If you want to fulfill a demanding need with a cloud services model, you can rent capacity from a provider as you need it. With a subscription such as Microsoft 365, if your organization brings on seasonal workers, depending on your license agreement with Microsoft, you may be able to increase or decrease the number of licenses as your headcount changes. You're only paying for what you need.

Scalable

Cloud service providers typically allow you to immediately increase or decrease resources or services, depending on demand.

Let's look at some examples:

- You host a website and, based on your usage metrics, you know that the busiest time is 9 A.M.–5 P.M. during weekdays. During the weekend, however, it is much less active. In this instance, you want to make sure you have enough servers or service instances to support your website visitors during specific busy times. You also want to decrease the server capacity outside of the busy hours to match your business demand. With the scalability of cloud services, you can meet the demand quickly and flexibly while maintaining minimal cost during off-peak times.

- You own a retail sporting goods store. You have estimated that you will need 10 seasonal workers on the floor to help assist shoppers. All of your staff need basic email, so you choose to provide everyone with Microsoft 365 Frontline Worker F1 licenses. Due to an upcoming winter festival and extended holiday season, your store is busier and you need to hire more workers. You can simply add additional F1 licenses to provide the new hires with emails without having to invest in additional infrastructure or other resources.

In both of those examples, you can use the flexibility of cloud services to scale to meet your organization's demand.

Quick

Scalability is a key differentiator of cloud services, but it's not very useful if it can't fit your business's schedule. It's critical to be able to *quickly* scale up or down:

- Cloud services enable you to quickly scale up your demand for website hosting resources to meet your peak load times, as well as allow you to scale down when you don't need the capacity. This frees your organization from having to spend capital on server, storage, or networking equipment.

- As your organization needs an email for additional staff, you can quickly add licenses in the Microsoft 365 admin portal and have mailboxes available for them almost immediately.

The speed of scalability is an important factor in evaluating cloud services for your organization.

Reliable

As a consumer, you expect services you access on the internet to be accessible when you want them. As a business customer, you demand reliability for your cloud services to ensure that your organization can continue to operate fully, whether that's internal operations, hosting e-commerce sites, or another public-facing service.

Resiliency, recoverability, and disaster recovery are high priorities in a cloud service provider's infrastructure design, which is why providers typically rely on a blend of highly available infrastructure designs. These architectures can include network load balancing, data replication, redundant hardware, multiple network paths, and data backups. In addition, service providers also publish **Service-Level Agreements (SLAs)** that outline their commitments and responsibilities in this regard (for more on Microsoft 365's SLAs, see *Chapter 16, Service Life Cycle in Microsoft 365*).

Data Resiliency in the Cloud

To read more about Office 365's data resiliency policies and procedures, please visit `https://docs.microsoft.com/en-us/office365/securitycompliance/office-365-data-resiliency-overview`.

When looking for cloud services providers, ensure your service providers have committed to providing a level of availability that meets your business requirements.

Secure

Security in this context addresses multiple concerns, both physical and logical.

From a physical security perspective, cloud service providers equip their data center facilities with hardware such as cameras, gates, locks, and equipment cages. They'll also implement personnel and procedures, such as guards and identification verification, to ensure only people who legitimately require access are allowed into the facilities. Some facilities even use X-ray machines, mantraps (interdependent locking and unlocking door systems), and biometric measures (handprints, retina scans, or fingerprints) at multiple stages to detect unauthorized individuals and prevent them from accessing a facility.

Securing the Physical Side of the Cloud

You can learn more about the security measures Microsoft implements at its data center facilities at `https://docs.microsoft.com/en-us/azure/security/fundamentals/physical-security`.

Just as importantly, computing service providers secure electronic data. To ensure the utmost security, providers implement multiple layers of logical security, including secure protocols and encryption to protect data that is both at rest (sitting on physical media) and in transit (as it is being transmitted between endpoints). These security measures help prevent unauthorized access to data. In the event of breaches of physical security, cryptographic technologies can be used to prevent attackers and thieves from being able to access the contents of stolen equipment.

Microsoft uses multiple logical security layers to protect data on disks and other media, as well as data being transmitted between servers, data centers, and end users.

> **Under Lock and Key**
>
> You can learn more about the security tools Microsoft uses in its environment at `https://docs.microsoft.com/en-us/office365/` `securitycompliance/office-365-encryption-in-the-` `microsoft-cloud-overview`.

Current

Cloud services are evergreen, meaning they are constantly under development and improvement. Both security updates and feature updates are constantly developed and deployed. In more traditional on-premises approaches, you might be waiting for security updates to be deployed on monthly, quarterly, or even yearly rhythms. Rather than waiting for the release of a security or feature update, spending the resources deploying said update, and then testing it, cloud service customers can focus on other operations, knowing that their environment is being maintained as part of their provider's commitment.

Features or new tools are made available to customers automatically, rather than you having to go through the process of reviewing, deploying, and potentially integrating features.

When using cloud computing services, organizations can spend more of their valuable resources driving or transforming the business, as opposed to *just keeping the lights on.*

We've gone through the six main benefits of cloud computing: cost-effectiveness, the ability to scale, speed, reliability, security, and always being current with the latest releases. In the next section, we'll look at using some use cases for cloud computing.

Uses of cloud computing

While we covered the benefits of cloud computing, you probably already started thinking of some use cases from your personal life, such as email or social media.

Let's start with a basic one from earlier: *storing your files in a cloud storage service such as OneDrive*. Some of these storage services are integrated and included with a purchase of a phone, while others may come with a subscription. Here, as mentioned previously, you are not spending money on a physical space to store these files; you are paying (or have paid) someone else to hold them for you. The benefits to you include costs and security: you don't have to buy or configure any extra equipment, it is inexpensive, and you can leverage password or identity protection to keep your files safe.

Audio and video streaming services are another great use case for cloud services. Consumers gain access to millions of songs, movies, and television shows for a low monthly or yearly cost. When an artist releases new tracks or a new episode of the latest television program becomes available, the consumer's subscription allows them access with no additional cost, so long as they are connected to the internet.

This type of service highlights several benefits: the cloud streaming service is always current with the latest content, the service scales automatically to accommodate both the growing amount of media as well as the increased number of subscribers without any effort or increased investment from the consumer, and the services are available on demand. Spotify, Amazon Prime Music, and Apple iTunes are all examples of cloud media streaming services.

For cloud computing examples in enterprises, let's look at use cases for a cloud service such as Microsoft 365. Suppose an organization onboards 20 or 30 new employees at the same time. In the on-premises architecture world, this might mean having to procure additional storage for both business and business files, as well as the email capacity. As a cloud service solution, Microsoft 365 allows you to scale quickly and efficiently. IT administrators can provide these mailboxes and storage resources by simply assigning licenses. The organization doesn't need to go through a lengthy procurement cycle for data center equipment to help support the new employees; this is all handled by the service provider. Cloud services can be advantageous to businesses from the perspective of being able to deploy services and resources more quickly by leveraging the investments, capabilities, and expertise of vendors.

> **Exploring Further**
>
> You can find even more potential use cases and examples of cloud computing at https://azure.microsoft.com/en-us/overview/examples-of-cloud-computing/.

We've covered three different examples of cloud computing, from relatable, everyday personal use to business scenarios. They reiterate the fact that cloud computing is everywhere. These use cases help to solidify your understanding of cloud computing.

Summary

In this chapter, we answered the question of what cloud computing is. Cloud computing allows you to access data, either personal or business, from any device, including your phone, tablet, or computer. We looked at the benefits of storing information this way and linked these benefits to a variety of popular use cases.

We also very briefly covered the power of Microsoft 365 as a business-oriented cloud computing service. It's critical to have this foundational understanding of cloud computing as it will help you answer cloud-related questions that may come up in MS-900.

In the next chapter, we'll continue exploring basic cloud concepts by discussing the different types of clouds, including public and private clouds. We'll also examine the different types of cloud services that are available, such as SaaS, IaaS, and PaaS, as well as what services Microsoft has to offer in each of those categories.

Questions

Use the following questions to test your knowledge of this chapter. You can find the answers in *Chapter 18, Assessments*:

1. Microsoft 365 is primarily an example of what kind of cloud computing?

    A. IaaS

    B. PaaS

    C. SaaS

    D. AaaS

2. Identify three of the benefits of cloud computing.

    A. Scalable

    B. Current

    C. Outdated

    D. Cost-effective

    E. Interactive

    F. Free

3. Identify two examples of CapEx.

   A. Microsoft 365 subscription

   B. Desktop computer

   C. Electricity

   D. Network cable

4. Identify two examples of OpEx.

   A. Microsoft 365 subscription

   B. Desktop computer

   C. Storage maintenance fee

   D. Storage area network system

5. CapEx generally refers to what?

   A. Capital expenditure

   B. Captain extra

   C. Capture extended

   D. Capital extended

6. When talking about cloud services, what does the term "scalable" mean?

   A. Able to build models.

   B. Able to add or reduce service capacity on demand.

   C. Able to resize organizational data structures.

   D. Services are deployed redundantly.

7. Identify three components that can contribute to a cloud service's reliability.

    A. Redundant hardware

    B. Multiple network paths

    C. Data backups

    D. Hybrid technologies

    E. Infrastructure-as-a-Service

    F. Identity-based security

    G. Identity-as-a-Service

8. Which two categories are most Microsoft Azure services placed in?

    A. Software-as-a-Service

    B. Architecture-as-a-Service

    C. Infrastructure-as-a-Service

    D. Identity-as-a-Service

    E. Services-as-a-Service

    F. Platform-as-a-Service

2
Cloud Deployment Models and Services

In *Chapter 1, Introduction to Cloud Computing*, we introduced cloud computing, along with some of its basic concepts and benefits, as well as real-life examples and use cases.

Now, we'll go a bit deeper by starting to examine the different types of cloud deployment models and cloud services that are available. We will cover three different deployment models: **private**, **public**, and **hybrid**. The goal is to understand the differences between the three, as well as the specific advantages of each. We will explore the three service model types and examine their differences and use cases. Specifically, we'll look at these industry-standard models and see that Microsoft has offerings that fit into each of those categories.

Then, we will discuss **Microsoft 365** in greater depth. You'll be prepared to identify where Microsoft 365 fits into an organizational strategy from the perspective of both cloud deployment and cloud service models. Finally, you will be provided with questions to answer that may show up on the **MS-900 exam**.

In this chapter, we will cover the following topics:

- Cloud deployment models
- Cloud service scenarios

By the end of the chapter, you should be able to describe each of the cloud deployment models, the four cloud service scenarios, and give some examples of each.

Cloud deployment models

When designing a technology strategy for their organization, business and technology architects need to choose where to invest their resources. Cloud deployment models answer the question, *where will we place our resources?* Hardware resources – such as servers, storage appliances, and network devices – all have to physically exist *somewhere*. When choosing a deployment model, architects also need to think about other aspects, such as serviceability and supportability, physical and logical security, redundancy and disaster recovery capabilities, business continuity concerns, ease of use, and performance.

Customers need to decide where they are going to put their equipment, which, in turn, defines where they will be storing their business-critical or potentially sensitive information. There isn't a one-size-fits-all design. Fortunately, there are several options, and organizations can choose the deployment model that makes the most sense for their business. Organizations typically choose from three options:

- **Public cloud**: This means using infrastructure and services provided by an external vendor.
- **Private cloud**: This means building and maintaining infrastructure on their own.
- **Hybrid cloud**: This means utilizing a combination of public and private cloud solutions.

In this section, we will explore each of those models more closely and identify the advantages and disadvantages of each.

Public cloud

Organizations can choose to leverage a public cloud to help achieve their business goals. A public cloud means that a service provider is responsible for provisioning, supplying, and maintaining resources such as application servers, networking hardware, and storage. There are public cloud options for specialized purposes, such as manufacturing resource planning and general ledger accounting, as well as more general purposes, such as file storage or email.

With public cloud solutions, you don't typically own anything except the actual data. You will probably share resources with others in some form of a **multi-tenant** environment. Multi-tenant configurations function much like an apartment or office building: everyone shares the same physical building, but each person or business has a small space allocated that they rent.

To translate this into cloud computing services, the service provider's infrastructure is the building, and your business's configuration and data are the office spaces. From a security perspective, you're responsible for granting keys to your office space. And when it comes to billing, you're only paying for the actual office space that you're leasing. You're not responsible for managing the relationship the building owner has with the utility companies, nor are you responsible for troubleshooting and fixing the plumbing or electrical service when something isn't working. Those are all part of your service agreement.

One of the primary benefits of a public cloud solution is that you are dividing the cost of the resources between all of the other organizations using the service. Because you are sharing resources with others, you're not responsible for the large capital expenditure required to procure equipment or software, nor are you responsible for deploying, troubleshooting, or updating the shared resources. Competition incentivizes service providers to provide redundancy and fault tolerance – features and capabilities that may cost organizations significantly were they to deploy and manage them themselves.

Public cloud solutions provide a lot of the benefits that we discussed in the previous chapter, including scalability, agility, and reliability. In public cloud deployments, the service provider takes on the risks and responsibilities of the system, and the customers pay a subscription fee that's typically proportional to their usage of the service. Service providers use their scale to obtain pricing benefits and discounts when purchasing and can invest in the expert, specialized talent required to support the platform. The subscribers are then able to focus more of their investment on their core business instead of investing in people to maintain infrastructure.

Looking back at the office building or apartment models, building maintenance is handled by the owner of the building as part of the lease; each business with office space has access to that specialized staff as opposed to having to hire and maintain their own building specialists. Public cloud solutions work in much the same way.

Microsoft's Azure and Microsoft 365 platforms are examples of public cloud platforms.

> **Jumping into the Public Cloud**
>
> To read more about the public cloud, please visit `https://azure.microsoft.com/en-us/overview/what-is-a-public-cloud/`.

Some organizations, however, have certain requirements or internal policies that might not allow them to use public cloud services. In those cases, private clouds are an alternative.

Private cloud

A private cloud essentially means that users connect to a restricted or secured private internal network. When an organization deploys a private cloud to meet their business objectives, they are responsible for virtually everything, from the disks that are used in the servers to network cables, switches and routers, firewalls, servers, storage appliances, and applications to the support staff, maintenance agreements for software and hardware, and building contracts.

When building and deploying a private cloud solution, you can restrict access to this private internal network to only employees or business partners. This level of control is a draw for many organizations. One of the benefits beyond access control and overall ownership is the ability to support unique business needs, such as legacy applications or particular regulatory and compliance requirements. With a private cloud solution, you control the storage of all the sensitive data in a data center you manage, and you can maintain physical access to it – something that isn't typically allowed with public cloud services. Private cloud deployments allow you to have much more control over your environment. You can implement an unlimited number of security procedures and protocols, and you can customize as much as you need, so long as your budget allows for it.

Some of those advantages, however, can also become drawbacks. For example, owning your hardware and software means you have the utmost physical control over it. It also means that you must secure the upfront financing and purchase the equipment and support contracts, which can influence your ability to deliver the finished product to your organization. Depending on your organization's timelines and objectives, you may need to budget time for internal procurement, external financing, delivery, installation, and configuration.

Outside of the physical procurement and deployment concerns, you also need to consider security requirements when building private cloud solutions. If your organization doesn't already have security access controls, protocols, and technology, you may need additional investment in remote access and networking technologies. If your private cloud will communicate externally with partners, vendors, or customers, you may also need to expand your network communications capacity with additional circuits, as well as staff or consulting resources to design and implement both the policies and technology.

Availability and redundancy are two additional key concerns for private cloud solutions that organizations must consider. If the private cloud is going to house business-critical data to support operations, you'll likely need to evaluate, purchase, and configure options for fault tolerance inside your data center, as well as geographically separated sites to ensure business operations continue in the event of localized outages or disasters.

Financial, healthcare, and public safety organizations have frequently decided to use private cloud solutions. They typically cite regulation and compliance requirements. Some municipalities and public sector organizations have data residency requirements (geographic requirements about storing data) that they feel can easily be met with private cloud solutions.

Diving Deeper into the Private Cloud

To read more about private cloud architectures, please visit `https://azure.microsoft.com/en-us/overview/what-is-a-private-cloud/`.

Most organizations, however, don't exclusively use public *or* private cloud solutions. They rely on a combined approach, called a *hybrid cloud*.

Hybrid cloud

The hybrid cloud combines the ideas of both public cloud and private infrastructure. With hybrid cloud solutions, organizations link their private cloud infrastructure with that of the public cloud service providers. In this scenario, organizations can have data residing in either cloud and, in some cases, can shift data and services between environments.

Properly designed and implemented hybrid cloud environments can create a seamless experience for users.

A common use of the hybrid cloud is to store non-sensitive data in a public cloud service while storing business-critical or sensitive customers in a private cloud infrastructure. Being able to use both of those services together can provide an advantage for organizations and can allow them to use the benefits of both cloud models. It's a model that can be used to save costs on general services (such as email) while introducing an organization to cloud services. The sensitive or critical line of business apps with more strict requirements can be kept on-premises or in a private cloud infrastructure until a cloud model can meet business requirements.

If configured appropriately, organizations can slowly transition on-premises or private cloud workloads to a public cloud service with little or no service interruption. Organizations can also start new projects in a cloud service or platform and leave their legacy private cloud or on-premises infrastructure in place rather than migrating it, letting it retire, or decommissioning it when it is no longer valuable or useful.

While being able to bridge the public and private cloud models has some advantages, it does introduce complexity. Having applications, services, or data split between two locations can introduce confusion and can be a disadvantage for hybrid cloud customers. This complexity can affect both the user and administration experiences, so it's important to architect hybrid cloud solutions in a way that directs users and administrators to the correct resources.

> **Resources for Hybrid Cloud Infrastructures**
>
> Check out the following link for more information on hybrid clouds: `https://azure.microsoft.com/en-us/overview/what-is-hybrid-cloud-computing/`.
>
> Microsoft Azure has hybrid cloud options as well, which you can read about at `https://azure.microsoft.com/en-us/overview/hybrid-cloud/`.

Here are some real-life examples of hybrid cloud solutions:

- Due to a global pandemic, an organization wants to start using **Microsoft Teams** for online meetings and chat. However, they continue to use their SharePoint Server 2010 and Windows-based file servers for the majority of their data. This organization decides to turn on Microsoft Teams and **OneDrive for Business** to enable meetings, instant messaging, and file sharing. In this scenario, users may need to be aware of which data is stored in which location or service and how to navigate to each service, as there's no direct integration between Microsoft Teams and the on-premises file server infrastructures.

- An organization that is slowly transitioning on-premises mailboxes to a service such as **Microsoft Exchange Online** and using Microsoft Teams for meetings and chat. The organization configures Exchange hybrid to allow for calendar interoperability between Exchange Online and **Exchange on-premises**. In this scenario, however, the hybrid configuration will allow users, regardless of their desktop client, to be able to locate the infrastructure hosting their calendars, messaging, and chat. Whether they are using Microsoft Exchange Server on-premises or Exchange Online or Microsoft Teams, their desktop clients can locate the appropriate services behind the scenes.

Now that we've discussed the three different cloud deployment models (public, private, and hybrid), we can move on to the different types of cloud service scenarios.

Cloud service scenarios

In the *Cloud deployment models* section, we answered the question *Where are we going to deploy our resources?* In this section, we'll address the questions *What type of resources are we going to use?* and *How much infrastructure management control do we want?*

Cloud computing services generally come in four forms:

- **Infrastructure as a Service (IaaS)**
- **Platform as a Service (PaaS)**
- **Software as a Service (SaaS)**
- **Serverless computing**

Your computing needs will drive what type of services you choose. Frequently, solutions can be built from any or all four types of services. It's important to identify what parts the organization wants to own or manage, what type of development the organization wants to do, and where the different points of responsibility will be.

Most organizations will end up utilizing some form of hybrid cloud deployment – perhaps linking some of their on-premises applications with cloud offerings or extending their on-premises data center with IaaS virtual server infrastructure.

This section will help you understand the types of services available. Knowing the capabilities of each will help you choose what is right for your business needs.

Infrastructure as a Service

All services (whether public or private cloud, hosted or on-premises) require a combination of computing power, network connectivity, storage resources, and applications. At its most basic level, you need a way to host the servers that run your apps, a way to connect your servers so that applications can exchange data, and the storage medium where your data resides.

Infrastructure as a Service (IaaS) is a model that allows you to configure those resources in the cloud. The following diagram depicts the core pieces that an IaaS offering typically provides – namely, the physical aspects of data center infrastructure:

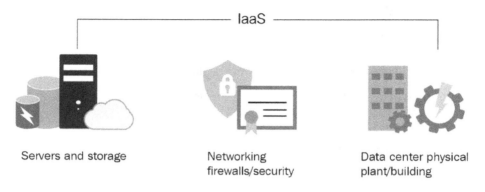

Figure 2.1 – IaaS

Every application has an entire IT infrastructure supporting it – servers, network switches, routers, firewalls, and data center buildings. An organization's IT department is typically responsible for most of this. When using traditional on-premises or private cloud deployment models, organizations typically have their own hardware, and they provision real or virtual server infrastructure (on that physical hardware) to help support their applications and services.

When using an IaaS platform, the IT staff are responsible for maintaining network connectivity to the service platform and the virtual infrastructure that's provisioned in the platform. The organization is no longer responsible for the physical hardware that hosts virtual machines or applications. In fact, with some IaaS service providers, even the operating system updates are handled by the platform.

Organizations might choose an IaaS scenario because they have custom-developed applications that they want to deploy without having to invest in their own equipment, or simply because the application they want to use doesn't have a public cloud service offering available. Customers can use IaaS to build entire data centers, complete with virtualized servers and applications, and manage configuration settings at a very fine-grained level.

Fundamentals of IaaS

For more information on the fundamentals of IaaS, visit `https://azure.microsoft.com/en-us/overview/what-is-iaas/`.

IaaS is frequently used to provide disaster recovery or site resilience at a low cost since it doesn't require upfront investment to obtain equipment. Customers also frequently use IaaS environments for development and testing scenarios due to the ability to rapidly build, destroy, and redeploy virtual infrastructure, as necessary.

Other popular uses for IaaS include the following:

- High-performance computer clusters or grid computing
- Website hosting
- File storage
- Big data analytics with custom tooling

> **Real-World Examples**
>
> Microsoft Azure Virtual Machines (`https://azure.microsoft.com/en-us/services/virtual-machines/`) is an example of an IaaS product.

IaaS providers typically bill customers based on a usage model – how many resources are configured and if they are activated or in use. For example, you may provision a virtual machine with two virtual processors, 8 GB memory, and 100 GB disk storage, and the provider will charge you a fixed fee per time unit (minute or hour). Just like the lights in a house, if you keep the virtual infrastructure turned on all the time, you will accrue charges.

In some cases, however, organizations don't want or need to manage the underlying virtual hardware and networking. That's where Platform-as-a-Service can help.

Platform as a Service

Platform as a Service (**PaaS**) is a slightly abstracted environment for developing and deploying cloud-based applications. In a PaaS model, the cloud service provider will provide all the things that IaaS does, plus operating systems, middleware, and any development or runtime tools that are necessary.

PaaS can be valuable to developers within an organization since the platform can provide services such as database management, development tools, scheduling, load balancing, and business analytics. Depending on the type of PaaS being used, developers may not need to be familiar with scaling or redundancy and availability concepts, as they might be managed by the service provider or implemented by simply selecting a few options in the platform.

The following diagram shows how PaaS provides a superset of features to IaaS. PaaS offerings include everything from IaaS, and then typically add operating system management and automation, deployment, and development tools.

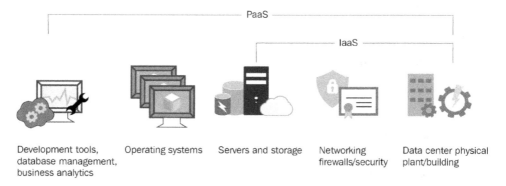

Figure 2.2 – PaaS

The application development life cycle includes the stages of building, testing, and deploying. PaaS enables developers to shorten their release cycles by utilizing tools that have already been made available on the platform. Developers don't need to spend time troubleshooting their infrastructure – they can simply build and deploy code iteratively and let the provider handle everything else.

Some popular use cases for PaaS include the following:

- Multi-platform testing

- Analytics

- Sophisticated development tools

- **Integrated Development Environment** (**IDE**) to support rapid build and deployment

> **Further Reading on PaaS**
>
> For more information on PaaS, visit `https://azure.microsoft.com/en-us/overview/what-is-paas/`.

Microsoft Azure Kubernetes Service (`https://azure.microsoft.com/en-us/services/kubernetes-service/`), Azure Cognitive Search (`https://azure.microsoft.com/en-us/services/search/`), Content Delivery Network (`https://azure.microsoft.com/en-us/services/cdn/`), and App Service (`https://azure.microsoft.com/en-us/services/app-service/`) are examples of some of Microsoft's PaaS offerings. These are tools, services, and platforms that developers can integrate into their product offerings.

Like IaaS, PaaS is also billed on a consumption model. Depending on your service provider, you may have access to billing calculators that help you estimate what the monthly charges will be, based on the number of environments you have running, the amount of data you process, and other metrics.

While IaaS and PaaS offer a lot of functionality and flexibility to build things the way you want, there are also scenarios where it doesn't make business sense to deploy and maintain infrastructure and applications.

Software-as-a-Service, another type of service, solves that problem by providing ready-to-use environments and services that organizations can start using immediately, with little or no configuration. Let's discuss this next.

Software as a Service

With both IaaS and PaaS offerings, organizations have a lot of fine-grained control over building, configuring, and deploying infrastructure and applications. With **Software-as-a-Service (SaaS)** applications, all of those low-level infrastructure and configuration management pieces are further abstracted from administrators and users.

SaaS products are fully deployed applications that are updated and managed by the service provider. When using SaaS applications, administrators usually don't have as many configuration tools available to them. The boundaries of what they can manage are well defined by the service provider. The following diagram shows how the delivery of applications is now managed by the cloud service provider:

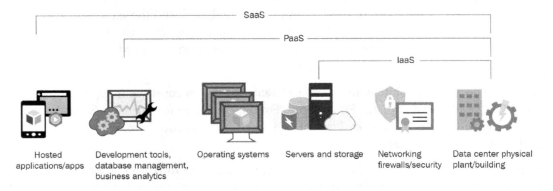

Figure 2.3 – SaaS

> **SaaS Fundamentals**
>
> To learn more about SaaS, visit `https://azure.microsoft.com/en-us/overview/what-is-saas/`.

Users typically only need an active internet connection to access SaaS applications.

SaaS applications are frequently designed as multi-tenant service offerings. Referring back to the building and office space example earlier in this chapter, SaaS applications have a shared infrastructure platform and software base, and each subscribing organization is segmented into its own space (frequently referred to as **tenants**).

In this type of architecture, each subscriber organization has a logical, software-defined boundary that prohibits accessing other subscribers' tenants. Other software technologies may be deployed to further insulate and isolate tenants from one another, such as data encryption or network access controls configured inside the tenant.

In the previous chapter, we identified a few cloud services (such as OneDrive and Spotify). These are examples of SaaS applications. As a consumer of these services, there is no way to control the amount of storage or networking that's allocated to yourself or others, nor can you update the infrastructure. Users connect to those services using a web browser or application on their devices and can only consume or create within the boundaries that the application allows.

Microsoft 365 is another example of a SaaS application. When users connect to the internet to access email with Microsoft 365, the Exchange Online SaaS application is responding. Microsoft 365 exemplifies the cloud service benefits outlined in the previous chapter: only the exact amount of service required is purchased, and the service provider is responsible for maintaining the application and its underlying hardware components. As a subscriber, the fee covers the servers, storage, and networking needed to provide the service.

While the Microsoft 365 suite is an example of SaaS, each of its constituent applications (Office Online, Power Automate, Power Apps, Forms, OneDrive for Business, SharePoint Online, Exchange Online, Tasks by Planner and To Do, Teams, and more) are *also* standalone examples of SaaS.

Other SaaS-based applications in the Microsoft family include **Office 365** (a subset of the Microsoft 365 suite) and **Dynamics 365**, a customer relationship and financial management tool.

SaaS products typically have a fixed price per license or unit included as part of the subscription fee. In some cases, there may be add-on services to expand capacity or services. For example, you may subscribe to a SaaS service such as Exchange Online and receive a 100 GB mailbox. It doesn't matter how full the mailbox gets, how much mail you send or receive, or how often you check your mail – the price will always be the same.

Finally, we'll tackle the newest entry in the cloud services scenario: **serverless computing**.

Serverless computing

Serverless computing is a bit of a misnomer. After all, the code and applications your business requires still have to run on *something*. With serverless computing, developers are fully isolated from the concepts of hardware and operating system management. Instead, the platform itself handles dynamically provisioning and allocating resources.

With serverless computing, code can be directly deployed to runtime environments without the developer having to manage anything except their code. Similar to other cloud service models, such as IaaS or PaaS, serverless computing offers organizations pay-per-use capabilities in an extremely cost-efficient model.

With IaaS or PaaS, you may pay to have environments running, even though they might not be fully utilized. Serverless computing, on the other hand, can frequently be purchased at a per-execution level, meaning that if your application isn't processing, it's not accruing costs.

Microsoft Azure Functions (`https://azure.microsoft.com/en-us/services/functions/`) and Amazon Web Services Lambda (`https://aws.amazon.com/lambda/`) are two commercial examples of serverless computing.

Depending on the business requirements (such as operational agility, regulatory, and financial), organizations may wish to leverage one or more of these cloud service scenarios.

Summary

In this chapter, we covered the three types of cloud deployments (public, private, and hybrid), as well as the four types of cloud service scenarios: IaaS, PaaS, SaaS, and serverless computing.

Knowing the difference between the private and public cloud, as well as the advantages of each in a hybrid deployment, is critical to helping organizations identify the best possible solutions. Furthermore, understanding the capabilities of each of the four cloud service models is also critical.

Each of the cloud deployment models and service scenarios has billing models as well. Mapping business requirements to IaaS, PaaS, SaaS, and serverless technologies can help organizations leverage each service appropriately and return the most value. SaaS and serverless computing options are frequently the most cost-effective (with a flat fee and transaction-based pricing) overall.

In the next chapter, we will begin exploring Microsoft 365's *core services*, such as Exchange Online and Teams. We will go over its features and administrative and end user experiences.

Questions

Use the following questions to test your knowledge of this chapter. You can find the answers in *Chapter 18, Assessments*:

1. Identify the three types of cloud deployment models.

    A. Private cloud

    B. Functional cloud

    C. Hybrid cloud

    D. Hosted cloud

    E. Public cloud

    F. Serverless cloud

2. In which deployment model is the customer organization responsible for acquiring, provisioning, configuring, and maintaining equipment?

    A. PaaS

    B. IaaS

    C. Private cloud

    D. Public cloud

    E. Serverless computing

    F. Functional computing

3. In which deployment model does the customer lease compute, networking, and storage resources?

    A. Public cloud

    B. Private cloud

C. Network cloud

D. Serverless cloud

4. Identify the three cloud service scenarios.

A. IaaS

B. SaaS

C. Serverless

D. Network cloud

5. Identify the three cloud service scenarios.

A. SaaS

B. Hybrid cloud

C. PaaS

D. Serverless

6. Azure Functions is an example of what type of cloud service?

A. SaaS

B. IaaS

C. PaaS

D. Serverless computing

7. Microsoft 365 is an example of what type of cloud service?

A. SaaS

B. Serverless computing

C. PaaS

D. IaaS

8. Virtual machines are an example of what type of cloud service?

A. SaaS

B. Serverless computing

C. PaaS

D. IaaS

9. OneDrive is an example of what type of cloud service?

    A. SaaS

    B. Serverless computing

    C. PaaS

    D. IaaS

10. What type of cloud deployment model uses a mix of private and public clouds?

    A. Serverless computing

    B. Hybrid cloud

    C. Relational cloud

    D. Containerized cloud

11. Identify two benefits of SaaS.

    A. The cloud solution provider is responsible for managing application and software updates.

    B. The customer connects over the internet.

    C. The customer is responsible for allocating hardware resources.

    D. The customer only pays for what they use.

12. Identify two popular uses of IaaS.

    A. Disaster recovery

    B. Serverless computing

    C. Multi-platform development

    D. High-performance compute clusters

13. What type of service is Dynamics 365?

    A. Serverless computing

    B. PaaS

    C. IaaS

    D. SaaS

14. Choosing a cloud deployment model primarily answers which question?

    A. When will my resources be available?

    B. Where will we place our resources?

    C. How will I secure my resources?

    D. How will I pay for my resources?

15. Choosing a cloud service scenario primarily answers what two questions?

    A. When will my resource be available?

    B. What type of resources are we going to use?

    C. How much infrastructure management control do we want?

    D. How will I secure my resources?

16. What type of service is Azure Cognitive Services?

    A. SaaS

    B. PaaS

    C. IaaS

    D. Serverless computing

17. SaaS subscription fees are typically what?

    A. A flat fee, regardless of service usage

    B. Billed on an hourly or monthly consumption model

    C. Billed on a transaction level

    D. Free

18. IaaS subscription fees are typically what?

    A. A flat fee, regardless of service usage

    B. Billed on an hourly or monthly consumption model

    C. Billed on a transaction level

    D. Free

19. Serverless computing subscription fees are typically what?

   A. A flat fee, regardless of service usage

   B. Billed on an hourly or monthly consumption model

   C. Billed on a transaction level

   D. Free

20. PaaS subscription fees are typically what?

   A. A flat fee, regardless of service usage

   B. Billed on an hourly or monthly consumption model

   C. Billed on a transaction level

   D. Free

21. Which two service scenarios are typically the most cost-effective?

   A. Serverless computing

   B. PaaS

   C. SaaS

   D. On-premises

   E. IaaS

Section 2: Microsoft 365 Core Services and Concepts

In this section, you'll explore the products, services, and components that make up Microsoft 365. Chapters in this section will familiarize you with the services in the Microsoft 365 platform, including Exchange, Teams, and SharePoint, and will help you understand the value proposition of the suite.

This section comprises the following chapters:

- *Chapter 3, Core Microsoft 365 Components*
- *Chapter 4, Comparing Core Services in Microsoft 365*
- *Chapter 5, Understanding the Concepts of Modern Management*
- *Chapter 6, Deploying Microsoft 365 Apps*
- *Chapter 7, Understanding Collaboration and Mobility with Microsoft 365*
- *Chapter 8, Microsoft 365 Analytics*

3
Core Microsoft 365 Components

In *Chapter 2, Cloud Deployment Models and Services*, we covered high-level cloud computing concepts, deployment models, and the different categories of services available. MS-900 primarily focuses on Microsoft 365, which is one of Microsoft's SaaS cloud offerings. If that still seems unclear to you, then it may be a good idea to go back to the first two chapters to brush up.

The objective of this chapter is to understand the core technologies that make up Microsoft 365.

In the exam, you might run into a variety of terms and product names, including **Exchange Online, SharePoint Online, Teams, Stream, Microsoft 365 Apps** (formerly **Office 365 ProPlus**), **Forms, Power Automate, Power Apps, Tasks by Planner and To Do**, and **Yammer**. All of these products are part of a broader suite called **Office 365**.

Added to that are products such as **Intune, Azure AD Premium**, and **Azure Information Protection**. Together, these products make up another suite: **Enterprise Mobility + Security**, or **EMS**.

Finally, there's **Windows 10 Enterprise**, which is the flagship desktop operating system.

These three products (Windows 10, Office 365, and EMS) make up **Microsoft 365**.

In this chapter, you will deep dive into these technologies and learn about five core service offerings that comprise Microsoft 365. You will need to know these well to pass the MS-900 exam.

In this chapter, we will cover the following topics:

- Understanding Windows 10 Enterprise
- Exploring Microsoft 365 Apps for Business
- Exploring Exchange Online
- Exploring SharePoint Online
- Introducing Microsoft Teams
- Discovering Microsoft Forms
- Introducing the Power Platform
- Discovering the features of Enterprise Mobility + Security

By the end of this chapter, you will be able to articulate all of the core services that make up Microsoft 365. It's important to have a solid understanding of the product suite – not only for the exam but also to understand the value proposition of the platform as a whole. This chapter will help you navigate through the different technologies that make up Microsoft 365 and understand their benefits.

Understanding Windows 10 Enterprise

Windows 10 Enterprise (soon to be **Windows 11**) is a core component of Microsoft 365. Windows 10 is Microsoft's latest **operating system** (**OS**). There are several different editions, including Home, Education, and Enterprise (as well as a few more, depending on your organizational vertical or country). In this book, we will focus on the Enterprise edition, as that is the edition of the product that's included as part of Microsoft 365.

Windows 10 Enterprise is the most current OS and is designed to be the best fit for mid- to large-sized organizations. It brings three very important improvements for both the IT administrators and the end users:

- **Management**
- **Productivity**
- **Security**

Let's look a little deeper at each of these areas.

Management

With Windows 10 Enterprise, managing hundreds (or even thousands) of devices has become significantly easier. IT administrators have the flexibility to customize the OS and secure corporate identities and applications using Azure Active Directory. Devices running Windows 10 can be managed through Intune (part of the EMS suite) or Microsoft **System Center Configuration Manager (SCCM)**.

Intune is Microsoft's cloud-based mobile device and application management platform. We'll dive deeper into Intune in *Chapter 7, Understanding Collaboration and Mobility with Microsoft 365*. SCCM (now a part of Microsoft Endpoint Configuration Manager) is an on-premises solution for managing devices such as servers, desktops, and mobile devices. Administrators can also use the platform to deploy software and updates, as well as collect system and application inventory. SCCM can also manage the health of a device or an application by leveraging native telemetry data.

In the previous versions of Windows, major OS updates were released on a yearly or biannual basis. Windows 10 can be delivered as part of Microsoft 365 and now follows a subscription service model (Windows as a Service). With this new servicing model, Microsoft releases more incremental feature updates twice a year. Windows 10 deployment and servicing will be covered in *Chapter 5, Understanding the Concepts of Modern Management*.

Productivity

Advanced technologies such as Microsoft's digital assistant, Cortana, and Focus Assist, Windows Ink, and Windows Mixed Reality help end users with their productivity. These built-in apps can help end users keep track of their priorities and reduce any distractions that may come up throughout the day by integrating with your schedule and reviewing your Office 365 application usage data.

> **Virtual Assistance**
>
> For more information on Cortana, please see `https://support.microsoft.com/en-us/help/17214/cortana-what-is`. You can also learn about Focus Assist (formerly called Quiet Hours) at `https://support.microsoft.com/en-us/help/4026996/windows-10-turn-focus-assist-on-or-off`.

Security

Security should be a priority for IT administrators. Windows 10 Enterprise's new security features, such as **Microsoft Defender for Endpoint (MDE**, formerly **Microsoft Defender Advanced Threat Protection**), **Windows Information Protection (WIP)**, and **Windows Hello for Business (WHFB)** are all technologies that can help secure an organization's data and mitigate risk. MDE is a threat protection offering that's part of Windows 10 Enterprise.

MDE is built into Windows 10 Enterprise and uses embedded sensors to detect anomalous behavior. MDE is a platform of technologies that protect computers, or endpoints, from cyber threats such as data breaches and makes additional security recommendations. MDE can offer automated investigations and remediation suggestions to help IT admins reduce manual effort and respond more quickly to emerging threats.

WIP uses security mechanisms to provide information protection services to curtail potentially sensitive or otherwise essential company data from leaving the environment.

Finally, WHFB helps with identity and access management by providing a two-factor authentication method for logging into devices. WHFB can leverage biometric data with unique device PINs to help secure devices and reduce some of the risks associated with credential phishing attacks.

While the exam won't focus much on configuring advanced security measures, it's a good idea to become familiar with the terminology and feature set.

> **Deep Dive into Windows 10 Security**
>
> For more information on Windows 10 Enterprise Security, please visit `https://docs.microsoft.com/en-us/windows/security/`.

Since Windows 10 Enterprise leverages other technologies from the Microsoft 365 suite, such as Intune, Office 365, and Azure Information Protection, it's important to understand how they all work together to provide a complete solution. These separate technologies not only appear in the MS-900 exam, but they are also imperative to your understanding of Microsoft 365.

In this section, we've discussed Windows 10 Enterprise and its management, productivity, and security features as part of the core Microsoft 365 technology. Next, we'll discuss Microsoft 365 Apps for Business.

Exploring Microsoft 365 Apps for Business

Many users' first experience of the power of business applications was with Microsoft Office. Originally launched in November 1990, Microsoft Office has become the premier productivity application suite for millions of users worldwide. The Microsoft Office experience has been reimagined and is a fully integrated part of the Microsoft 365 platform. Microsoft 365 Apps for Business includes all of the desktop applications you've become familiar with, including Word, Outlook, Excel, Access, PowerPoint, OneNote, and Publisher.

Traditionally, Office was a static product, licensed on a per-device or per-user basis. With Microsoft 365, the Office application suite has been transformed into an evergreen product with continuous updates and feature developments, leveraging the best of the Microsoft cloud. Like other parts of the Microsoft 365 platform, Microsoft 365 Apps for Business is subscription-based software. The following is a screenshot of Microsoft Word, one of the business productivity applications of the Microsoft 365 Apps for Business subscription:

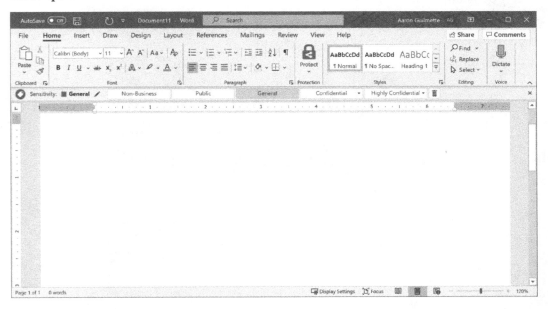

Figure 3.1 – Microsoft Word

Microsoft 365 Apps for Business is natively integrated with other parts of the Microsoft 365 ecosystem, including OneDrive for Business, SharePoint Online, Azure Information Protection, and Exchange Online. We'll cover Microsoft 365 Apps for Business in depth in *Chapter 6, Deploying Microsoft 365 Apps*.

Next, we'll look at Exchange Online.

Exploring Exchange Online

If you've used Outlook before, you might have some familiarity with Exchange Online. Exchange Online, an essential part of Office 365, is the cloud version of Exchange Server. Exchange Online is a messaging collaboration tool that allows you to email your colleagues and clients, organize tasks, schedule meetings, view calendars, and manage contacts.

You can do all of this through a desktop application such as Outlook by using a web browser, or from a mobile device.

Exchange Online for users

Let's discuss some of the basic Exchange Online end user features!

Each user has an Exchange Online mailbox. This allows users to send and receive emails. Users may be required to preserve or archive content so that administrators can enable a variety of mailbox archiving and retention policies.

When a user views their mailbox using Outlook on the web, they will have an experience similar to the one shown in the following screenshot:

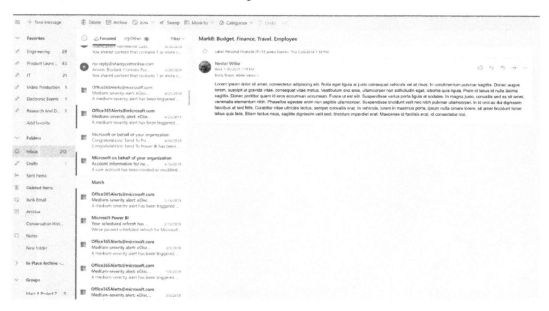

Figure 3.2 – Microsoft Outlook

Users can schedule meetings, events, and appointments through Exchange Online's calendaring features. Each user can keep track of their schedule, as well as check for free/busy times for other coworkers or resources. Certain users may also opt to delegate access to their calendars. An example might be a CEO delegating the management of their schedule and calendar to an administrative assistant. Here is a screenshot of a user's calendar via the monthly view:

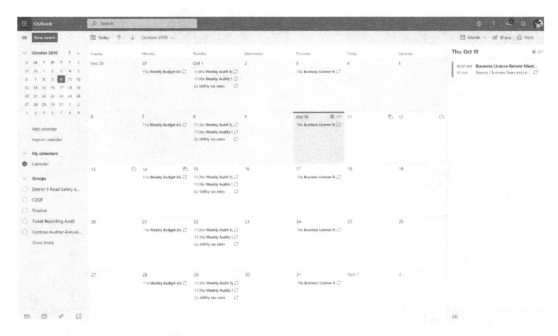

Figure 3.3 – Microsoft Outlook Calendar view

Like other messaging platforms, Exchange Online allows users to attach files to messages. Frequently, organizations have multiple users that need to work together on projects or share a job role. For example, an organization may want to have a general email address such as `sales@contoso.com` that potential customers can use to contact sales staff. In this case, a shared mailbox might be useful. Exchange Online supports shared mailboxes (where multiple people can access one mailbox).

> **More on Mailbox Licensing**
>
> While shared mailboxes do not incur any license fees themselves, each user who accesses a shared mailbox must be individually licensed.

Exchange Online also has a feature called **Microsoft 365 Groups** (previously known as **Office 365 Groups**) that functions like both a shared mailbox and a distribution list. You can see an example of a Microsoft 365 Group as it is displayed in Outlook in the following screenshot:

Figure 3.4 – Microsoft 365 Groups in Outlook

> **Connecting to Exchange Online**
>
> As we mentioned previously, Outlook is available as a desktop client application, as well as a browser-based application. Mobile clients are also available. You can learn more about the mobile clients for iOS and Android at `https://products.office.com/en-us/outlook-mobile-for-android-and-ios`.

Microsoft 365 groups are used heavily throughout the Microsoft 365 system.

Now that you've become familiar with some of the features of the end user experience, let's see what Exchange Online looks like from an administrator's point of view.

Exchange Online for administrators

As an Exchange Online administrator, you will have access to the **Exchange admin center** (**EAC**). You can access the EAC from either the Microsoft 365 admin center (`https://admin.microsoft.com`) or by navigating directly to either `https://outlook.office365.com/ecp` or `https://admin.exchange.microsoft.com`.

There, you can configure mail flow rules, such as email forwarding or adding text and notifications to messages. Administrators can also configure message encryption settings to help secure confidential communications.

The administrators of a messaging system should be concerned with message hygiene configurations to manage spam and suspected malware. Exchange Online uses a mail protection gateway, **Exchange Online Protection** (**EOP**), to trap these threats. Message hygiene settings (including configuration options for spam, phishing, and malware filtering) are managed through the EAC.

Organizations may opt to configure an Exchange hybrid environment. Exchange Online hybrid allows user mailboxes to be moved between the on-premises and Office 365 environments. Building on your knowledge from *Chapter 2, Cloud Deployment Models and Services*, you can see that Exchange Online hybrid is an example of a hybrid cloud deployment model.

Exchange hybrid configuration settings are configured in the EAC, as shown here:

Figure 3.5 – Exchange admin center

If your organization needs to meet regulatory compliance requirements, you'll likely configure many of those features in the *Microsoft 365 compliance center* (`https://compliance.microsoft.com`). This can be used to configure retention and data loss prevention policies. The compliance center can also be used to conduct eDiscovery activities for content stored throughout the Microsoft 365 service (including content stored in Exchange Online, SharePoint Online, and Microsoft Teams). The compliance center also gives you access to alerting, logging, and auditing data, as shown in the following screenshot:

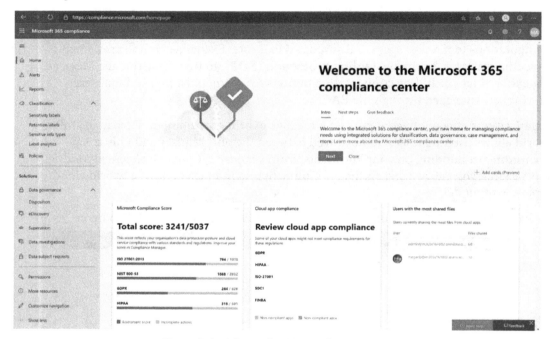

Figure 3.6 – Microsoft 365 compliance center

Accessing the compliance center requires a separate set of permissions. This enables organizations to separate and delegate administrative roles.

In this section, we covered Exchange Online's features. Furthermore, we divided Exchange Online between the end user's experience and IT administrator configurations. It's important to familiarize yourself with both aspects, such as Outlook mobile for the end user and retention policies for the IT administrators. MS-900 will contain questions regarding Exchange Online features but, more importantly, you should be able to demonstrate your knowledge of this core Microsoft 365 service.

Next, let's explore SharePoint Online.

Exploring SharePoint Online

SharePoint Online (SPO), another essential part of Office 365, is a web-based collaboration and communication platform. Many organizations use SPO as an intranet.

SharePoint has two core design methodologies: classic and modern. Classic SharePoint is based on the older, on-premises versions of SharePoint Server, while modern SharePoint is a reimagining of the service, which relies heavily on responsive design elements and Microsoft 365 groups.

Regardless of which design methodology you choose (classic or modern), the underlying SharePoint technologies are largely the same. Content in SharePoint Online is organized hierarchically. This starts at the organizational or tenant level. From there, you have smaller groupings of content called **site collections**. Site collections, as the name implies, contain **sites**. A site collection can contain one or more sites.

With classic SharePoint, each site collection is generally a security boundary and contains one or more related sites. Classic architecture generally relies on a traditional web navigation hierarchy. For example, you might need to navigate to a Finance site collection, and then select a Purchasing site to locate a requisition document.

However, with modern SharePoint, each Microsoft-365 connected site is a site collection with a security membership. Modern SharePoint sites can be linked via a mechanism called **hubs**.

In either design strategy, sites contain multiple content elements, such as pages, calendars, media, and document libraries. A simple classic SharePoint architecture is shown in the following diagram:

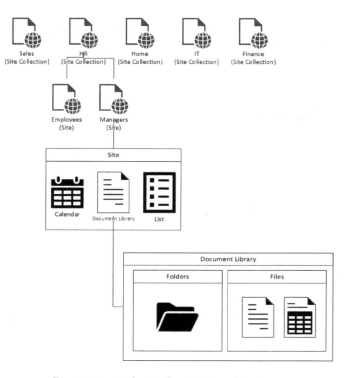

Figure 3.7 – A classic SharePoint architecture

Sites and site collections can be created to meet a variety of business and design needs.

There are several different templates available for creating sites that meet your organization's needs, such as team-based collaboration, wikis, and sophisticated search experiences. Organizations can create sites for groups of people that collaborate often.

SPO is also the foundation for other Microsoft 365 cloud services, such as Microsoft Teams and **OneDrive for Business (ODFB)**. ODFB is a personal storage space for files.

In the next section, we'll discuss three SPO use cases:

- Team site collaboration
- Communication sites
- ODFB

As we mentioned previously, SPO sites are created using templates. The two most popular site templates in modern SPO are **team sites** and **communication sites**.

Team site collaboration

Users can create documents, news posts, events, lists, and more, and then store the content in SPO.

End users can collaborate with other coworkers or even partners from other organizations securely using a SharePoint **team site**. Team sites allow you to create or upload files and then share them with your teammates easily. You can also use SharePoint team sites to manage lists, apps, and web pages.

The following screenshot shows an example of a team site's landing page:

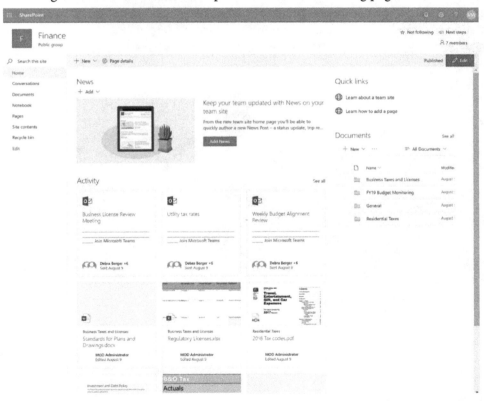

Figure 3.8 – SharePoint team site

Team sites have several features, including document libraries and web components that can easily be customized. Team sites are primarily designed in such a way that everyone can contribute or update content.

> **Team Sites in Depth**
>
> For more information on team sites, please visit `https://support.office.com/en-us/article/What-is-a-SharePoint-team-site-75545757-36c3-46a7-beed-0aaa74f0401e`.

There may be instances, however, where you don't want users to be able to contribute anything. In that case, a communication site might be a good fit.

Communication sites

Whereas team sites are designed for everyone to contribute, **communication sites** have a different focus. Communication sites are geared toward presenting the information. You can use a communications site to showcase content, images, links to other sites, and reports. The default communications site template allows you to format all this information in a modern layout, as shown in the following screenshot:

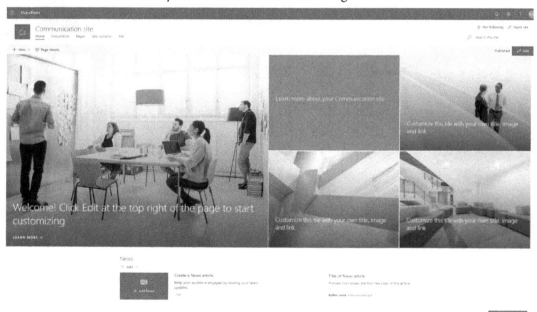

Figure 3.9 – SharePoint communications site

> **Communication Sites in Depth**
>
> For more information on communication sites, please visit `https://support.office.com/en-us/article/What-is-a-SharePoint-communication-site-94A33429-E580-45C3-A090-5512A8070732`.

In some situations, though, neither a team site nor a communication site may be appropriate to store some types of data, such as personal files. Next, we'll look at using OneDrive for Business to address that need.

OneDrive for Business

OneDrive for Business (ODFB) is a personal storage space for end users. The following screenshot shows an end user's view of OneDrive for Business:

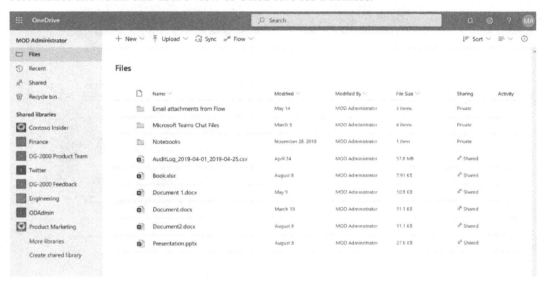

Figure 3.10 – OneDrive for Business

As we mentioned previously, ODFB is built on SPO. A user's ODFB storage space is their own SPO site. End users can deploy a client to their Windows or macOS devices, which will allow them to synchronize a copy of their data from the service locally. This can be used to enable offline support.

Similar to Outlook, SharePoint and ODFB also have apps available for mobile devices that run on iOS or Android.

External sharing

One of the things that differentiates SharePoint Online (and Microsoft 365 experience, overall) from on-premises environments is the ability to grant collaborators access to interact with documents in your environment. SharePoint Online has a robust sharing interface to send invitations to users at other organizations. Access can be managed inside the SharePoint Online interface. Both internal and external collaborators can work on a document at the same time.

SharePoint Online for administrators

SharePoint Online (and, by extension, ODFB) also has a robust set of administration tools that allow you to manage site provisioning, search, sharing, and permissions. The current SharePoint admin center is shown in the following screenshot:

Figure 3.11 – SharePoint admin center

Compliance and eDiscovery tasks are managed inside the compliance center, similarly to other Office 365 suite applications. As SPO provides the storage infrastructure for many Microsoft 365 services, it's important to become familiar with its concepts (especially around permissions, sharing, and external access).

SPO is also an integral part of Microsoft's collaboration hub, Teams, which we will cover next.

Introducing Microsoft Teams

Microsoft Teams, a relatively new service in Office 365, is the collaboration hub for teamwork within your organization. It's based on Microsoft 365 Groups, which, as you learned previously, incorporates Azure Active Directory, SPO, and Exchange Online features.

Teams builds on the Microsoft 365 Groups framework to allow users to chat, host, and conduct meetings, share and collaborate on files, deploy bots and connectors to external services, and make calls. We will discuss the infrastructure later in this chapter, but it's important to understand the basic capabilities of Microsoft Teams first.

Let's take a look at some of the features of Teams.

Chat

The first Teams feature we'll explore is chat. Teams users can conduct both one-to-one (or peer-to-peer) chats and group chats. You can see a sample of the chat interface here:

Figure 3.12 – Microsoft Teams chat

Teams users can communicate via rich text with personal mentions, reactions (such as a like button), and popular social media animations such as GIFs, memes, and stickers. Users can also share files in the context of their chat.

Files shared through Teams chat are first uploaded to the sender's OneDrive for Business. The recipient receives a sharing link to the file in the sender's OneDrive for Business.

> **Teams and OneDrive**
>
> As we mentioned previously, a Microsoft Teams peer-to-peer file transfer stores the files shared in a chat in the sender's OneDrive for Business. If users do not have OneDrive for Business provisioned, they will be unable to share files via chat.

Files

The **Files** tab within Teams will direct you to all the files you can access, whether they've been shared in a Teams channel or are located in ODFB, as shown in the following screenshot:

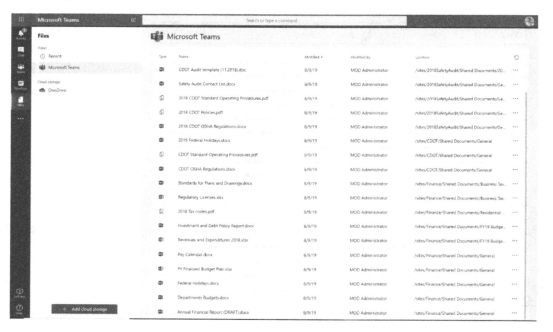

Figure 3.13 – Files in Microsoft Teams

Additionally, you can connect to a third-party cloud storage provider and view those files in Teams. The ability for users to connect to third-party storage providers can be managed through the Microsoft Teams admin center.

Calls and meetings

Teams is also a full voice conferencing and calling platform. In addition to chat, end users can make calls to both Teams users and those on traditional phone systems, as well as host online meetings and events. Teams allow users to initiate PC-to-PC calls through the Teams client, dial out to and receive calls from the **public switched telephone network (PSTN)**, and conduct impromptu meetings via the **Meet now** functionality. You can see an example of a Teams meeting in the following screenshot:

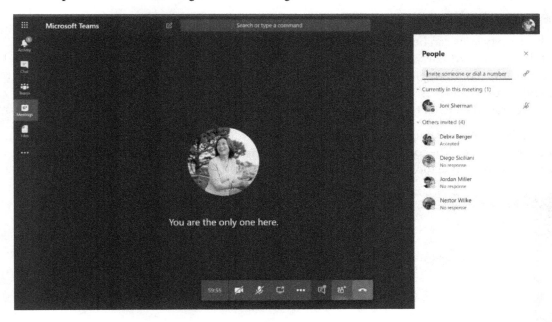

Figure 3.14 – Teams meeting

You can also bring Microsoft Teams into your meeting rooms. Users can leverage Teams Rooms systems to start sharing screens, present content, and collaborate with remote participants. Teams Rooms systems are audio and video conferencing devices capable of creating and hosting end-to-end meeting experiences.

Additional information regarding the limits and specifications of calls and meetings can be found at `https://docs.microsoft.com/en-us/microsoftteams/limits-specifications-teams#meetings-and-calls`.

Live events

Microsoft Teams also allows users to produce streaming broadcast events called **Teams live events**. A live event is a one (or few)-to-many meeting. Organizations might choose to use these for town hall meeting-style broadcasts from management or during a product launch. Live events can have multiple presenters, host up to 10,000 attendees, and can be recorded for later viewing.

Apps

Third-party apps can be critical to an organization's day-to-day operations. Hundreds of first- and third-party apps can be integrated right into the Teams client via bots and connectors. For example, users can use connectors and webhooks to get data from social media sources, such as Twitter, and post directly to Teams conversation channels or incorporate data from their sales pipeline tools.

With these integrations, users can accomplish their work using these apps without leaving the Teams client. The following screenshot shows the **Apps** tab, which can be used to add and configure these tools:

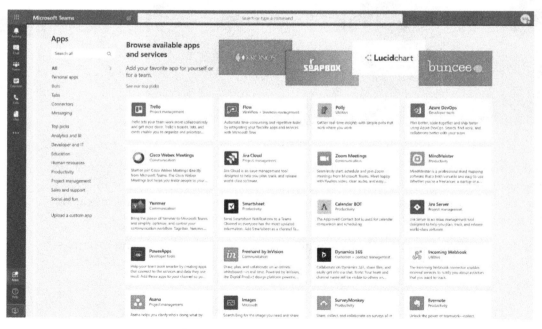

Figure 3.15 – Microsoft Teams apps

Multi-platform access

In addition to being accessible from modern browsers, Microsoft Teams is available across all devices, including Windows 10, macOS, iOS, and Android. You can download the Teams client for those devices from `https://products.office.com/en-us/microsoft-teams/download-app`, as shown in the following screenshot:

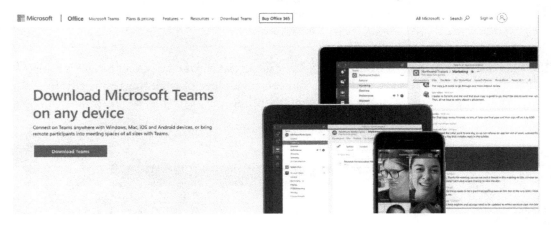

Figure 3.16 – Downloading the Teams client

Microsoft has also released a Linux client, available in DEB and RPM formats. Detailed instructions for installing Microsoft Teams for Linux are available at `https://docs.microsoft.com/en-us/microsoftteams/get-clients#linux`.

Teams for administrators

As Teams administrators, you'll need to think about a lot of settings to provide the most productivity and security for your environment, including the following:

- Meeting room devices
- Meeting, messaging, and app policies
- Telephony options, such as phone numbers, audio conferencing licenses, call queues, and auto-attendants
- External and guest access policies

Additionally, you'll want to familiarize yourself with the different migration paths and coexistence modes, especially if you're integrating with or migrating from Skype for Business.

> **Note**
>
> Organizations that have currently deployed Skype for Business Online should start planning their Teams migration as soon as possible. Skype for Business Online was retired on July 21, 2021. This announcement does not affect the Skype for Business on-premises server. For more information and the official announcement, please visit `https://support.microsoft.com/en-us/help/4511540/retirement-of-skype-for-business-online`.

The Teams admin center (`https://admin.teams.microsoft.com`) provides tools to manage all of those settings and more. You can get an idea of what the Teams admin center looks like by looking at the following screenshot:

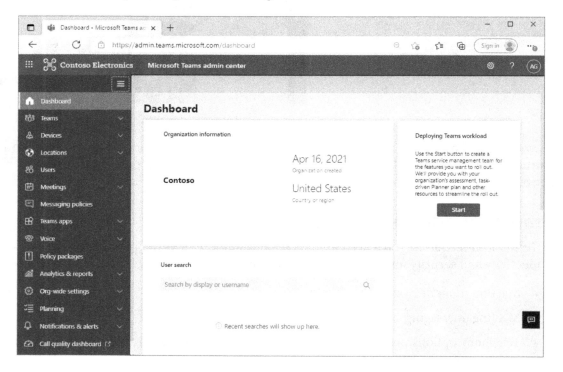

Figure 3.17 – Teams admin center

As you can see, Microsoft Teams brings together the features of the entire Microsoft 365 ecosystem. It allows the user to communicate via chat, meetings, share, and integrate with other apps, all from a single tool.

Next, we'll look at one of the newer products in the Microsoft 365 suite – *Forms*.

Discovering Microsoft Forms

Microsoft Forms is a survey tool that allows creators to ask a variety of questions and compile answers. Forms allows you to gather data through multiple-choice questions, text answers, date fields, and various rating methodologies. Respondents even have the opportunity to upload files.

The following screenshot shows an example of the Forms creation process:

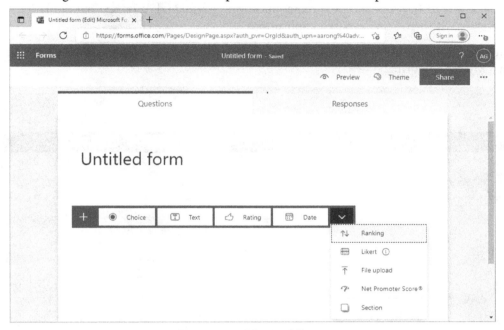

Figure 3.18 – Microsoft Forms

Surveyors can review the answers to the questions, download the output of responses, or even send questions to database tables for further analysis.

Introducing the Power Platform

The **Microsoft Power Platform** comprises several modular tools, each of which can stand alone, integrate into other Power Platform or Microsoft 365 ecosystem tools, or connect to third-party applications and datasets.

Power Platform tools are primarily designed to be low-code or no-code tools that allow people without development backgrounds to create applications, workflows, and data visualizations. Power Platform's tools share configuration objects called *connectors*, which are used to define the inputs, outputs, and other information that are used to connect to applications and services.

The three main components of the Power Platform are **Power Automate**, **Power Apps**, and **Power BI**.

Power Automate

Power Automate is a workflow engine that allows users and administrators to automate common business scenarios. Power Automate can be used to connect Microsoft 365 apps, databases, spreadsheets, or files to other applications, perform data or text manipulation, and interact with web service-based applications.

The following screenshot shows an example of a Power Automate flow that processes data from a Microsoft Form:

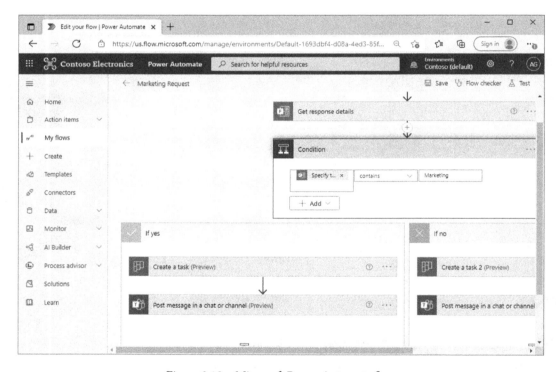

Figure 3.19 – Microsoft Power Automate flow

Power Automate allows users to create flows (the Power Automate nomenclature for a workflow process). A flow generally comprises one or more connectors, as well as conditions (where content or variables can be compared and evaluated) and actions. Flows can be configured to be automated (triggered by an event or notification), scheduled to occur at specific intervals, or manually.

Microsoft recommends using Power Automate in place of SharePoint Workflows and SharePoint Designer.

Power Apps

Power Apps is a low-code application development platform. Like Power Automate, it can use the concept of connectors to integrate with data sources and repositories. Power Apps allows users to create applications that can take input, file, or data uploads, as well as allow data entry and manipulation. Power Apps can be divided into three categories:

- **Canvas**: Canvas apps are what many people think about when they think of Windows object-oriented development. With canvas apps, developers drag and drop components onto a blank screen (or canvas), and then add actions to buttons. Canvas apps are not responsive by design (as their layout is determined when you start building the app), though certain elements can be moved around and made to render suitably on multiple platforms.

- **Model-driven**: With model-driven apps, the application is based on how data is stored and represented in the Common Data Service or the Dataverse, a structured data service available in the Microsoft 365 ecosystem. Most user interface components are context-sensitive and are limited based on the types of data objects you choose to include in the app. Model-driven apps are more common for scenarios that require complex business logic. Model-driven apps are responsive by design.

- **Portal**: Portal apps are designed to be rendered as web browser experiences and are useful for both internal and external users. Model-driven and canvas apps typically require an authenticated user account, and while portal apps can leverage authentication, they can also be anonymous (since they're presented on the internet). Portal apps, such as model-driven apps, are based on the Dataverse and are responsive by design.

Power Apps can call Power Automate flows to execute specific tasks. Power Apps can also be used to build applications that are integrated into the Microsoft Teams user interface. The following screenshot shows an example of the Power Apps canvas, which is used to build applications:

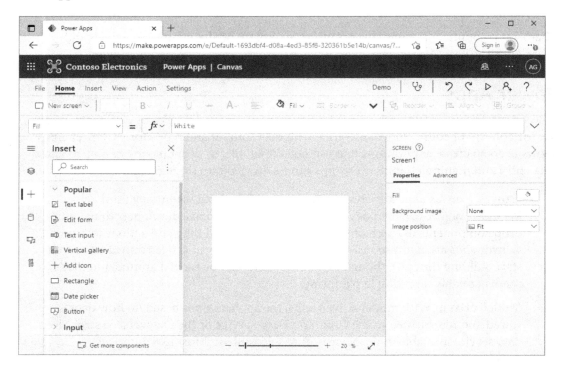

Figure 3.20 – Power Apps canvas

While designing applications is outside the scope of the MS-900 exam, it's important to know the different kinds of apps that can be built (canvas, model-driven, and portal).

Power BI

While Power Apps and Power Automate are generally used for data creation or processing, Power BI is used to visualize and represent data. Power BI is a visual data reporting tool.

Power BI can bring in data from a variety of sources (SQL, Excel, flat files, and more) and then render it in a myriad of ways to create endless dynamic reports. The following screenshot shows an example of a Power BI dashboard:

Figure 3.21 – Power BI dashboard

In addition to displaying data, Power BI also allows you to build complex queries and reports, import and manipulate data models, and even use **artificial intelligence** (**AI**) to ask sophisticated natural language questions.

The Power Platform offers a broad array of application development and processing capabilities, as well as content visualization capabilities. Power Apps can be used for data input and processing, to trigger Power Automate flows, and even display content from Power BI.

Next, we'll shift gears and look at the features of the Enterprise Mobility + Security suite.

Discovering the features of Enterprise Mobility + Security

Enterprise Mobility + Security (**EMS**) is Microsoft 365's security solution. It's an identity-driven, holistic approach to help address today's security threats. EMS licensing comes in two tiers: E3 and E5. Because identity is the crux of Microsoft 365's model, it's important to have a basic understanding of **Azure Active Directory** (**AAD**).

For the sake of the MS-900 exam, it's important to cover the basic elements of EMS.

AAD Premium

AAD has two licensing levels: **Premium 1** and **Premium 2**.

AAD Premium 1 (AADP1) is part of EMS E3. It allows you to use features such as **multi-factor authentication** (**MFA**), dynamic groups for license and application assignment, and conditional access. MFA is a security protocol that prompts users to verify their credentials using a second method, such as biometrics or a one-time-use passcode.

Dynamic Group Management allows administrators to determine group membership based on a user or a device's **Active Directory** (**AD**) properties and make licensing or assignment changes automatically.

Conditional Access is an AAD tool that helps enforce company policy. For instance, the company policy requires end users to sign in only from specific locations. Conditional Access can be configured so that when an end user is within that location boundary, access is granted. Otherwise, access is blocked.

With **AAD Premium 2** (part of EMS E5), organizations can enforce risk-based sign-in policies for MFA, as well as use leaked credential detection to determine whether compromised user credentials are available on the dark web.

Microsoft Intune

Microsoft Intune is a mobile management platform that encompasses both device (**mobile device management**, or **MDM**) and application (**mobile application management**, or **MAM**) capabilities. Intune allows you to manage a device remotely. MDM can be useful, for example, when a user loses their work phone. Once the loss has been reported, an administrator can remotely wipe that device, preventing the data from being compromised by an unauthorized party.

Intune device management also allows administrators to determine if the device meets certain security controls (such as being up to date with device updates or having encryption enabled) and make access decisions based on that. MAM extends similar controls down to the managed applications, allowing administrators to require additional passwords and enforce data storage controls. Intune is supported on Windows, macOS, iOS, and Android devices. Intune is managed from the AAD portal.

Azure Information Protection

Azure Information Protection (**AIP**) is included with both EMS E3 and E5. AIP helps organizations protect files by applying labels that allow or enforce specific actions according to company policy. AIP builds on technology from **Azure Rights Management** (**ARM**) to help define and apply these classification rules.

A few common examples include using the protection of the rights to prevent message recipients from forwarding an email message, preventing recipients from using the **Reply All** button, or applying watermarks to protected documents.

While AIP Premium 1 (included with EMS E3) requires users to manually apply protection to their content, AIP Premium 2 (included with EMS E5) allows organizations to automate the classification and enforcement actions.

Microsoft Cloud App Security

Microsoft Cloud App Security (**MCAS**) is a **cloud access security broker** (**CASB**) solution that can be connected to Office 365 and other SaaS applications to provide sophisticated analytics and security response actions. MCAS be used to detect shadow IT applications in your environment, as well as evaluate risk factors. MCAS is included as part of EMS E5.

Microsoft Advanced Threat Analytics

Microsoft **Advanced Threat Analytics** (**ATA**) captures on-premises network authentication and authorization traffic and analyzes it for attack patterns and suspicious behavior. ATA is included with both EMS E3 and EMS E5.

Privileged Identity Management

Privileged Identity Management (**PIM**) is a feature that allows users to use an access elevation request process to perform administrative tasks. Rather than having users configured with static administrative roles, PIM provides a mechanism for users to either automatically self-elevate or request privilege elevation for a time to perform administrative duties. With this configured, an organization can reduce the risk of having always-on administrative access. PIM is included as part of EMS E5.

Microsoft Defender for Identity

Microsoft Defender for Identity (previously known as Azure Advanced Threat Protection or Azure ATP) is a security product designed to provide insights, analytics, and alerting for suspicious activities, including lateral movements through Pass the Hash, Kerberos Golden Ticket, or other attempted exploits. Defender for Identity is included as part of EMS E5.

Microsoft Defender for Office 365

Formerly Office 365 ATP, **Defender for Office 365** includes threat detection and analytics primarily targeted at email-based threats. Defender for Office 365 Plan 1 is included with EMS E3 and includes the Safe Links and Safe Attachments features, which evaluate content for and links in a sandbox for threats.

Defender for Office 365 Plan 2, included with EMS E5, expands that protection with end user-focused threat training campaigns, the threat explorer, and automated investigation and response capabilities.

Windows Server Client Access Rights

This benefit is a usage right that grants users the ability to access software deployed on-premises without additional license purchases. This benefit is included with both EMS E3 and EMS E5.

It's important to understand the capabilities of the EMS suite, specifically features such as MFA and Conditional Access, for the MS-900 exam.

Summary

This chapter covered the core technologies that make up Microsoft 365. We learned about some of the advanced features of Windows 10 Enterprise and then covered four parts of the Office collaboration platform (Microsoft 365 Apps for Business, Exchange Online, SPO, and Teams). Finally, we discussed the breadth of capability in the EMS suite, Microsoft's holistic security platform, and identified which licenses cover which products and features.

After reading this chapter, you should be able to list the core Microsoft 365 services, along with two or three of the key features of each. For example, you should be able to identify Microsoft Teams and that some of its key features are meetings, chat, and file sharing.

In the next chapter, we will talk more about the advantages of having to deploy these cloud-based services over traditionally managed on-premises software.

Further reading

The following links provide more information on the EMS feature set:

- Multi-factor authentication: `https://docs.microsoft.com/en-us/azure/active-directory/authentication/concept-mfa-howitworks`

- Conditional Access: `https://docs.microsoft.com/en-us/azure/active-directory/conditional-access/overview`

- Microsoft Cloud App Security: `https://docs.microsoft.com/en-us/cloud-app-security/what-is-cloud-app-security`

- Microsoft Advanced Threat Analytics: `https://docs.microsoft.com/en-us/advanced-threat-analytics/what-is-ata`

- Windows Client Access License: `https://www.microsoft.com/en-us/licensing/product-licensing/client-access-license`

- EMS E5 capabilities and licensing: `https://www.microsoft.com/en-us/microsoft-365/enterprise-mobility-security/compare-plans-and-pricing`

- Microsoft Defender for Identity: `https://docs.microsoft.com/en-us/defender-for-identity/what-is`

Questions

Answer the following questions to test your knowledge of this chapter. You can find the answers in *Chapter 18*, *Assessments*:

1. Identify three core components of Microsoft 365.

    A. Enterprise Mobility + Security

    B. Windows 10 Enterprise edition

    C. Windows 10 Professional edition

    D. Office 365

    E. Windows Server 2019

    F. Windows 10 Home edition

    G. Azure Sentinel

    H. Azure IoT

2. Which Microsoft 365 feature utilizes biometrics?

    A. Windows Defender ATP

    B. Windows Hello for Business

    C. Windows Advanced Biometric Scanner

    D. Azure Information Protection

    E. Windows Information Protection

3. Exchange Online is primarily used for what?

    A. Creating and filling out online forms

    B. Composing spreadsheets

    C. Email and calendaring tasks

    D. Recording brief videos

4. The _____ can be used to configure data loss prevention policies.

    A. Microsoft 365 admin center

    B. SharePoint Online admin center

    C. Matter center

    D. Compliance center

5. Exchange Online hybrid is an example of what kind of cloud deployment model?

    A. Service cloud

    B. Hybrid cloud

    C. Private cloud

    D. Public cloud

6. Where would you perform an eDiscovery search for data stored in SharePoint Online?

    A. Microsoft 365 admin center

    B. SharePoint Online admin center

    C. eDiscovery center

    D. Matter center

    E. Compliance center

    F. Azure Security Center

7. Audit logs for Microsoft 365 can be accessed from which location?

    A. Microsoft 365 admin center

    B. SharePoint Online admin center

    C. Compliance center

    D. Compliance manager

    E. Azure Audit Log center

8. You need to perform an eDiscovery search for content in Exchange Online. Which tool should you use?

    A. Microsoft 365 admin center

    B. SharePoint Online admin center

    C. Compliance center

    D. eDiscovery center

    E. Exchange Online in-place Discovery and Hold

9. What are the two most popular site templates in modern SharePoint Online?

    A. Team site

    B. Hub site

    C. Collaboration site

    D. Communication site

    E. Project site

    F. Wiki site

10. OneDrive for Business is part of Exchange Online.

    A. True

    B. False

11. OneDrive for Business is part of SharePoint Online.

    A. True

    B. False

12. OneDrive for Business is part of Teams.

   A. True

   B. False

13. OneDrive for Business has native clients available for which of the following platforms?

   A. Android

   B. iOS

   C. Linux

   D. Windows

   E. macOS

14. What can you use to apply classification labels and actions to files?

   A. Label manager

   B. Azure Information Compliance

   C. Azure Information Protection

   D. Data Loss Prevention Manager

15. Microsoft Cloud App Security is an example of what type of product?

   A. Cloud app security proctor

   B. Cloud app security manager

   C. Cloud app security broker

   D. Cloud app security modeler

   E. Cloud app security proxy

16. You need to prompt users to enter a value from a one-time pass token when they log on to Office 365 applications. Which type of technology should you use?

   A. Azure Information Protection

   B. Multi-factor authentication

   C. Private Identity Storage

   D. Federated Identity Manager

   E. Privileged Identity Management

17. Which tool's primary purpose is to collect data in the form of surveys?

    A. Power Automate

    B. Power BI

    C. Microsoft Forms

    D. Power Flow

    E. Power Apps

    F. Microsoft Surveys

    G. Infopath

18. Which Power Platform tool can be used to create data visualizations?

    A. Power Pivot

    B. Power BI

    C. Power Automate

    D. Power Table

    E. Power Query

    F. Power Apps

19. Identify the three types of Power Apps.

    A. Model-driven

    B. Canvas

    C. Visual

    D. Portal

    E. Enterprise

    F. Responsive

20. Which two types of Power Apps are responsive by design?

    A. Canvas

    B. Portal

    C. Model-driven

    D. Responsive

    E. Enterprise

    F. Dataverse

21. Microsoft Teams is a full-featured telephony platform.

   A. True

   B. False

22. Which product is the new *hub for teamwork*?

   A. Microsoft Staffhub

   B. Microsoft Kaizala

   C. Microsoft Teams

   D. Microsoft SharePoint Hubs

23. Microsoft Teams allows up to _____ participants in a Live Event.

   A. 250

   B. 300

   C. 5,000

   D. 10,000

   E. 25,000

4

Comparing Core Services in Microsoft 365

In *Chapter 3*, *Core Microsoft 365 Components*, we covered the core technologies that make up Microsoft 365. Microsoft 365 consists of Windows 10 Enterprise, Office 365, and **Enterprise Mobility + Security (EMS)**.

In this chapter, we will begin by discussing the benefits of the cloud, specifically with reference to Windows 10 Enterprise management. Then we will address some high-level considerations when migrating from Exchange and SharePoint on-premises to their corresponding services in the Microsoft cloud. Finally, we will cover the benefits of Microsoft Teams and security in the cloud.

By the end of this chapter, you will be able to explain the difference between core services in Microsoft 365 and their on-premises counterparts. The topics we'll be examining are as follows:

- Understanding Windows 10 Enterprise management
- Evaluating Exchange options
- Evaluating SharePoint options

- Evaluating Teams
- Addressing security concerns

Understanding Windows 10 Enterprise management

In this section, we will go over from a high level what it takes for administrators to manage Windows devices and how that process changes for Windows 10 Enterprise. Microsoft 365 has new features that help ease the management of today's Windows 10 devices.

In this new, modern operating system, it's important to understand the new ways to manage devices. When making the transition from older Windows operating systems to Windows 10, an organization needs to make a decision on what tools to use to manage devices, and whether those tools will exist in an on-premises or cloud deployment.

Let's begin by looking at traditional management strategies.

Traditional Windows operating system management

In the past, Microsoft would typically release a new operating system on a multi-year cycle. For example, Windows 2000 Professional was released in February 2000. Windows XP was released in October 2001, Windows Vista in January 2007, followed by Windows 7 in October 2009, Windows 8 in August 2012, and finally, the first edition of Windows 10 in July of 2015.

Notice there was an eight-year span from XP to 7 where no new desktop operating system was released. For many business and enterprise customers, desktop operating system updates were frequently tied to hardware refresh cycles. Compatibility testing, for example, could take months to complete. An operating system refresh also usually meant a significant amount of downtime for users.

Here's an example of the deployment life cycle in a legacy management scenario whenever an operating system was released:

- First, requirements gathering. Administrators had to make sure the existing hardware was capable of running the new operating system and applications. If not, this meant budgeting for hardware upgrades, potentially adding months to an upgrade cycle.

- Once the hardware requirements were satisfied, the next step was configuring a system to be representative of what would be deployed to users. The reference system would have to be configured with the appropriate drivers and applications and then tested to ensure stability and capability. Once the configuration was validated, it would then be captured as an image: a point-in-time snapshot of the operating system, drivers, updates, applications, and settings that would get deployed on subsequent machines.

- As time went on, the image would become stale. Administrators would then have to re-create the baseline image, update the operating system, drivers, and applications, and then recapture it.

This process would normally get repeated for every brand and type of device: a unique image for each model of desktop or laptop device. Fortunately, there's a new approach with Windows 10 Enterprise management.

Modern Windows 10 Enterprise management

Now, let's talk about a more modern management platform.

Many large organizations already own a software deployment platform, such as **System Center Configuration Manager** (commonly referred to as **Configuration Manager**, **SCCM**, or just **CM**). It's typically used to manage devices such as desktops, laptops, and servers, as well as applications and updates. Just like in the past, CM can be used to manage Windows 10 devices.

However, there's also an option to integrate the device management platform and Intune with CM. This configuration is called **co-management**. Co-management allows you to leverage both an existing CM deployment as well as Intune, and gain benefits from both services. For example, you can deploy settings to co-managed Windows 10 devices from CM, while utilizing Conditional Access policies that leverage device compliance status from Intune.

Co-management brings several features to Windows 10 management, including the following:

- Conditional Access policies using device compliance
- Intune-based remote actions such as remote control, device restart, and factory reset
- Centralized visibility of device health
- The ability to link users, devices, and apps with **Azure Active Directory** (**AAD**)
- Modern, internet-based provisioning experience with Windows Autopilot

Let's have a look at some of the co-management features in more depth.

Conditional Access policies using device compliance

We've already touched on Conditional Access policies as a means to secure access to resources in the Microsoft 365 ecosystem. When you connect an existing CM deployment with Intune, you gain the ability to use device health and compliance as a condition. With Intune co-management, for example, you can determine whether devices are compliant with your current compliance policies, such as non-rooted or jailbroken devices or ensuring application updates are applied.

> **Conditional Access Deep Dive**
>
> For more information on Conditional Access policies with device compliance, see `https://docs.microsoft.com/en-us/configmgr/comanage/quickstart-conditional-access`.

Intune-based remote actions

Since the Microsoft 365 suite depends on access to the internet and the Microsoft cloud to deliver services, ensuring you have access to remote devices is key to ensuring user productivity and security. Co-management gives you the ability to perform a number of remote actions on managed devices, including the following:

- Deleting data on lost or stolen devices
- Restarting devices
- Renaming devices
- Gathering device inventory
- Performing immediate policy synchronization
- Performing remote control activities
- Removing factory-installed OEMs with Fresh Start reboot
- Performing a factory reset

> **Co-management with Intune and SCCM**
>
> To learn more about the Intune remote action benefits from a co-managed deployment, see `https://docs.microsoft.com/en-us/configmgr/comanage/quickstart-remote-actions`.

Centralized visibility of device health

Maintaining device health is critical to maintaining both user productivity and environment security. Since Intune is a cloud-based service, it can communicate with devices that are not on a corporate or organizational network. Intune bridges the gap between the client health monitoring tool CCMEval for the times when devices aren't on a managed network and enables auto-remediation for common health issues.

> **Client Health Management with CM**
>
> For more information regarding management and visibility of client health with a co-managed CM deployment, see `https://docs.microsoft.com/en-us/configmgr/comanage/quickstart-client-health`.

Ability to link users, devices, and apps with AAD

As we've discussed throughout this book, identity is the basis of security in Microsoft 365. It's the single most important entity and controls access to data, applications, and resources. With an Intune co-managed CM deployment and hybrid AAD joined devices, you get additional benefits:

- Automatic device licensing
- Self-service password reset
- Self-service BitLocker recovery
- Enterprise state roaming
- Device-based Conditional Access
- Windows Hello for Business
- Single sign-on to cloud-based resources

You can learn more about the hybrid AD benefits of co-management here: `https://docs.microsoft.com/en-us/configmgr/comanage/quickstart-hybrid-aad`.

Modern, internet-based provisioning experience with Windows Autopilot

Without on-premises infrastructure, you have the option to deploy your Windows 10 devices remotely using Windows Autopilot. Windows Autopilot is a collection of technologies that provides administrators and end users alike with a modern experience when deploying, repurposing, or resetting devices.

Autopilot, together with Intune, creates a cloud management experience. One of the benefits of an Autopilot deployment is the ability to drop-ship new devices from manufacturers directly to field staff. When the remote worker receives the device, they simply have to boot it, connect to the internet, and enter their AAD identity. The Autopilot framework allows the laptop to identify that it belongs to a specific Microsoft 365 tenant and begin the AAD device join process. During this process, it downloads software and policies assigned to the user.

However, with co-management, this experience can be even better. Co-management allows administrators to ensure that all devices have the same end state, including Intune device enrollment (which provides the additional previously mentioned co-management features) as well as the CM client for any on-premises management activities. You don't have to maintain specific device images as you did with legacy deployment models since Autopilot leverages the **Original Equipment Manufacturer** (**OEM**)-optimized edition of Windows that is pre-installed on the device. During the autopilot enrollment, devices are automatically upgraded to Windows 10 Enterprise and all of the Enterprise-based features are enabled.

Autopilot with CM also enables streamlined device upgrade processes from previous versions of Windows.

When deploying devices using Autopilot, the following steps are required:

- **Register devices**: When purchasing devices from supported OEMs, the OEM performs the device registration. When purchasing from resellers, distributors, or partners that are members of the **Cloud Solution Partners** (**CSP**) program, they can also register the devices on behalf of the customer:

  - Existing devices running Windows 10 can be automatically enrolled if they are using a **Mobile Device Management** (**MDM**) service such as Intune.

  - Existing devices may also be manually enrolled by capturing the hardware ID and uploading it to the Windows Autopilot service.

- **Create device profiles**: Profile settings need to be set up to adjust experiences such as skipping the **End User License Agreement (EULA)** page, automatically setting up work or school accounts, or disabling local admin account creation.

- **Create user/group or device-based profiles and configure and customize the device using Intune**: This can help meet business needs such as installing certain group- or department-specific applications or configuring specific settings, as shown in the following screenshot:

Figure 4.1 – Create an Intune profile

- **Boot the devices**: Connect to the internet and sign in using an Azure identity to complete the configuration.

In order to use all the modern co-management capabilities and features, CM must be updated to the current branch.

We have covered some of the differences between the legacy or traditional Windows management techniques and modern Windows management, including Intune and CM, as well as the benefits of shifting to modern operating system management.

Next, we'll begin looking at transitioning existing on-premises productivity applications such as Exchange and SharePoint to the Microsoft 365 platform.

Evaluating Exchange options

Many organizations have existing on-premises Exchange deployments and may be evaluating whether to upgrade to the next version of the on-premise edition or migrate to a cloud-based service such as Exchange Online. As it is when transitioning other services from traditional to cloud-based subscriptions, it's important to weigh the risks and benefits, such as cost, security, accessibility, mobility, growth, maintenance, and compliance.

Once an organization has decided to make the transition to Exchange Online, its next step is determining a migration strategy. Functionally, it's important to look at the following:

- How many users', shared, and resource mailboxes need to be migrated?

- What is the volume of data that must be migrated?

- How much bandwidth will be required?

- What services and features are you currently using, and what is the cloud-based equivalent?

- Is any data currently subject to litigation or retention policies, and does it need to be preserved?

- What mobility options need to be available?

- What is the least disruptive approach?

- Are there any features that won't be available or restrictions and limitations to work around?

- How will it be secured?

- Can any (or all) of the on-premises system be decommissioned?

Understanding the capabilities of Exchange Online and its migration paths is crucial for a successful transition.

From a feature perspective, it's important to note that organizations using Exchange Unified Messaging will need to select a new solution, whether that's moving towards an on-premises solution such as Skype for Business or a cloud solution such as Microsoft Teams with Phone System. Exchange Online still supports public folders and several types of shared and resource mailboxes. For organizations that synchronize their identity from an on-premises Active Directory, Microsoft recommends that at least one on-premises Exchange server is left to handle management tasks. You can learn more about this recommendation at `https://docs.microsoft.com/en-us/exchange/decommission-on-premise-exchange`.

Once the feature and capability questions have been answered, it's time to identify migration strategies. Exchange supports the following native migration paths:

- **Cutover**: All mailboxes will migrate over from on-premises to Office 365 over a few days. This also means that the mailboxes will be managed in Office 365. Cutover migrations support 2,000 mailboxes at a time but are really recommended for less than 150 mailboxes.

- **Staged**: Batches of mailboxes will move from on-premises to Office 365.

- **Hybrid**: Mailboxes can either be on-premises or in Office 365 and can be moved between environments. Deploying a hybrid environment allows a single, feature-rich, and consistent end user experience. Hybrid deployments require at least one server running Exchange 2010 Service Pack 3 or later. For organizations that manage identity on-premises and synchronize it with AAD Connect, Exchange hybrid is the only supported method for managing mailboxes.

- **G Suite Migration**: Microsoft now provides a native G Suite migration tool if the source environment is the Google G Suite platform.

- **IMAP**: If your source environment is not Exchange-based and doesn't rely on G Suite, you may consider using an IMAP-based migration. **IMAP** stands for **Internet Message Access Protocol** and is a standard interface used by a variety of third-party hosting platforms. Exchange also provides IMAP-based access to mailboxes, but it's far better to use a native Exchange migration. IMAP migrations frequently have limitations around contact and calendar folders, since those are typically extensions to the IMAP protocol and not part of the standard.

- **Third-party tools**: If your environment isn't compatible with performing a native Exchange-based migration or the built-in G Suite or IMAP-based migration methods don't meet your needs, there are a number of third-party products that can also be used to perform migrations. You can also find some additional guidance for other deployment scenarios using the Microsoft 365 Migration Advisor at `https://aka.ms/MailSetupAdvisorFromEDA`.

The type of migration you can perform depends on several factors:

- Source environment (Exchange Server-based, non-Exchange based, or hosted)

- Number of users

- Type of data being migrated (user or resource mailboxes, email, calendars, contacts, personal archives)

- Types of email clients (current or legacy versions of Outlook, third-party mail clients, mobile devices)

Once the overall migration methods have been determined, you need to decide what steps must be completed to successfully complete a migration process. A high-level project plan might look like the following:

- Configuring the test or trial environment
- Configuring the production environment
- Configuring coexistence tools and methods
- Conducting test migrations and feature testing
- Testing third-party or on-premises application integrations
- Conducting pilot migrations and feature testing
- Establishing the migration schedule and logistical considerations

Part of the logistical considerations includes how to select users for migration, depending on their work role, business functions, or even internal political pressure. There may be considerations about how to configure environments for security and end user or data center components that need to be upgraded in order to facilitate a smooth transition experience.

As previously mentioned, Microsoft recommends using the native hybrid migration configuration whenever possible. It provides the best end user experience. Some examples of features provided by a hybrid migration are as follows:

- The ability to move mailboxes between cloud and on-premises environments
- Automatic updating of user devices without the need to reconfigure Outlook mail profiles
- Fully functional address book
- Cross-premises permission delegation
- Fully functioning free/busy and calendaring features
- The ability to complete migrations when it is convenient for the business
- Little change for service desk/user provisioning practices

Other migration methods may require additional work, configuration, or coexistence software, and may not provide the best overall experience for users.

Now that we've discussed some of the considerations for migrating to Exchange Online, we'll look at migrating to SharePoint Online.

Evaluating SharePoint options

In addition to Exchange Server, many customers have also deployed SharePoint Server. SharePoint, as we discussed in the previous chapter, is a document management and collaboration platform.

When we discussed **SharePoint Online** (**SPO**) in the previous chapter, we discussed the two main types of site layouts: *team sites* and *communication sites*. These are considered modern site templates, whereas templates such as *enterprise wiki* and *development sites* are considered part of the classic site technology. The on-premises edition, SharePoint Server 2019, also has the concept of modern site layouts. Both on-premises and cloud SharePoint deployments can have a mix of SharePoint classic and modern sites. Microsoft 365's new products and services, such as Teams and Planner, utilize Microsoft 365 Groups, which rely on modern site templates.

While both classic and modern sites support many of the same features, there are some important differences:

- User interface elements and layouts (classic versus modern, responsive layouts).
- Web parts are available.
- Site architecture concepts (classic site collection and site hierarchies versus modern hub site associations).
- Search experiences (refiners, search dictionaries, and so on).

The MS-900 exam (and this book) won't cover all of the differences between classic and modern site architectures but suffice to say that modern groups and modern sites make up Microsoft's identity, group, security, and collaboration strategy for a number of the cloud-based tools available on the Microsoft 365 platform.

Unlike Exchange Server, which has a direct migration path to Exchange Online through hybrid mailbox moves, SharePoint Server does not have the ability to do native site or document library migration to SPO. SharePoint *does* have hybrid and cross-premises capabilities, as shown here:

Feature	SPO and SharePoint Server without hybrid	SharePoint Server with hybrid
OneDrive for Business	OneDrive for Business is available in Office 365 for licensed users, but there is no link to it from SharePoint Server. If users have been configured with My Sites or OneDrive sites on-premises and have a license in Office 365, they will have two sites to manage separately.	OneDrive links in SharePoint Server direct users to OneDrive for Business in Office 365. No content migration is performed as part of hybrid; content migration must be performed separately.
Site following	The SPO followed sites listing tracks followed SPO sites. If you've deployed MySites, a second followed sites list in SharePoint Server tracks followed SharePoint Server sites.	Followed sites from both locations are consolidated in the SPO followed sites list. SharePoint Server links to the followed sites list redirect users to the SPO followed sites list.
Document following	If you've deployed MySites, the followed documents list in SharePoint Server tracks followed SharePoint Server documents.	There is no corresponding hybrid document-following feature. If you use hybrid OneDrive for Business, the SharePoint Server followed documents list will be hidden from users, though you can still favorite SharePoint Server documents if you have Delve enabled.
Profiles	Users have separate profiles in SPO and SharePoint Server.	Profiles continue to exist in both locations, but SharePoint Server links to users' redirected profiles in Office 365.
Extensible app launcher	Users see different app launchers in Office 365 and in SharePoint Server.	Their app launchers are still separate, but the SharePoint Server app launcher includes tiles from Office 365.

Feature	SPO and SharePoint Server without hybrid	SharePoint Server with hybrid
Hybrid self-service site creation	There are separate self-service site creation experiences in SharePoint Server and SPO.	The default SharePoint Server site creation page is redirected to the SPO Group Creation page, allowing users to create sites in SPO instead.
Search	There are separate search indexes and search centers for SharePoint Server and Office 365. Users must search from each individual to find relevant content.	Search results between the two locations are combined with either cloud hybrid search or federated search options.

Table 4.1 – SharePoint Hybrid features

SharePoint content migrations can be achieved using a number of mechanisms, depending on the type of content being migrated and the destination:

- On-premises file server shares can be migrated to SPO sites using the **SharePoint Migration Tool** (**SPMT**).

- On-premises user home directories can be migrated to OneDrive for Business using SPMT.

- On-premises SharePoint Server 2010 and 2013 sites and document libraries can be migrated to SPO using SPMT.

- Third-party tools to migrate on-premises or cloud-based content to SPO and OneDrive for Business.

- On-premises business workflows may be able to be migrated, or they may need to be recreated if particular workflow options or features are not available in SPO. Microsoft Power Automate (formerly Flow) can be used to recreate or extend many workflows.

New Migration Tools

In October 2019, Microsoft acquired the cloud-based **Mover**, a tool that can migrate workloads from a number of cloud-based sources to SharePoint Online. For more information on the acquisition, please see http://www.mover.io.

While migrations to Exchange Online are purely administrator-driven, content migrations to SPO or OneDrive for Business may be either administrator or end user-driven (or a combination of both). Organizations should determine a strategy that covers the following areas:

- What SharePoint hybrid features will be configured (such as hybrid search, hybrid OneDrive, and hybrid user profiles)?

- Will sites and site collections be migrated?

- If sites and site collections are migrated, will they be migrated as-is or redeveloped with hub sites and modern site architecture?

- Will end user home directories or existing SharePoint MySites or OneDrive sites be migrated to OneDrive for Business?

- Are there any workflows that need to be evaluated and potentially recreated?

- Are there any legacy custom apps that could be redeveloped with Power Apps or Power Automate?

- Are there any dashboards or visualizations that may require features such as Gateways or Business Connectivity Services?

The process of configuring and migrating content to SPO, as well as configuring SharePoint hybrid options, is outside the scope of the MS-900 exam. However, it's important to be able to identify features of a SharePoint hybrid configuration and what migration options exist.

Now that you've seen what SharePoint migration options are available, let's examine Teams.

Evaluating Teams

Microsoft Teams is the collaboration hub that brings together many Office 365 services, integrating internal content, tools, and external data into a single interface. Unlike Exchange or SharePoint, Teams is cloud-only and doesn't have an on-premises counterpart. It's an all-new service that builds on familiar services such as Exchange, Skype for Business, and SharePoint as well as new constructs and services such as Microsoft 365 Groups and Planner.

In the previous chapter, we introduced Teams and its core features, such as chat, meetings, calls, connectors, bots, and file sharing. Microsoft Teams works with a core Office 365 architectural component, Microsoft 365 Groups, and stores content in both Exchange Online and SPO. In the rest of this section, we'll look at how Teams, Exchange Online, and SPO work together to provide the optimal Teams experience.

The following diagram illustrates how Office 365 technologies come together with Teams:

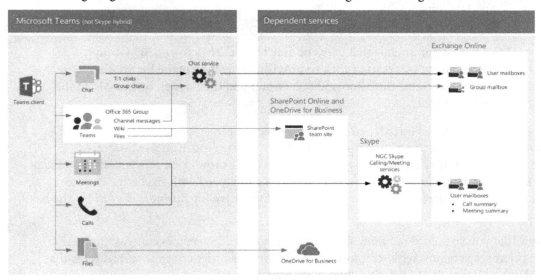

Figure 4.2 – Microsoft Teams services

A Microsoft 365 Group is the security boundary for Microsoft Teams. When you create a team, you are creating a Microsoft 365 Group and attaching Teams features to it. The group dictates who has access to the Team, which in turn controls who can access documents and conversations or participate in meetings.

As the preceding diagram shows, a team is based on a Microsoft 365 Group, which in turn maps certain features and capabilities to other Office 365 services:

- Conversations and messages are stored in the Microsoft 365 Group's connected mailbox.

- Channel files are stored in the Microsoft 365 Group's connected SharePoint site.

A team can be public or private. If a team is public, anyone in the organization is able to search for and join it. Private teams aren't visible, and users will need special permission or an invitation to join. In addition, a team (whether it's public or private) can be configured to have external members.

In order for Teams to function optimally, you need the following:

- Users should have mailboxes in Exchange Online. Teams is also supported when Exchange is configured in a hybrid with mailboxes on-premises, but cloud users still require a Teams license.

- Users must have a SharePoint license with OneDrive available for file sharing inside 1:1 chat to work.

- SPO resources must be available.

- Microsoft recommends that users be able to create Microsoft 365 Groups. Some organizations restrict this, so provisions must be made for another team or process to create the Microsoft 365 Group and then assign ownership to the correct end user.

There are a number of interdependencies for specific features, as detailed here: `https://docs.microsoft.com/en-us/MicrosoftTeams/exchange-teams-interact`. While specific feature dependencies don't show up in MS-900, it's important to know that Microsoft recommends all users be configured with Exchange Online mailboxes and SharePoint Online licenses with OneDrive for Business sites to get the best Teams experience.

Now that you've seen how some of the core Microsoft 365 services compare to their on-premises versions, we'll shift towards cloud-only security controls and features that make the Microsoft 365 offering even more compelling.

Addressing security concerns

As organizations move to the cloud, one of the concerns they face is security. Fortunately, Microsoft has invested in developing a full range of security controls that can be configured and deployed. We've already discussed multi-factor authentication briefly. In this section, we'll learn about how additional security controls and features, such as Conditional Access, access reviews, and Cloud App Security can improve an organization's overall security posture.

Conditional Access

Conditional Access is a set of security rules used to describe conditions for granting or blocking access to managed data and resources. Common conditions include network location (on or off a corporately managed network), geolocation to particular localities, using a managed or company-owned device, and group membership.

Using those types of conditions as factors for granting access can mean that a user can get access to a resource when meeting the parameters, or when introducing additional conditions (such as multi-factor authentication). Such scenarios might include allowing someone to access data only when they're on the network or to prompt for multi-factor authentication when they log in from an IP range located outside your current country. Maybe you want to grant someone access if they're remote, but you also want to restrict their access to web browser sessions only so they can't download content to an unmanaged device. Or possibly, if you detect someone logging in from two different IP addresses with very different geolocations in a short amount of time (for example, New York and then Ireland), you may wish to prompt for multi-factor authentication or deny them altogether.

Conditional Access Deep Dive

Detailed configurations for Conditional Access are beyond the scope of the MS-900 exam, but you should familiarize yourself with the concepts of using multiple conditions or controls to manage access to applications and services. You can learn more about common scenarios for Conditional Access at `https://docs.microsoft.com/en-us/intune/protect/ conditional-access-intune-common-ways-use`.

Depending on your organization and the type of data it manages, there may be several different scenarios that you need to enable to ensure your organization's data is secure.

Access reviews

One of the more cumbersome parts of technical administration is the management of security controls such as group memberships. As people move throughout an organization, their roles change, and frequently, they'll gain access to new applications or tools to do their new role, but the access they had for their previous role won't get removed.

Access reviews and entitlement management are features of AAD Premium Plan 2 that allow organizations to implement a review process that can wait for administrator or reviewer input, but also take automated actions, such as removing a user's access to an application. You can implement one-time or recurring access reviews and configure access reviews so that a group owner or designated reviewer can review the assignments and take action. Access reviews also support self-service reviews, allowing users to attest that they still need access to a group or application.

Cloud App Security

Microsoft Cloud App Security is a **Cloud Access Security Broker (CASB)** with features including log collection, API connectors, and reverse proxy. As a CASB, it is able to provide visibility and control over any integrated applications. It's fully integrated with the Microsoft 365 stack and can plug into thousands of third-party applications as well.

Cloud App Security's features are broken into four main pillars. They are as follows:

- **Discover and manage the use of shadow IT (unapproved applications or services)**: Cloud App Security can identify the cloud apps and services used by an organization. Cloud App Security can provide analytics around usage patterns and the risk levels of more than 16,000 SaaS apps.

- **Protect sensitive information regardless of location**: By connecting business applications to Cloud App Security, you can discover sensitive data stored in non-Microsoft services and use built-in policies to apply controls such as data encryption across cloud apps.

- **Protect against cyber threats and anomalies**: Detect unusual behaviors across cloud apps to identify risky situations, ransomware, and potential compromises. Cloud App Security allows you to define and customize risky behaviors using built-in templates and then automate remediation actions.

- **Assess the compliance of cloud apps**: Cloud App Security can assess your cloud apps for compliance. Cloud App Security can enforce non-compliant apps to comply with your organizational policies regarding data leaks.

Cloud App Security's discovery features are included in AAD Premium Plan 1, and its enforcement and automation features are part of AAD Premium Plan 2.

The EMS suite's features should very much be considered as a means to improve visibility and manageability across the security spectrum.

Summary

In this chapter, we compared the current state of Windows devices, Exchange, and SharePoint management with the capabilities that come with Microsoft 365, including modern management, co-management, and hybrid scenarios. In addition to comparing the features of Windows 10, Exchange, and SharePoint, we also looked at what makes Teams a unique, cloud-only application, and how to secure its infrastructure with the EMS suite's features.

In the next chapter, we will learn about **Windows as a Service** (**WaaS**) and its deployment and release models.

Questions

Use the following questions to test your knowledge of this chapter. You can find the answers in *Chapter 18, Assessments*:

1. CASB stands for which of the following?

   A. Cloud app service broker

   B. Cloud app security broker

   C. Cloud app service buffer

   D. Cloud app system buffer

2. Identify two pillars of Microsoft Cloud App Security:

   A. Block bulk email campaigns.

   B. Trigger Access Reviews.

   C. Discover and manage the use of shadow IT.

   D. Assess compliance of cloud apps.

3. You are the security administrator for your organization. You need to ensure that people accessing the system from outside your corporate network are using company-managed devices. Which tool should you use to meet the requirement?

   A. Access reviews

   B. Conditional Access

   C. Multi-factor authentication

   D. On-premises data gateway

4. You are the security administrator for your organization. You need to ensure that group memberships are periodically checked, and you want to delegate the management of this to group owners. Which tool should you use to meet the requirement?

   A. Conditional Access

   B. Access reviews

   C. Privileged Identity Management

   D. Privileged Authentication Management

5. System Center Configuration Manager can integrate with Intune using a feature called _____.

    A. System connection

    B. Co-location

    C. Co-management

    D. Hybrid management

6. Identify two features of an Exchange hybrid deployment:

    A. All mailboxes are either in-cloud or on-premises.

    B. Requires third-party tools to complete the migration.

    C. Allows cross-premises calendaring and free/busy availability.

    D. Move mailboxes easily between on-premises and the cloud.

    E. 10 additional free shared mailbox licenses.

7. Which of these is NOT part of a SharePoint hybrid deployment?

    A. Migrating document library content

    B. Hybrid search

    C. Document following

    D. User profile redirection

8. Microsoft Teams replaces what on-premises product?

    A. SQL Server.

    B. Team Foundation Server.

    C. It doesn't replace any product.

    D. Windows for Workgroups.

9. What are the three requirements for Microsoft Teams to function optimally?

    A. Exchange Online license

    B. Microsoft 365 Apps license

    C. SharePoint Online license

    D. Microsoft Teams license

10. With Configuration Manager and Intune configured for co-management, which two Intune remote actions are available?

   A. User reset

   B. Factory reset

   C. Remote control

   D. Application reset

5
Understanding the Concepts of Modern Management

In *Chapter 4*, *Comparing Core Services in Microsoft 365*, we covered modern Windows 10 Enterprise management, Exchange Online, Exchange Server features, SharePoint Online, and SharePoint Server features, as well as hybrid and migration considerations. Then, we covered how Teams integrates with Microsoft 365 Groups, Exchange Online, and SharePoint Online. Finally, we covered security features such as **multi-factor authentication (MFA)** and Conditional Access to elevate protection on cloud services.

In this chapter, we will introduce the **Windows-as-a-Service (WaaS)** model and the Windows deployment and release model. We will also introduce **Azure Virtual Desktop**, or, as it used to be referred to, Windows Virtual Desktop. Then, we will be navigating the Microsoft 365 admin center for tasks such as managing licensing, monitoring service health, and creating and monitoring a service request.

The following topics will be covered in this chapter:

- Understanding the WaaS model
- Understanding the Windows deployment and release model

- Introducing Azure Virtual Desktop
- Navigating the Microsoft 365 admin center
- Navigating the Microsoft 365 portal

Understanding the WaaS model

In *Chapter 4, Comparing Core Services in Microsoft 365*, we reviewed how Windows deployment and servicing has been managed historically. To summarize, Microsoft traditionally released operating system feature updates once every 2 to 4 years. Due to the significant feature and capability changes, operating system upgrades would frequently require significant amounts of testing to ensure hardware and application compatibility. This tedious update and refresh cycle could consume organizations for months or years.

WaaS is Microsoft's modern way to keep operating systems current and secure, as well as ensuring a smooth path to deploy security updates and release incremental features.

In today's landscape, the traditional model of releasing feature upgrades or enhancements would not be practical. Today, there are constant cyber-attack attempts and ever-developing threats, meaning organizations must be in a position to continuously adopt new defensive strategies. From a security perspective, organizations need to be able to respond more quickly to emerging threats. And, from a productivity and business point of view, organizations need to be able to adopt new technologies more quickly to attain a competitive advantage.

With the release of Windows 10, WaaS allows IT administrators to receive incremental updates that will help to reduce the time to deploy throughout an organization. WaaS provides organizations with a methodology to deploy operating system updates and enhancements in a streamlined fashion, efficiently keeping devices current.

Types of updates

With a new update model for Windows 10 comes new some terminology around the type of software that is delivered. First, there are two types of updates:

- **Feature updates**: Feature updates are bite-sized chunks released twice a year—once in March and then again in September. Any new feature releases such as improvements in a specific built-in application, visual refresh, or user experience enhancement in the operating system are deployed as feature updates.

- **Quality updates**: Quality updates denote the mandatory monthly release that contains both security and non-security maintenance fixes. There may be servicing stack updates that are included with quality updates. The servicing stack includes components that help update the device to the latest Microsoft security fixes. These updates are cumulative, which means it contains the previous month's quality update. This cumulative nature means that no matter when you choose to deploy the WaaS model, you'll have all of the quality updates to that point.

Let's get started with servicing tools in the next section.

Servicing tools

Next, there are **servicing tools**. Servicing tools are a mechanism that IT administrators can use to push updates. Microsoft provides four options for IT administrators to use:

- Windows Update
- Windows Update for Business
- Windows Server Update Service
- System Center Configuration Manager

They are explained as follows:

- **Windows Update**: Windows Update Standalone Installer is available for Windows 10 and uses the Windows Update API to install packages onto a client device. Windows Update Standalone Installer requires manual feature update deferrals and cannot approve updates. It will support Delivery Optimization.

> **More about Delivery Optimization**
>
> Delivery Optimization is a peer-to-peer sharing mechanism in which devices on the same network act as a distributed cache to reduce pressure on the bandwidth. For more information on Delivery Optimization, please visit `https://docs.microsoft.com/en-us/windows/deployment/update/waas-delivery-optimization`.

- **Windows Update for Business (WUfB)**: WUfB uses Intune or Group Policy to control how and when Windows 10 devices are updated. WUfB has more controls than Windows Update Standalone in that it allows Group Policy configuration options and the ability to push feature and quality updates as well as non-Microsoft driver updates. WUfB also includes the ability to deliver updates for other Microsoft products. Microsoft's published recommendations for the best experience with Windows Update are to make sure devices have at least 10 GB of free space and allow devices access to the Windows Update service.

- **Windows Server Update Service (WSUS)**: WSUS requires an on-premises server such as Windows Server 2012 R2, Windows Server 2016, or Windows Server 2019. Like WUfB, WSUS allows the servicing of Windows and other Microsoft applications. However, one advantage of WSUS is that it provides a single place for an organization to service Windows with more flexible controls such as approving updates and choosing when to deliver them. WSUS requires some planning and on-premises resources to deploy.

> **Deep Dive on WSUS Options**
>
> Refer to this page for more information and how to configure relevant Group Policy settings for managing updates through WSUS: `https://docs.microsoft.com/en-us/windows/deployment/update/waas-manage-updates-wsus`.

- **System Center Configuration Manager**: Of all of the servicing tools, System Center Configuration Manager provides IT administrators with the most control as they can control both quality and feature updates in addition to the other device, server, software management, and reporting capabilities. Configuration Manager can also use BranchCache and peer cache to distribute updates to remote clients more effectively. Configuration Manager also provides tools such as Desktop Analytics to provide insight around planning for and managing Windows 10 devices.

> **More on Desktop Analytics for Windows 10**
>
> For information on Desktop Analytics and its role in Windows 10 deployments, please visit `https://docs.microsoft.com/en-us/configmgr/desktop-analytics/ready-for-windows`.

Hardware compatibility has also traditionally been a barrier to upgrading operating systems. However, Windows 10 has the same minimum requirements as Windows 7. For organizations looking to upgrade from Windows 7 to Windows 10, their devices are most likely already supported and capable.

Now that you have an understanding of the feature and quality updates as well as updating methodologies, we'll move to the next section. Next, as an extension of this section, we will also introduce servicing channels and deployment rings to explain the deployment and release model.

Understanding the Windows deployment and release model

With the continual release of updates, IT administrators may have concerns about how to control these releases to an organization. Common questions include *"Can I get a preview of upcoming features?"* and *"How can I control which users or devices receive updates first?"*.

These issues are addressed with the concepts of the Windows deployment and release model, which uses the concepts of servicing channels and deployment rings to answer these questions.

Servicing channels

Servicing channels are a way to determine how often end users get feature and quality updates pushed to their Windows 10 devices. Servicing channels can be divided into the following three groups:

- **Windows Insider Program for Business (WIP)**: WIP is for those who are eager to get the latest updates. This may be a group of IT administrators or even end users who are willing to test features before they're made available to everyone. WIP has three rings: Windows Insider Fast, Windows Insider Slow, Windows Insider Release Preview. WIP is on a monthly release cadence and requires registration. Once registered, updates can be managed through Group Policy Configuration Manager, Windows Update for Business, or another device management platform. Microsoft recommends you have at least a few devices enrolled in WIP.

- **Semi-Annual Channel (SAC)**: After common issues are fixed, private builds are then made public and available for deployment. Then, the latest build is available for the rest of the public. SAC versions are released twice a year, once in September/ October and then again in March/April. IT administrators can defer or delay these new builds from the SAC up to 365 days. They can use this opportunity to first deploy the latest public builds to a pilot group of users and test before pushing it out to the rest of the organization. SAC builds have an 18-month life cycle. So, it's highly recommended that organizations stay within the time frame of support. SAC is recommended for enterprise customers running Windows 10 on their end user devices.

- **Long-Term Servicing Channel** (**LTSC**): Devices that do not need as many feature updates and receive just quality updates can subscribe to LTSC. It is designed for special or single-purpose devices, such as ATMs, medical equipment, and kiosks. LTSC editions do not have access to services and features such as Microsoft Edge, Store, Calendar, or OneNote. The core applications that aren't included aren't supported, even if you attempt to install them via side loading. LTSC is not the recommended nor preferred channel for enterprises.

More on Windows Servicing Channels

For more information on features, limitations, and recommendations regarding servicing channels, visit `https://docs.microsoft.com/en-us/windows/deployment/update/waas-overview`.

Next, we'll talk about deployment rings.

Deployment rings

While servicing channels determine the update cadence, **deployment rings** are the mechanism used to specify who will be receiving software from a particular servicing channel. Deployment rings can be used to configure pilot groups for new releases. A common best practice is to include a handful of users from every department in each deployment ring.

The following table illustrates an example of how an organization might structure servicing channels and deployment rings for their users:

Deployment ring	Servicing branch	Weeks after SAC release
Preview	WIP	Pre-SAC release (monthly)
Ring 1 – Pilot IT	SAC	SAC + 0 weeks
Ring 2 – Pilot business users	SAC	SAC + 4 weeks
Ring 3 – Broad IT	SAC	SAC + 6 weeks
Ring 4 – 10% of business users	SAC	SAC + 8 weeks
Ring 5 – 90% of business users	SAC	SAC + 10 weeks until all devices deployed

Table 5.1 – Deployment rings

As you can see from *Table 5.1*, Windows Insiders get the earliest builds. Then, pilot IT users get it upon release. Once IT is satisfied that it is working, they begin releasing to pilot business users. Pilot business users are a representative cross-section of the organization who can test in conjunction with their daily application usage and workflow.

After pilot users have verified that it has been successful for them, the deployment can proceed through the rings until the rest of the computers are updated.

Now, we'll shift the focus from the desktop to the virtual desktop.

Introducing Azure Virtual Desktop

Azure Virtual Desktop (AVD) was previously known as **Windows Virtual Desktop (WVD)**.

> **Terminology Update**
>
> In this book, we will use the terms Azure Virtual Desktop and AVD, though the MS-900 exam may still have some references to either Windows Virtual Desktop or WVD.

AVD is a service that deploys Windows desktop and Microsoft 365 apps in Azure. Virtualizing in such a way allows users to log in from any device to access remote desktops and apps. IT administrators do not have to worry about installing software on the local device. In short, AVD helps provide a flexible, secure, and consistent experience for all end users.

In this section, we will introduce AVD and the specific benefits of this service. Then, you can decide whether to pursue this option for your organization.

Benefits of AVD

The benefits of virtualization, specifically AVD, can be divided into two main categories: end user and administration. End user benefits include ease of use and flexible accessibility. From an administrative perspective, security, management simplification, high performance, and costs are of high importance. Let's go over each of them.

End user benefits

Imagine you are working for a financial institution and your organization is bringing in 150 interns for the summer season. These interns are expecting a smooth introduction and onboarding experience into the organization. AVD is a great option to onboard these end users because they can access their virtualized desktop from any HTML 5 browser. That means many of the interns can have a macOS computer, a Windows device, or a Linux machine. As long as these devices have an **HTML 5-supported browser**, such as Microsoft Edge, Google Chrome, Apple Safari, or Mozilla Firefox, the end users can navigate to `https://rdweb.wvd.microsoft.com/arm/webclient` and log in with the provided credentials. From a mobile device perspective, end users can go to the Apple Store or the Google Play Store, download the **Microsoft Remote Desktop** app, log in with the provided credentials, and now the interns have access to their resources on the go.

From an end user perspective, we covered two main benefits: flexible accessibility and ease of use. Now let's look at the administrative benefits using the same scenario.

Administration benefits

As mentioned previously, security, management simplification, high performance, and costs are very important for IT admins. Let's go over how AVD can address these issues.

First, you can secure your virtualized desktops by using role-based access control to make sure users are only accessing data they are allowed to access. Additionally, you can enable security measures such as MFA and conditional access to secure user sign-ins. Finally, because AVD is virtualized, sensitive information leaking from the local device is a lot less likely to happen because all the data lives in the virtual desktop.

You can automate a lot of the machine provisioning through Azure. This will help expedite the process of readying the environment for an additional 150 interns for the summer. Azure also lets you provision multiple environments with the same configuration. This helps with that consistent end user experience, and the actual provisioning process can be streamlined through the cloud. AVD also allows **multi-sessions** in Windows 10. That means you can have multiple interns logged into one virtual machine at the same time.

To provide top performance on these virtualized desktops, you can use Azure's services. By adding **load balancing**, Azure will distribute and spin up resources to meet demand, if necessary.

That leads to the topic of cost. Azure Reserved Virtual Machine Instances, a one-year or three-year subscription, is available and can save more money than the pay-as-you-go model. Paying for this subscription is also flexible, as there are monthly and yearly options.

IT admins will still have to manage identities, apps, and different images (Windows 10 with various versions, Windows 7 Enterprise, Windows Servers). IT admins will also have to configure networking policies and make sure the organization environment has all the infrastructure pieces, such as Azure Active Directory and an Azure subscription.

However, there are many business needs and specific scenarios in which AVD might be a good fit for the organization.

Now that we've gone through AVD, let's go into navigating the Microsoft 365 admin center.

Navigating the Microsoft 365 admin center

After purchasing a Microsoft 365 subscription, the organization's staff will have access to the Microsoft 365 admin center. There are basic tasks IT administrators should know how to do. Roles are critical to consider within an organization as well, so this section will also contain a table of the roles available in the Microsoft 365 admin center, and a short description of each.

In this section, we will go over the Microsoft 365 roles available in the admin center and then cover some of the common tasks as an administrator, such as checking billing and service health statuses.

Roles

There are a handful of essential administrator-related tasks in the admin center. Each task can be completed by users with certain administrative roles. For example, the Global Administrator role has access to everything within the Microsoft 365 admin center and can delegate additional roles. The most commonly delegated roles include the service administration roles, such as Exchange admin or Teams admin, though there are many others designed for specific groups, such as helpdesk or billing users.

Microsoft has updated the names of some roles and has changed the visibility of some items, choosing to display them only in the Azure portal or hidden from view entirely. The following table is a complete list of roles currently available in the Microsoft 365 admin center, with roles visible in the Azure portal designated:

Role	Description
Application Admin	This role has full access to enterprise apps, app registrations, and app proxy settings.
Application Developer	This role can create app registrations and consent to app access on their own behalf.
Attack Payload Author	Create payloads for the attack simulator.
Attack Simulation Administrator	Create and manage attack simulations, including creating payloads, configuring and launching simulations, and reviewing reports.
Authentication Admin	This role can require users to register or reregister authentication for non-password credentials, such as multi-factor authentication.
Authentication Policy Administrator	Configure and manage authentication methods policies, multi-factor authentication settings, and password protection policies.
Azure AD joined device local administrator	Users with this role become local computer administrators on Windows 10 devices joined to Azure AD. This role does not grant rights to manage objects in the directory (Azure-only role).
Azure Information Protection Admin	This role manages labels for the Azure Information Protection policies, activates protection policies, and manages protection and classification templates.
Billing Admin	This role makes purchases and manages subscriptions. Billing admins also can manage service requests and monitor service health.
Cloud App Security Administrator	Configure and manage Cloud App Security.
Cloud Application Admin	This role has full access to enterprise applications and application registrations. The role has the same permissions as the Application Administrator, except for being able to manage Application Proxy.

Role	Description
Cloud device admin	This role enables, disables, and deletes devices in Azure AD and can read Windows 10 BitLocker keys. Cloud device administrators cannot manage any other properties of a device.
Compliance admin	This role manages compliance and data governance policies, audits, and regulatory requirements across the Microsoft 365 compliance center, Microsoft 365 admin center, Compliance Manager, Azure, Intune, and the Office 365 Security & Compliance Center.
Compliance data admin	This role tracks data and audits in the Microsoft 365 compliance center, Azure, Intune, and the Microsoft 365 admin center. Data compliance administrators can also track, assign, and verify compliance activities in the Compliance Manager.
Conditional Access admin	This role manages Azure Active Directory Conditional Access settings, but not the Exchange ActiveSync Conditional Access policy (users must be a Global administrator to deploy the Exchange ActiveSync Conditional Access policy).
Customer Lockbox access approver	Manages (approves or denies) Customer Lockbox requests and can turn the Customer Lockbox feature on or off.
Desktop analytics admin	This role can access and manage Desktop management and Office Customization and Policy tools and services.
Directory readers	Users can read all basic directory properties and information (Azure-only role).
Directory Synchronization Accounts	This role is only for use with the AAD Connect service. It is not intended for any other purpose and should not be assigned to users (Azure-only role; now hidden from view in Azure and Microsoft 365 admin portals).
Directory Writers	This is a legacy role designed for applications that do not support the modern Consent Framework for application role delegation. It should not be assigned to users (Azure-only role).

Role	Description
Dynamics 365 Administrator	This role has full access to Microsoft Dynamics 365 Online. This role also grants permission to open and manage service requests and monitor service health.
Exchange Administrator / Exchange Service Administrator / Exchange Online Administrator	This role has full access to Exchange Online creates and manages mailboxes and groups.
Exchange Recipient Administrator	Manage recipients, message tracking, and migration tasks.
External Identity Provider admin	This role configures identity providers for use in the direct federation. Users in this role can manage the federation between AAD and other external identity providers.
Global Administrator / Company Administrator	This role has unlimited access to all management features and most data in all admin centers. Only users with the Global administrator role can assign other administrator role delegations. The role is identified as Company Administrator in PowerShell.
Global Reader	This has read-only access to all management features and settings in most admin centers. There are some limitations currently around the role. The Global reader role isn't supported in SharePoint or OneDrive admin centers or features such as Privileged Identity Management, Customer Lockbox, or Sensitivity Labels.
Groups Admin	This role creates groups and manages all group settings, such as naming and expiration policies, across admin centers.
Guest Inviter	This role manages Azure Active Directory B2B guest user invitations when the Members can Invite setting is configured as No.
Helpdesk Admin	This role resets passwords and reauthenticates for all non-admins and some admin roles (Directory readers, Guest inviter, Helpdesk administrator, Message center reader, and Reports reader), manages service requests, and monitors service health. This role was previously called Password Administrator.

Role	Description
Hybrid Identity admin	This role has full rights to manage AAD Connect cloud provisioning.
Identity Governance Administrator	Manage AAD entitle management features.
Insights Administrator	This role has full access to the Microsoft 365 Insights application and features, can read AAD properties and monitor service health, and can manage service requests.
Insights Business Leader	This role has the ability to read Microsoft 365 Insights application reports and insights.
Intune Administrator / Intune Service Administrator	This role has full permissions within Microsoft Intune, as well as the ability to create and manage groups. This role is identified as Intune Service Administrator in the Microsoft Graph API, the AAD Graph API, and AAD PowerShell and Intune Administrator in the Azure portal.
Kaizala Admin	This role has full access to all Kaizala management features and the ability to open and manage service requests.
Knowledge Administrator	This role can configure the knowledge network and content understanding features.
Knowledge Manager	Users with this role can create and manage content and content centers as well as maintain the structure of knowledge and taxonomies inside the term store.
License Admin	This role assigns and removes licenses from users and edits the usage location of user objects. This role cannot purchase, update, or renew subscriptions or billing.
Message Center privacy reader	This role has access to all messages in the Message center, including data privacy messages, and gets email notifications on privacy-related messages. Only users assigned the Global Administrator or Message Center Privacy Reader roles can read data privacy messages. This role cannot create or manage service requests.

Role	Description
Message Center reader	This role reads and shares regular messages in the Message center, gets weekly email digests, and has read-only access to users, groups, domains, and subscriptions. This role cannot read data privacy messages in the Message center, nor can it create or manage service requests.
Office apps admin	This role manages cloud-based policies for Office and self-service downloads. Users in this role can manage the What's New content that users see in their Office apps, as well as create and manage service requests and monitor service health.
Password admin	Resets passwords for all non-admin users (as well as some users with admin roles assigned—the primary exception being Global Admin).
Power BI Administrator	Users with this role have full permissions for the Power BI service, as well as the ability to create and manage support tickets and monitor service health.
Power Platform Admin	This role has full access to all Power Platform apps, including Microsoft Dynamics 365, Power Apps, data loss prevention policies, and Microsoft Power Automate (formerly Microsoft Flow).
Printer admin	Manages network printers and print connectors, and configures printer access and queues.
Printer tech	Users with this role can register and unregister printers as well as update printer status.
Privileged Authentication Admin	Users granted the Privileged Authentication Administrator role can set, reset, and manage non-password credentials for all users (including Global admins), and can update passwords for all users. Users with this role can also force users to re-register against existing non-password credentials such as MFA tokens and revoke the remember MFA on the device setting, prompting for MFA on the next login of all users.

Role	Description
Privileged Role Admin	This role manages role assignments in AAD as well as Privileged Identity Management and Administrative Units. This role doesn't grant any specific user, group, or device management privileges, though members of this role can grant themselves any other role that does have those privileges.
Reports Reader	This role reads usage reporting data from the reports dashboard and Power BI adoption content pack. Reports Reader also grants the ability to read Azure sign-in reports and use the Microsoft Graph reporting API.
Search admin	This role has full access to Microsoft (activated through the Microsoft 365 admin center Services & add-ins page), assigns the Search Administrator and Search Editor roles, and manages editorial content. This role also grants permission to monitor service health and manage service requests.
Search editor	This role can create, edit, and delete content for Microsoft Search, such as bookmarks, Q&A, and locations. This role does not permit managing service requests.
Security admin	This role grants permission to manage security-related features in AAD Identity Protection, Azure Security Center, Azure Information Protection, the Office 365 Security & Compliance Center, Cloud App Security, Intune, and the Microsoft 365 admin center. This role also can see service health.
Security operator	This role grants permission to read security-related features in AAD Identity Protection, Azure Security Center, Azure Information Protection, the Office 365 Security & Compliance Center, Cloud App Security, Intune, and the Microsoft 365 admin center. This role also can see service health as well as respond to alerts in the Identity Protection portal.

Role	Description
Security reader	This role grants permission to read security-related features in AAD Identity Protection, Azure Security Center, and Identity Protection center. Azure Information Protection, the Office 365 Security & Compliance Center, Cloud App Security, Intune, and the Microsoft 365 admin center. This role also can see service health. The only difference between this role and the Security Operator role is that the Security Reader role cannot manage alerts or respond to alerts.
Service Administrator / Service Support Admin	This role creates and manages service requests for Azure, Microsoft 365, and Office 365 services. The role is also granted permission to monitor service health. This role is identified as both the Service Support Admin and as Service Administrator.
SharePoint Administrator	This role has full access to SharePoint Online and can manage Office 365 groups. It creates and manages service requests and can monitor service health.
Skype for Business Administrator	The Skype for Business Administrator role has full access to all Teams and Skype features. Users with this role can also modify Skype user attributes. The role can create and manage service requests and monitor service health.
Teams Administrator / Teams Service Administrator	This role has full access to the Teams and Skype admin centers and can manage Office 365 groups. Creates and manages service requests and can monitor service health. It is displayed as both Teams Administrator and Teams Service Administrator.
Teams Communication Admin	This role manages the voice and telephony features of Microsoft Teams, such as the ability to assign telephone numbers and manage voice and meeting policies. This role also grants access to the call analytics toolset.
Teams communication support engineer	This role uses call troubleshooting tools in the Microsoft Teams and Skype for Business admin centers. Users with the Teams Communication Support Engineer role can view full call record information for all participants. It cannot create or manage service requests.

Role	Description
Teams communication support specialist	This role uses call troubleshooting tools in the Microsoft Teams and Skype for Business admin centers. It cannot create or manage service requests.
Teams Device Administrator	Users with the Teams Device Administrator role can configure and manage devices used for Microsoft Teams, such as Teams Rooms, Teams Displays, and phones.
Usage summary reports reader	This role allows users to read usage reports and the Productivity Score. The role cannot access user details.
User Administrator	Users with this role can reset user passwords, as well as create and manage users and groups. It can create and manage service requests and monitors service health. User Administrators cannot reset the passwords of Global Admins.
Windows Update Deployment Administrator	This role allows users to create and manage all aspects of the Windows Update for Business deployment service.

Table 5.2 – Admin center roles

Most organizations do not use all of their specialized roles. However, they are available if the organization requires a tighter level of granularity. A new feature called *Custom Roles* allows organizations to create even more fine-grained control as well.

> **Deep Dive into Role Assignments**
>
> For more information on the available roles, please visit https://docs.microsoft.com/en-us/azure/active-directory/users-groups-roles/directory-assign-admin-roles.

Next, we'll review some common tasks related to the Microsoft 365 admin center.

Common tasks

One of the most common tasks available as an administrator is to create and manage service requests and monitor service health. Another operational activity would include viewing the bill or the invoice details, licensing, and checking the Message center.

Let's review each of these common tasks!

Billing

As a global administrator or billing administrator, you can navigate to the **Billing** page to view your bill or invoice details. To access billing features, launch the Microsoft 365 admin center (`https://admin.microsoft.com`) and select **Billing** from the navigation menu. You may need to select **Show all** at the bottom to see all of the menu options.

The **Billing** menu has several options, as depicted in the following screenshot:

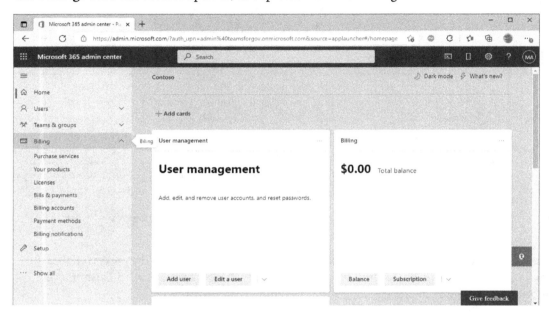

Figure 5.1 – Billing

From these options, you can purchase new services, review aggregate license details, and manage invoices and payment methods.

Licensing

The licensing view shows general information on the SKUs and licenses available in the tenant, as well as aggregate usage details. Go to **Licenses** to view different product licenses available to the tenant. To view general license details, launch the Microsoft 365 admin center (`https://admin.microsoft.com`) and select **Billing** from the navigation menu, and then select **Licenses**. You may need to select **Show all** at the bottom to see all of the menu options.

Once the **Licenses** page is displayed, you will see a list of the services available in your tenant, similar to what is shown in the following screenshot:

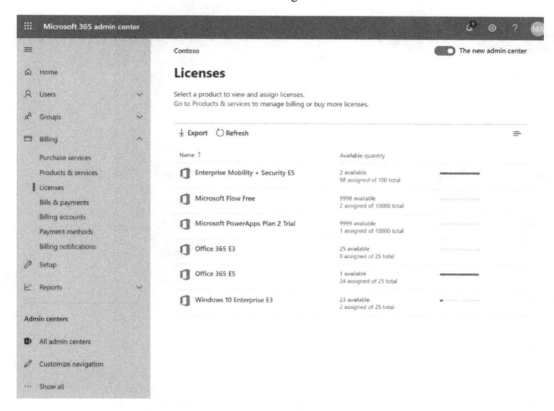

Figure 5.2 – Licensing

If a user is a member of one of the roles that can manage user licenses, they can also assign the licenses by following these steps:

1. Launch the Microsoft 365 admin center (`https://admin.microsoft.com`).

2. From the navigation menu on the left, select **Users** | **Active Users**.

3. Select one or more users, and then select **Manage product licenses**.

4. Use the toggles for each license to assign licenses or sublicense service plan features. Click **Add** or **Save** (depending on the type of modification being made), as the following screenshot indicates:

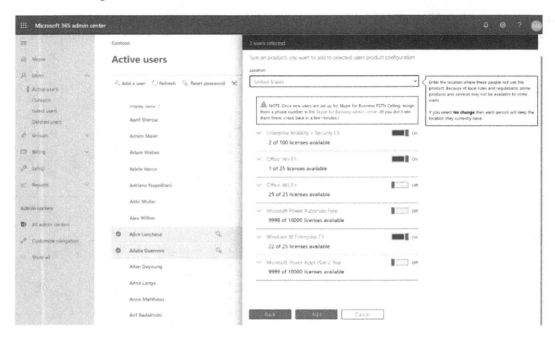

Figure 5.3 – Manage licenses

License changes are effective immediately, though some services may take a few minutes to provision or enable (such as mailbox creation or OneDrive for Business site creation).

Service health

Many roles support viewing the health status of the service. The service health dashboard can be accessed using the following process:

1. Launch the Microsoft 365 admin center (`https://admin.microsoft.com`).
2. From the navigation menu on the left, select **Health | Service health**:

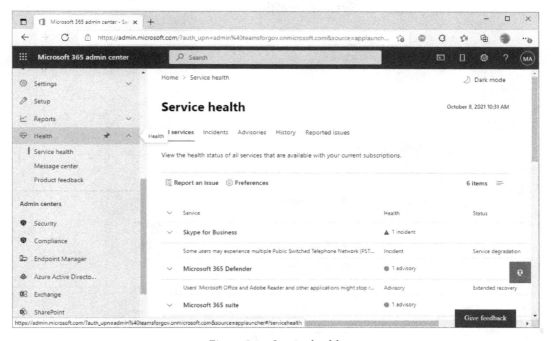

Figure 5.4 – Service health

3. Select the **Incidents**, **Advisories**, or **History** tabs to filter and organize events, as displayed in the following screenshot:

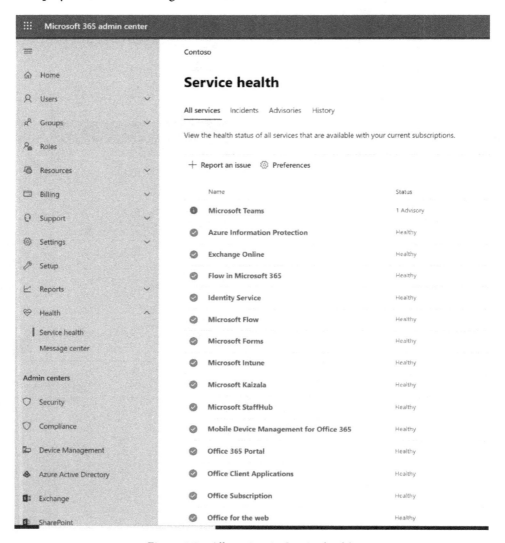

Figure 5.5 – All services in Service health

Status Definitions and Explanations

For a list of status definitions, visit `https://docs.microsoft.com/en-us/office365/enterprise/view-service-health#status-definitions`.

Events, services, and notifications can be viewed, sorted, and filtered.

Message center

Microsoft makes its product announcements in several places, such as blogs, news articles, and events, and the Microsoft 365 Message center. Follow the steps given here to access the Message center:

1. Launch the Microsoft 365 admin center (`https://admin.microsoft.com`).

2. From the navigation menu on the left, select **Health | Message center**, as shown in the following screenshot:

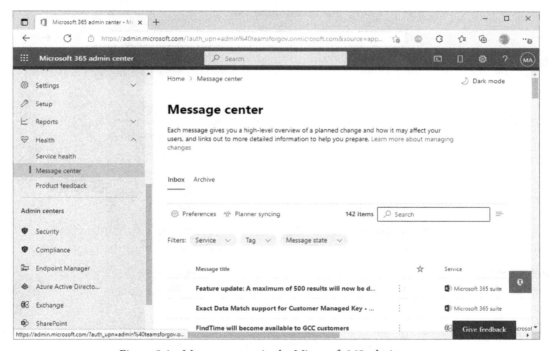

Figure 5.6 – Message center in the Microsoft 365 admin center

Administrators can filter by high-importance, unread, and dismissed messages, as well as search and sort, as shown in the following screenshot of the **Message center** page:

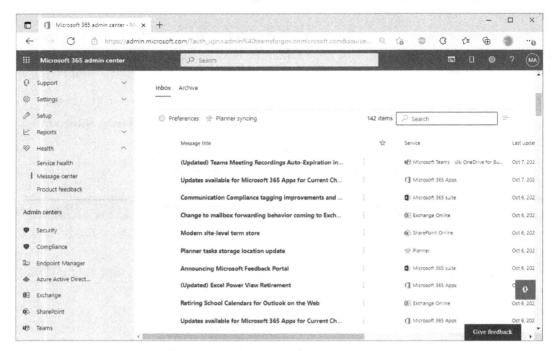

Figure 5.7 – Messages in the Message center

Notifications for upcoming changes and features are posted here. Some periodically require administrative intervention, so be sure to monitor the Message center regularly.

The Message center also includes a new area, **Product feedback**, that allows administrators to review feedback that users have submitted about products.

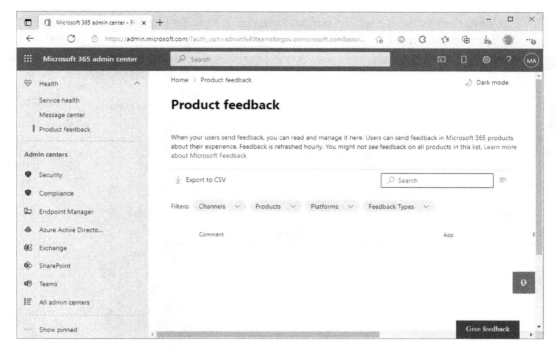

Figure 5.8 – Product feedback

Using the feedback option in many Microsoft 365 apps and experiences, users can submit product feedback. For more information on how Microsoft uses feedback, see `https://docs.microsoft.com/en-US/microsoft-365/admin/misc/feedback-user-control?view=o365-worldwide`.

Service ticket

Should support issues arise, you can open a service ticket with Microsoft. Resources will be assigned to assist you. Follow these steps to initiate a service ticket:

1. Log in to the Microsoft 365 admin center (`https://admin.microsoft.com`) with an account that has one of the roles required to create a support ticket.

2. Click **Support** in the navigation bar, and then click **New Service Request** to launch the **Support Assistant**:

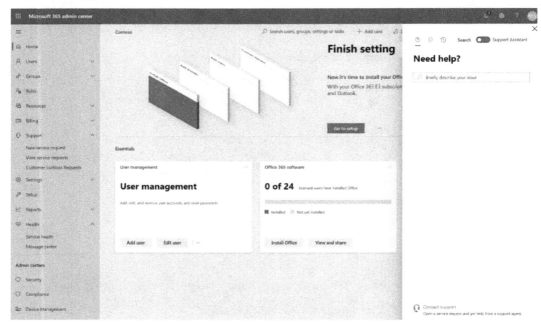

Figure 5.9 – Service ticket

3. If the support assistant is unable to answer your question, select the link at the button to contact support.

Administrators can also see past service requests as well.

Additional Self-Help Tools

While not specifically in the Microsoft 365 admin center (and not part of the MS-900 exam), it's good to note that Microsoft does provide additional self-help troubleshooting guides for Exchange, Outlook, Teams, and SharePoint.

Teams: `https://docs.microsoft.com/en-us/microsoftteams/troubleshoot/teams-administration/admin-self-help-diagnostics`

SharePoint Online: `https://docs.microsoft.com/en-us/sharepoint/troubleshoot/diagnostics/sharepoint-and-onedrive-diagnostics`

Exchange and Outlook: `https://docs.microsoft.com/en-us/exchange/troubleshoot/administration/self-help-diagnostics`

Now that you've seen some of the basic features of the admin center, let's take a look at the Microsoft 365 portal user experience.

Navigating the Microsoft 365 portal

Users will navigate to the Microsoft 365 portal when accessing services and applications through a web browser. The address for the Microsoft 365 portal is `https://portal. office.com`, though some organizations may decide to create referrals or redirections from other sites they manage. When a user logs in, they see a landing page similar to the following:

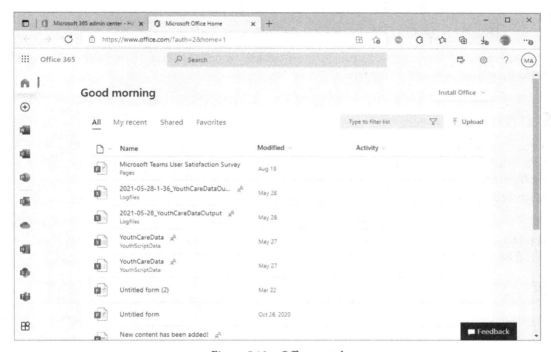

Figure 5.10 – Office portal

The home page has several features, including the following:

- There's a search bar at the top of the page that allows users to search for applications and files.

- There is an **Install Office** link to install Microsoft 365 apps. Users can select to install apps for 32-bit or 64-bit platforms as well as multiple languages.

- There are tiles or icons for all of the applications that they are licensed to use.

- There's a list of files, organized into categories:

  - **Recent** shows files that a user has recently accessed across various services.

  - **Pinned** shows files that a user has pinned (similar to marking something as a favorite in a browser).

  - **Shared with me** lists the files those other users have granted them permissions to access, as well as items that they have pinned (similar to saving as a browser favorite).

  - **Discovery** shows files that may be relevant to you, based on Office Graph signals.

  - There's a list of recently accessed OneDrive files.

  - There are frequently visited or followed SharePoint sites.

Now we have covered both the administrator and user interfaces to the Microsoft 365 platform, as well as some of the features of both.

Summary

In this chapter, we discussed the new WaaS model for delivering Windows, including the feature updates, quality updates, servicing channels, and deployment rings. Understanding the deployment methodology is important from both the MS-900 exam perspective as well as the real-world management perspective.

Additionally, we introduced Windows Virtual Desktop, now referred to as **Azure Virtual Desktop**, or **AVD**. We covered the benefits of AVD and how some business needs may be served best with this service.

Then, we covered some of the features of the Microsoft 365 admin center, including the various security roles and basic administrator tasks. Finally, we took a tour of the Microsoft 365 end user interface so you can understand how users will see and interact with the service.

In the next chapter, we will discuss some of the differences between Office 2016 and Microsoft 365 Apps (formerly known as Office 365 ProPlus), as well as how to begin deploying the application suite.

Questions

Use the following questions to test your knowledge of this chapter. You can find the answers in *Chapter 18, Assessment*:

1. When deciding when users will get a Windows release, what concept would apply?

   A. Service branch

   B. Service channel

   C. Deployment ring

   D. Windows Insiders

2. What are the three primary servicing channels?

   A. Windows Insiders

   B. Semi-Annual Channel

   C. Long-Term Servicing Channel

   D. Monthly Channel

3. Which role has access to nearly every feature and role in the Microsoft 365 service by default?

   A. Enterprise admin

   B. Domain admin

   C. Global admin

   D. Azure admin

4. Which of these describes a feature update?

   A. Anything new, such as improvements in a specific built-in application, visual refresh, or user experience

   B. Monthly release that contains both security and non-security maintenance fixes

   C. Security releases only

   D. Non-security releases only

5. Which of these describes a quality update?

    A. Anything new, such as improvements in a specific built-in application, visual refresh, or user experience

    B. Monthly release that contains both security and non-security maintenance fixes

    C. Security releases only

    D. Non-security releases only

6. Application Administrators can administer aspects of the Application Proxy.

    A. True

    B. False

7. Cloud Application Administrators can administer aspects of the Application Proxy.

    A. True

    B. False

8. Which of the following tasks is *not* part of the License Administrator role?

    A. Remove licenses from users

    B. Assign licenses to users

    C. Edit usage location on user objects

    D. Purchase licenses

9. Which of the following tasks is *not* part of the Message center reader role?

    A. Access to regular messages in the Message center

    B. Access to data privacy messages in the Message center

    C. Read-only access to users and groups

    D. Read-only access to subscriptions

10. Which of the following tasks is *not* part of the Customer Lockbox Access Administrator?

    A. Approves Customer Lockbox requests

    B. Denies Customer Lockbox requests

    C. Enables or disables the Customer Lockbox feature

    D. Create and manage service requests

11. Which role should only be used for the AAD Connect Service Account?

    A. Global admins

    B. Company administrators

    C. Directory synchronization accounts

    D. Password admins

12. Which role has full access to full call record information?

    A. Teams Communication Support Engineer

    B. Teams Communication Service Engineer

    C. Skype Communication Support Engineer

    D. Skype Communication Service Engineer

6
Deploying Microsoft 365 Apps

Microsoft 365 Apps for enterprise is the new enterprise, government, and education subscription-based edition of the familiar Office application. The applications you're familiar with (Word, Excel, Outlook, Access, PowerPoint, and OneNote) are still part of the Microsoft 365 Apps package. This book will refer to this as Microsoft 365 Apps.

In *Chapter 5, Understanding the Concepts of Modern Management*, we introduced the concept of **Windows as a Service** (**WaaS**) and the Windows deployment and release model for Windows 10. In this chapter, we will shift the discussion to Office desktop applications. Similar to the WaaS model, Microsoft 365 Apps has unique considerations. In this chapter, you'll learn about the deployment and licensing options for Microsoft 365 Apps and how to choose the right options for your organization.

One of the core differences between traditional retail or volume perpetual license editions and the Office subscription model is the concept of channels in Microsoft 365 Apps. Like Windows 10, Microsoft 365 Apps has update channels and release cadences to understand.

Microsoft 365 Apps has both deployment and licensing differences from traditional software, both of which we will address in this chapter:

- Licensing and activating Office editions
- Deploying Office editions

Let's get started!

Licensing and activating Office editions

While the software components are very similar between the various Office editions, it's important to note that there are different licensing and acquisition methods. In this section, we'll look at the following differences:

- Licensing Office Professional 2016 (and later)
- Licensing Microsoft 365 Apps

Licensing and activating Office Professional 2016

Traditionally, Office products have been licensed with what is known as a **perpetual license**. This means that you purchase it once and you're never obligated to make another payment again unless you want to upgrade to a new version or need support for it. If Office 2016 or later meets your needs, you can purchase it once through a channel (such as a retail or volume license) and then continue to use that edition until you no longer have a means to run the software, whether that's next month, next year, or a decade from now.

There are some benefits to this licensing model, as follows:

- It's a fixed cost and can be capitalized easily from an accounting point of view.
- The software can be licensed per device or user, depending on which scenario is most beneficial to the organization.

Some of the drawbacks of this model, however, include the following:

- It's possible to let the software grow stale and unsupportable.
- The software is a legacy architecture and requires complex migration planning to upgrade.
- It's very easy to under-license and over-deploy.
- Organizations may be responsible for paying for costs and penalties for *all* the licenses that are deployed (even if the media is stolen or taken home by an employee).

As such, Microsoft is shifting from perpetual licensing models to subscription-based models such as Microsoft 365 Apps.

Licensing and activating Microsoft 365 Apps

From a licensing perspective, Microsoft 365 Apps is part of the Microsoft 365 subscription. Because it's a subscription, it has certain important requirements and features. They are as follows:

- Licensing is user identity-based, meaning a user must have an Azure AD account and have a Microsoft 365 Apps license associated with it.

- Microsoft 365 Apps can be installed on up to five different computers (Windows PC or Mac), five tablet devices, *and* five mobile phones with one single-user license, for a total of 15 installations. Users activate their subscription by signing in with their tenant credentials.

- Microsoft 365 Apps *does* support a shared computer activation configuration. Scenarios where this might be useful include if users share workstation devices (such as shift workers) or have been configured to use non-persistent virtual desktop environments.

- Microsoft 365 Apps is activated over the internet, so the licensing service that's deployed on the computer must be able to reach the internet to check in every 30 days and verify that the user still has a valid subscription. If the status cannot be verified, or if the user remains offline for more than 30 days, OPP goes into reduced functionality mode.

> **Exam Tip**
>
> This is important and will show up on the exam. If a device is offline for more than 30 days, the Microsoft 365 Apps suite will be in reduced functionality mode. In reduced functionality mode, users can *only view* or *print* their documents. Other features such as edit or create will be unavailable.

When looking at this, a few benefits emerge:

- Since licensing is user-based, so it's very easy to understand how many licenses need to be acquired. Users get a total of 15 that they can tie to their user account.

- When a user leaves the organization, their identity is typically deactivated, and their license is returned to the organization's pool. There's no need to worry about licensed *installations in the field* as they will stop working in 30 days.

- The update servicing mechanism is built-in by default, so installations will always be up to date and in a supported state.

The only potential drawback is for organizations that like to maintain their software as an *asset* since the subscription is an operating expense instead of a capital expense.

As you can see, there are some important choices to make when deploying technologies, updating and servicing methodologies, as well as choosing a product and licensing model that achieves your organization's business needs.

Next, we'll look at the technical differences between the products.

Deploying Office editions

As we discussed in *Chapter 3*, *Core Microsoft 365 Components*, Microsoft 365 Apps contains the same applications (Outlook, PowerPoint, Word, Excel, Publisher, and Access) as the traditional Office software package. In that sense, **Microsoft 365 Apps** and Office 2016 and later editions are very similar. Microsoft 365 Apps is also available in both 32-bit and 64-bit versions. Microsoft recommends the 64-bit editions for new deployments, but you'll need to verify which edition is right for your organization based on your hardware and third-party plugin compatibility requirements.

While they have many similarities, there are some differences. We'll start with Office Professional.

Deploying Office Professional

Microsoft Office has been available as a traditional, Windows Installer-based media package for quite some time. However, Office Professional 2016 is the last Windows Installer-based version of the Office suite. All future versions (including Office 2019 and Office 2021) will be based on a newer deployment architecture called **Click-to-Run** (**C2R**), which we'll discuss later.

All Office media packages up to this point have relied on fixed installers, meaning that all of the software components are present on the media at the time of installation. Any updates or service packs are normally applied either after the installation has been completed or slipstreamed (downloading the updates and manually integrating them into the deployment package). Microsoft would publish updates or service packs that would need to be downloaded and applied individually.

From a feature perspective, Office Professional is normally only updated when another version of the product suite is released. Office Professional is serviced through a traditional release cadence, meaning that new features only become available with a new version.

While the C2R deployments *do* support side-by-side installations, it only applies to different versions (for example, Microsoft 365 Apps can be deployed side by side with Office 2010 Professional). You cannot simultaneously install the Windows Installer-based edition and C2R edition of the same Office build on a computer.

You can use traditional methods to deploy and update Office Professional, such as Group Policy or **System Center Configuration Manager (SCCM)**.

Installation Note

The **Office Customization Tool (OCT)** is only used with MSI-based installers, such as Office 2016 and earlier. If you have newer media (such as Office Professional 2019), you'll need to use the steps for the **Office Deployment Tool (ODT)**.

Let's go over some examples of each.

Group Policy

If your organization doesn't have a software distribution platform, you can use Active Directory Group Policy to deploy the Windows Installer-based builds of Office Professional. Follow these steps to do so:

1. Create a network share on a server that's accessible to all computers that you will deploy Office Professional on. You'll need to enable the Share and NTFS permissions to allow Authenticated Users and Domain Computers.

2. Copy the contents of the Office media (extracted ISO image, extracted compressed EXE, or CD/DVD media) to the share.

3. If desired, run the Microsoft OCT by running `setup.exe /admin` in the folder where you copied the media in the previous step to choose which product options you want to install or configure.

Note

The OCT allows you to configure product keys, accept the **End User License Agreement (EULA)**, configure additional network sources, provide the organization name to be used in the registration process, and some additional security and setup options.

---

4. Select **Create a new Setup customization file** and click **OK**:

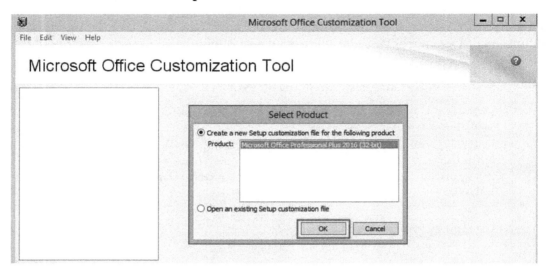

Figure 6.1 – Microsoft OCT

You'll want to configure the unattended installation settings inside the OCT.
If you don't want to run the OCT, you'll need to edit the configuration file manually
to support a Group Policy-based installation.

5. If you did not use the OCT to edit the configuration file, you'll need to edit it
    manually. The config.xml file is located in the source files folder where
    you copied the media. By default, it will be in \\server\share\Office16\
    ProPlus.WW\config.xml. Locate the line that contains the <!-- <Display
    Level --> element and update it with the following settings:

```
<Display Level="none" CompletionNotice="no"
SuppressModal="yes" AcceptEula="yes"/>
```

Create a .bat script in Notepad that contains the path to the installation media and
configuration file and save the file. For example, the contents of the script might be
as follows:

```
@ECHO OFF
SET LOCATION="C:\Program Files (x86)\Microsoft Office\
root\Office16"
IF NOT EXIST ""%LOCATION%\MANIFEST.XML"" \\server\share\
Office16\setup.exe /config \\server\share\Office16\
ProPlus.WW\Config.xml
```

> **Advanced Batch Script for GPO Deployment**
>
> A more complex example of the previous script sample is available at
> `https://aka.ms/BatchOCT`.

6. On a domain controller, launch the Group Policy Management Console (`gpmc.msc`).

7. Create a new Group Policy object in the Group Policy Objects container and edit it.

8. Navigate to `Computer Configuration\Policies\Windows Settings\` `Scripts (Startup/Shutdown)` and double-click on **Startup**:

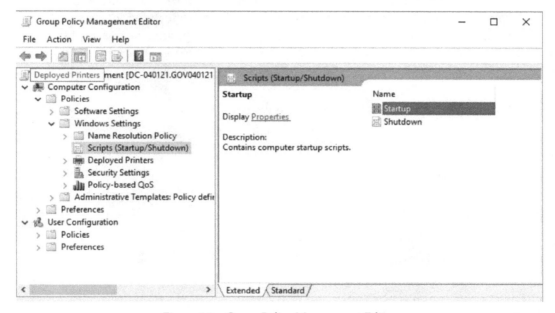

Figure 6.2 – Group Policy Management Editor

9. Click **Show Files...** to open the GPO folder under `SYSVOL`.

10. Copy the file you saved in *Step 5* to this folder and click **OK**.

11. In **Group Policy Management Editor**, select **File | Close**.

12. Link the GPO to a container that has one or more computers that you want to install Office 2016 on.

After configuring a Group Policy and linking it to a container that has computers in it, restart one of the computers. Group Policy should trigger the Office installation.

System Center Configuration Manager

If your organization has a software deployment tool such as SCCM, you can follow these steps to deploy the Windows Install-based editions of Office as well:

1. Create a network share that will be accessible to you for the entire configuration process on SCCM.

2. Copy the contents of the Office media (extracted ISO image, extracted compressed EXE, or CD/DVD media) to the share.

3. Run Microsoft OCT by running `setup.exe/admin` in the folder where you copied the media in the previous step to choose which product options you want to install or configure. The OCT allows you to configure product keys, accept the EULA, configure additional network sources, provide the organization name to be used in the registration process, as well as some additional security and setup options. You'll want to configure the unattended installation settings inside the OCT.

4. Select **Create a new Setup customization file** and click **OK**:

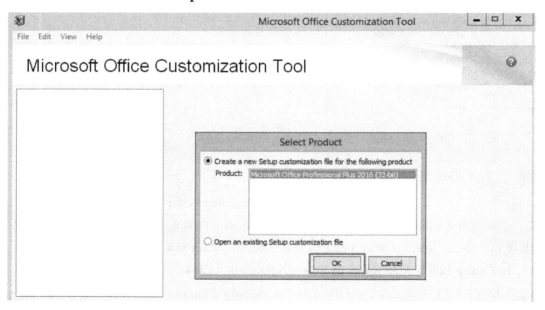

Figure 6.3 – OCT

5. Select **Modify Setup properties**. Add a new property called SETUP_REBOOT with a value of Never and click **OK**:

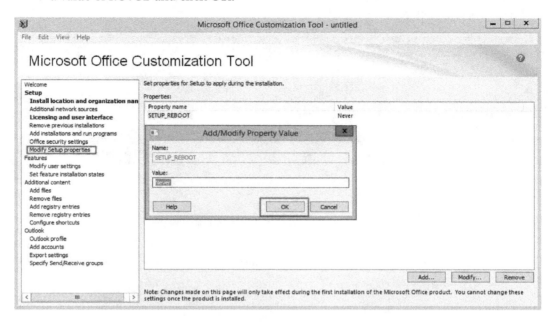

Figure 6.4 – Microsoft OCT

6. Perform any additional customizations and save the file in the \Office 2016\ Updates folder.

7. Launch the SCCM console.

8. Expand **Application Management**, right-click **Applications**, and select **Create Application**.

9. Select **Automatically detect information about this application from installation files**, provide the path to the installation media (typically in the form of \\server\ share), and click **Next**:

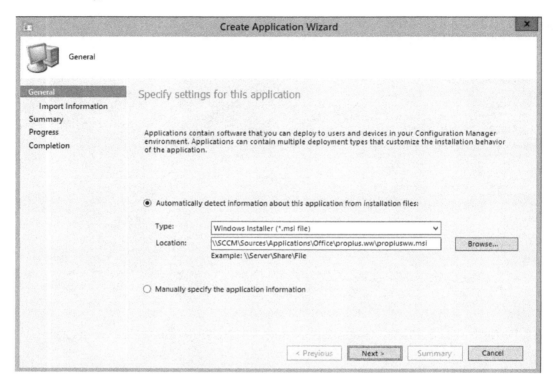

Figure 6.5 – Configuring application settings

10. On the **View imported information** page, click **Next**.

11. On the **Specify information about this application** page, edit the information as necessary. Select **Install for system** under **Install behavior** and click **Next**:

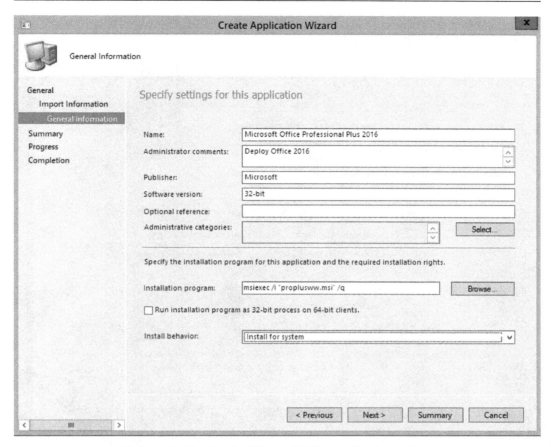

Figure 6.6 – Configuring Microsoft Office application settings

12. Click **Close** after the wizard completes.

13. Right-click the Office 2016 application and select **Properties**.

14. Select the **Deployment Types** tab, select the MSI file, and click **Edit**.

15. On the **Content** tab, set the content location to the folder root (removing `ProPlus.ww`) and click **Apply**:

Figure 6.7 – Configuring Microsoft Office application settings

16. On the **Programs** tab, update the installation program value to `setup.exe`. Then, click **OK**.

17. Right-click on the Office 2016 application, select **Distribute Content**, and select a distribution point that you wish to make the content available to.

18. Deploy the Office 2016 application to the desired collection.

After following these steps, the Office 2016 Professional suite should be installed on the desired computers.

Deploying Microsoft 365 Apps

Whereas older versions of the Microsoft Office suite were deployed as Windows Installer packages, newer versions of Office Professional (starting with the 2019 version) and all versions of Microsoft 365 Apps are packaged with C2R technology.

> **Product Detail**
>
> Visio and Project are *not* included with Microsoft 365 Apps. These products are available separately for purchase.

C2R installations are primarily designed to use the Microsoft **Content Delivery Network** (**CDN**) to stream the installation media to endpoints. C2R deployments can also be configured to cache content on a local network share to minimize the internet bandwidth for clients.

> **The Microsoft 365 Content Delivery Network**
>
> Microsoft uses a distributed CDN to deliver content and updates for Microsoft 365 Apps. Individual clients typically need access to the CDN to install the Microsoft 365 Apps software, obtain updates, and download shared files (such as icons and images) for the Office 365 service. Depending on your organization's requirements, you can configure local servers to host the Microsoft 365 Apps content updates.

Part of deploying Microsoft 365 Apps is determining which update cadence (referred to as a *channel*) you will be deploying to users, as you'll see in the next section.

Servicing and update channels

Like Windows 10, Microsoft 365 Apps uses **update channels**. Update channels are used to determine how software updates are scheduled for endpoints. There are three update channels:

- **Current Channel**: Users in the Current Channel will receive updates for the newest Office features on a monthly cadence. Updates may include performance improvements and security updates. Microsoft recommends configuring a small percentage of your users as a Current Channel as a way to test upcoming features for your organization. Builds in the Current Channel release are supported until the next Current Channel release is available. This channel is not recommended for business users who have a heavy reliance on macros, embedded application integrations, or third-party app integrations as part of their daily role.

- **Monthly Enterprise Channel**: If you have users that are looking for the newest features and are willing to provide feedback on behalf of the organization to Microsoft regarding new features, you can select this channel. It's not intended for broad distribution. Monthly Enterprise Channel builds are released on the second Tuesday of the month and are supported for 2 months.

- **Semi-Annual Enterprise Channel**: The Semi-Annual Channel is the default channel for Microsoft 365 updates. Users in this channel will receive feature updates twice a year – one in January and another in July. These updates will include new feature updates that have previously been available to those in the Monthly Enterprise Channel. While security updates are part of this update as well, critical security updates are deployed during the normal security update release cycle, once a month. Microsoft recommends configuring most of your users for this channel, including users that rely heavily on line-of-business applications, plugins, or custom and complex macros. Support for semi-annual releases lasts 14 months, starting from the initial release.

Once you have selected an update and servicing cadence for Microsoft 365 Apps, you'll need to decide on how to deploy the software to endpoints.

Deployment methods

As we mentioned earlier, Microsoft 365 Apps uses C2R packaging. There are four ways to deploy Microsoft 365 Apps. Let's go over each method here (in order of complexity):

- **Self-install from the cloud**: This is the simplest option – allowing end users to self-configure Microsoft 365 Apps on their workstations. They can click a download link directly in the Office 365 portal to initiate the installation process.

- **Deploy from the cloud with the ODT**: Administrators can use Microsoft's ODT to deploy Office from the Office CDN. In this scenario, an administrator can connect the client devices to the Office CDN using the ODT for distributing media. The ODT will help IT administrators determine Microsoft 365 App configurations such as language, update channel, and products (exclude Word or include Visio, for example). This can be a good option for mobile devices that are not connected to a corporate network very often or for remote workers.

- **Deploy from a local source with the ODT**: With the local source option, administrators can use their infrastructure to create a local source repository to store the latest Office updates and services. In this local source infrastructure, administrators maintain current updates for each of the channels. The ODT is then used to control which configurations are delivered to endpoints.

- **Deploy from a local source with Configuration Manager**: Finally, if organizations have a current version of SCCM, they can use it to deploy and update Microsoft 365 Apps. Since the Configuration Manager already has a dedicated service for Microsoft 365 Apps (Office 365 Client Management), the ODT is not required.

Now that you understand some of the deployment options, let's look at some configuration examples.

Self-installing from the cloud

The cloud is the default mechanism for deployment and updates. To configure a cloud deployment, users only need to click the **Install Office** button on the portal. Users must have administrative rights on their devices. For self-installations, follow these steps:

1. Navigate to the Microsoft 365 portal and sign in (`https://portal.office.com`).

2. Select the **Install Office** dropdown and select **Office 365 apps**:

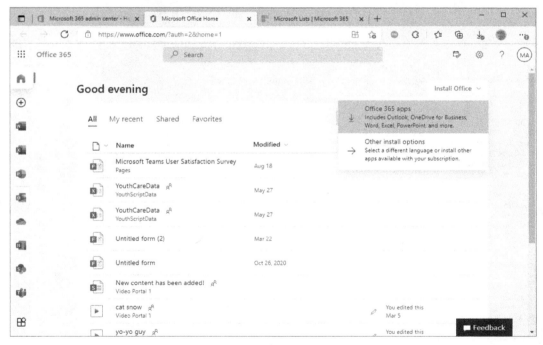

Figure 6.8 – Selecting apps to install

3. Follow the prompts to install the software.

By default, the setup will install the 64-bit version of Microsoft 365 Apps (if you have a 64-bit system). You can also select the **Other install options** link and select other download options, such as the 32-bit version of the Microsoft 365 Apps suite. You may need to do this if you already have existing 32-bit Office applications installed or need to use add-ins or plugins that only support 32-bit deployments.

Deploying from the cloud with the ODT

In this scenario, you'll be creating a configuration file that will be executed on user desktops. This configuration file will instruct the installer to configure specific applications, as well as use the Office CDN to obtain media. To create the configuration, you'll need to use the ODT, which you can obtain from the Microsoft Download Center: `https://go.microsoft.com/fwlink/p/?LinkID=626065`. Follow these steps to get started:

1. Create a network share, such as `\\server\share\Office365ProPlus`, that all users will have to be able to access.

2. Download the ODT and double-click to extract the files to the previously created network share. Agree to the license terms and click **Continue**:

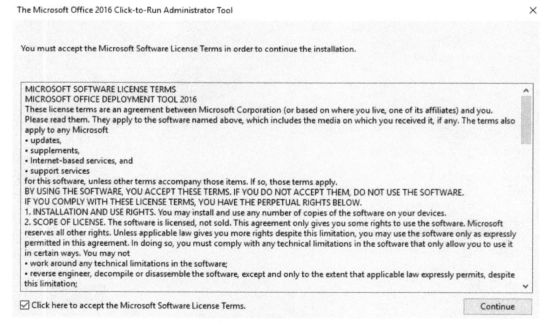

Figure 6.9 – The Microsoft Office 2016 C2R Administrator Tool

3. Open a browser and launch the OCT (`https://config.office.com`). Sign in if necessary.

4. Using the OCT, you can either create a custom configuration or download existing base configurations that you can then reimport and customize. In this example, expand **Customization**, select **Device Configuration**, and select + **Create**:

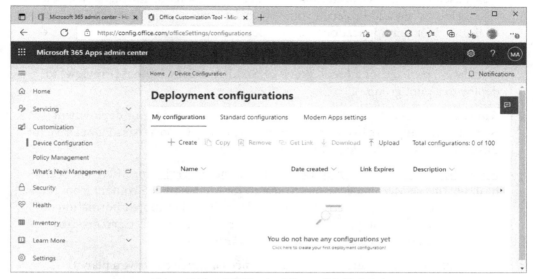

Figure 6.10 – OCT in the Microsoft 365 portal

5. Select the Office Suite and the options you want:

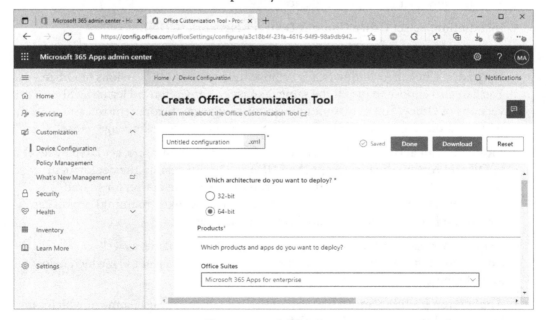

Figure 6.11 – OCT options

The recommended settings are as follows:

- **Products**: Select Microsoft 365 Apps for Enterprise (this tool can also be used for C2R-based volume license editions, as well as Microsoft 365 for Business). You can also include Visio and Project if you plan to deploy those applications. Users must be licensed for any applications that are deployed.

- **Update channel**: Choose **Semi-Annual Enterprise Channel** to configure the installation package for a broad group or **Semi-Annual Channel (Preview)** to deploy to a pilot group.

- **Apps**: You can decide which apps you will enable as part of your deployment. By default, all apps are installed except for the legacy Groove-based OneDrive for Business client and the Skype for Business client.

- **Features**: You can enable or disable the Background service for Microsoft Search in Bing. This service enables users to search for Microsoft 365 content from their browser search bar. By default, this setting is enabled. For more information on Microsoft Search in Bing, see `https://docs.microsoft.com/en-us/deployoffice/microsoft-search-bing`.

- **Language**: Here, you can include all the Office language packs you plan to deploy. Microsoft recommends selecting the **Match operating system** option to automatically install the same languages that are in use by the operating system, as well as any user on the client device.

- **Installation**: Select **Office Content Delivery Network (CDN)**.

- **Updates**: Select **CDN** and set **Automatically check for updates** to **On**.

- **Upgrades**: Choose to automatically remove the previous MSI versions of Office. You can also choose to install the same language as any removed legacy MSI versions of Office. You may want to inventory languages before removal and reinstallation, depending on how you choose to select Office language packs.

- **Licensing and activation**: To silently install Office for your users, set **Display level** to **Off** and **Automatically accept the EULA** to **On**. By default, the deployment is configured for **user-based** activation. You can select the option for shared computer activation if desired (and configured license token roaming) or you can use Group Policy to manage Shared computer activation.

- **General**: You can set a default company or organization name, as well as a description of the particular configuration (such as *Sales team v1*), which helps identify this configuration file.

- **Application preferences**: Define any additional Office settings (some of which can be managed through ADMX templates).

6. Click **Done** when you're finished.

7. Click **Download** to download the XML file to the network location where you'll save the media, such as \\server\share\Office365ProPlus.

8. On a workstation where you wish to deploy Microsoft 365 Apps, launch an elevated Command Prompt and type the following, replacing the network path and filenames with yours: \\server\share\Office365ProPlus\setup.exe / configure\\server\share\Office365ProPlus\FullDeployment.xml.

Once the installation has been completed, verify that it works correctly. If everything has worked as intended, you can then instruct users to run that command or deliver the command line using a method such as Group Policy Computer Startup Scripts. For more information on using this method, go to https://docs.microsoft.com/en-us/DeployOffice/deploy-office-365-proplus-from-the-cloud.

Deploying from a local source with the ODT

In this scenario, you'll be creating a configuration file that will be executed on user desktops. This configuration file will instruct the installer to configure specific applications, as well as to use the local media source where we've saved the installation media. To create the configuration, you'll need to use the ODT, which you can obtain from the Microsoft Download Center at https://go.microsoft.com/fwlink/p/?LinkID=626065.

Let's get started:

1. Create a network share, such as \\server\share\Office365ProPlus, that all users will have access to.

2. Create a network folder for each channel that will be deployed with this method. In this example, we're going to deploy the Semi-Annual Channel, so we'll create a folder called \\server\share\Office365ProPlus\SemiAnnualChannel.

3. Download the ODT and double-click to extract the files to the previously created network share. Agree to the license terms and click **Continue**.

4. Open a browser and launch the OCT (https://config.office.com). Sign in if necessary.

5.   Using the OCT, you can either create a custom configuration or download existing base configurations that you can then reimport and customize. In this example, expand **Customization**, select **Device Configuration**, and select **+ Create**:

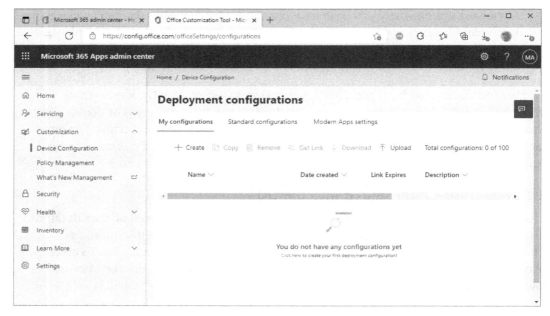

Figure 6.12 – Office customization

6.   Select the Office Suite, and any additional applications and channel options that you want. The recommended settings are as follows:

- **Products**: Select Microsoft 365 Apps (this tool can also be used for C2R-based volume license editions, as well as Office 365 for Business). You can also include Visio and Project if you plan to deploy those applications. Users must be licensed for any applications that are deployed.

- **Update channel**: Choose **Semi-Annual Enterprise Channel** to configure the installation package for a broad group or **Semi-Annual Enterprise Channel (Preview)** to deploy to a pilot group.

- **Language**: Here, you can include all the Office language packs you plan to deploy. Microsoft recommends selecting the **Match operating system** option to automatically install the same languages that are in use by the operating system, as well as any user on the client device.

- **Installation**: Choose the local source, and then enter the path we created in *Step 1*: `\\server\share\Office365ProPlus\SemiAnnualChannel`.

- **Updates**: Select **CDN** and set **Automatically check for updates** to **On**.

- **Upgrades**: Choose to automatically remove the previous MSI versions of Office. You can also choose to install the same language as any removed legacy MSI versions of Office. You may want to inventory languages before removal and reinstallation, depending on how you choose to select Office language packs.

- **Licensing and activation**: To silently install Office for your users, set **Display level** to **Off** and **Automatically accept the EULA** to **On**. By default, the deployment is configured for **user-based** activation. You can select the option for shared computer activation if desired (and configured license token roaming) or you can use Group Policy to manage shared computer activation.

- **General**: You can set a default company or organization name, as well as a description of the particular configuration (such as *Sales team v1*), which helps identify this configuration file.

- **Application preferences**: Define any additional Office settings (some of which can be managed through ADMX templates).

7. Click **Done** when you're finished.

8. Click **Download** to download the XML file to the network location where you'll save the media, such as \\server\share\Office365ProPlus.

9. Launch the Command Prompt and type the following, replacing the network path and filenames with yours: \\server\share\Office365ProPlus\setup.exe /download \\server\share\Office365ProPlus\FullDeployment-LocalSource.xml.

The /download switch that's specified will cause the ODT to download the installation media to the location you previously specified in the OCT (in this example, this is \\server\share\Office365ProPlus\SemiAnnualChannel).

Once the files have been downloaded, you can deploy them to a test workstation using the following command:

```
\\server\share\Office365ProPlus\setup.exe /configure \\server\
share\Office365ProPlus\FullDeployment-LocalSource.xml
```

Once the installation has been completed, verify that it works correctly. If everything has worked as intended, you can instruct your users to run that command or deliver the command line using a method such as Group Policy Computer Startup Scripts.

> **App Deployment Deep Dive**
>
> For more information on using this method, go to `https://docs.microsoft.com/en-us/DeployOffice/deploy-office-365-proplus-from-a-local-source`.

Deploying from a local source with Configuration Manager

With this method, you'll be configuring new application deployments for an existing SCCM installation.

> **Background Knowledge Required**
>
> This section assumes that you have a working knowledge of configuring SCCM settings, collections, and applications. The MS-900 exam doesn't require that you have deep knowledge of SCCM, though it does require some knowledge of its concepts and terminology.

From a best practice perspective, Microsoft makes these recommendations:

- Use the Current Branch of Configuration Manager to deploy Microsoft 365 Apps.

- Enable peer cache on your client devices, which will provide benefits during both initial deployment and updating.

- Deploy Office using the Office 365 Client Management Dashboard and Office 365 Installer wizard.

- Ensure your endpoints have internet access so that they can complete the Microsoft 365 Apps activation process.

- Ensure that the Configuration Manager server can reach `https://config.office.com` on port `443`.

- If Enhanced Security Configuration for Internet Explorer is enabled on the Configuration Manager server, add `https://*.office.com` and `https://*.officeconfig.msocdn.com` to Trusted Sites.

> **Configuration Best Practice**
>
> Before configuring the application, you should identify or configure a collection with at least one device so that you can test the configuration.

To configure Microsoft 365 Apps for deployment, follow these steps:

1. Create a share on the Configuration Manager where you will store the Microsoft 365 Apps setup files, such as `\\server\share\Office365ProPlus`.

2. In the Configuration Manager console, expand **Software Library | Overview** and select **Office 365 Client Management**.

3. Select **Office 365 Installer** and wait for the Office 365 Client Installation wizard to start.

4. On the **Application Settings** page, provide a name and description for the app (such as Microsoft 365 Apps) and enter the target download location for the files that you created in *Step 1*.

5. Click **Next**.

6. On the **Office Settings** page, select **Go to the Office Customization Tool**. As we mentioned previously, ensure that the Configuration Manager server can reach `https://config.office.com`.

7. Configure the settings for this Office 365 installation. Microsoft recommends the following options:

   - **Software**: Select Microsoft 365 Apps. You can also include Visio and Project if you plan to deploy those applications. Users must be licensed for any applications that are deployed.

   - **Update channel**: Choose **Semi-Annual Enterprise Channel** to configure the installation package for a broad group or **Semi-Annual Enterprise Channel (Preview)** to deploy to a pilot group.

   - **Languages**: Select this option to include the language packs you plan to deploy to the system.

   - **Upgrades**: Choose the option to automatically remove all the previous MSI versions of Office.

   - **Licensing and activation**: To silently install Office for your users, set **Display level** to **Off** and **Automatically accept the EULA** to **On**. By default, the deployment is configured for **user-based** activation. You can select the option for shared computer activation if desired (and configured license token roaming) or you can use Group Policy to manage Shared computer activation.

   - **General**: You can set a default company or organization name, as well as a description of the particular configuration (such as *Sales team v1*), which helps identify this configuration file.

- **Application preferences**: Define any additional Office settings (some of which can be managed through ADMX templates).

- **Application settings**: Define any additional Office settings. Ensure you select the default Office formats.

8. Once you have selected the required options, click **Submit**.

9. On the **Deployment** page, click **Yes** to deploy the application. When you're ready, select **Next**.

10. On the **General** page, select the test collection you previously identified or created.

11. Complete the wizard.

Using these steps, SCCM will configure the clients so that they automatically update from the Office CDN. You can go through an additional process to enable the Configuration Manager so that it manages the update cycle for Microsoft 365 Apps applications as well.

> **Managing Updates with Configuration Manager**
>
> For more information on managing updates with Configuration Manager, go to `https://docs.microsoft.com/en-us/DeployOffice/ manage-office-365-proplus-updates-with- configuration-manager`.

By now, you should have a good idea about the deployment differences between Microsoft 365 Apps for enterprise and Office 2016. There are many more methods that you can use to deploy and manage Microsoft 365 Apps, which is especially advantageous for organizations with workforces that have varied network configurations or have remote workers that don't often connect to corporate resources.

Summary

In this chapter, we learned about the differences between Microsoft 365 Apps for enterprise (formerly Office 365 ProPlus) and the legacy Office 2016 MSI-based platform. One of the core differences between them is the product packaging and architecture, with the legacy Office 2016 editions being available as MSI-based installers and both the Office 2019+ editions, as well as the Microsoft 365 Apps editions, being only available as C2R installations.

We covered the four different installation options for Microsoft 365 Apps, including self-service and IT-driven deployments. You also learned about the update servicing methodology, along with the channels and differences between traditional Windows Installer-based installations and the new C2R technology.

By completing this chapter, you should be able to explain the benefits and advantages a Microsoft 365 Apps subscription has over the traditional perpetual license of Microsoft Office.

In the next chapter, we'll discuss the collaboration and mobility options that are available with Microsoft 365, including how the Microsoft 365 options enable remote and mobile working scenarios for modern organizations.

Questions

Answer the following questions to test your knowledge of this chapter. You can find the answers in *Chapter 18, Assessments*:

1. You are the administrator of your organization. You need to deploy a Microsoft 365 Apps configuration that allows users to get updates twice a year. Which option should you choose?

    A.   Current Channel (targeted)

    B.   Monthly Enterprise Channel

    C.   Semi-Annual Enterprise Channel

    D.   Semi-Annual Enterprise Channel (Preview)

2. You have several users who are part of the Office Business Insiders program. They need to be configured to receive the latest stable Microsoft 365 Apps updates. Which option should you choose?

    A.   Current Channel

    B.   Current Channel (Preview)

    C.   Beta Channel

    D.   Semi-Annual Enterprise Channel

3. You are assisting a user in troubleshooting their Microsoft 365 Apps installation. The user reports that while they can print or view documents, they cannot create a new document or edit an existing one. What are the two most likely causes of this issue?

    A.   The user does not have a subscription to Microsoft 365 Apps.

    B.   The user's document is read-only.

    C.   The user's profile is corrupt.

    D.   The Microsoft 365 Apps activation service has been unable to connect to the internet for 30 days.

4. Which two options best describe Microsoft 365 Apps licensing?

    A. It is a subscription.

    B. It is a perpetual license.

    C. It is per user-based.

    D. It is device-based.

5. Which two options best describe Office 2016 Professional licensing?

    A. It is a subscription.

    B. It is a perpetual license.

    C. It is per user-based.

    D. It is per user or per device-based.

6. Microsoft 365 Apps uses the Windows Installer platform.

    A. True

    B. False

7. Identify the technology platform used for Microsoft 365 Apps.

    A. Windows Installer

    B. MSI

    C. Click-to-Run

    D. Run-Anywhere

8. Identify the tool that's used to configure the options for the Office installation.

    A. Office Deployment Tool

    B. Office Configuration Tool

    C. Office Customization Tool

    D. Office Installation Tool

9. The Microsoft 365 Apps configuration XML file can be configured through which of
    the following?

    A.   `https://configure.office.com`

    B.   `https://config.office.com`

    C.   `https://config.office365.com`

    D.   `https://configure.office365.com`

10. Identify two Microsoft 365 Apps requirements.

    A.   Azure Identity

    B.   Microsoft 365 Apps subscription license

    C.   Office perpetual license

    D.   KMS server

7
Understanding Collaboration and Mobility with Microsoft 365

In *Chapter 3, Core Microsoft 365 Components*, and *Chapter 4, Comparing Core Services in Microsoft 365*, we discussed the core technologies that make up Microsoft 365: Exchange Online, SharePoint Online, Teams, Windows 10, and the Enterprise Mobility + Security suite. *Chapter 6, Deploying Microsoft 365 Apps*, covered the basics of deploying the Microsoft 365 Apps software platform.

In this chapter, we will bring all those technologies together to highlight effective collaboration with Microsoft 365. We will be focusing on enterprise mobility, device management, and application management within an organization. This chapter will be split into two sections: the first will concentrate on effective collaboration with different parts of Microsoft 365, while the second will cover the benefits of enterprise mobility and device and application management.

These two sections will bring all the Microsoft 365 technologies together so that you can be equipped to address and think critically to meet an organization's collaboration, productivity, and security needs. Being able to evaluate and understand the scenarios presented here is critical for effectively using the Microsoft 365 platform as well as completing the MS-900 exam.

In this chapter, we will cover the following topics:

- Discussing effective collaboration with Microsoft 365

- Understanding enterprise mobility and device and application management

Discussing effective collaboration with Microsoft 365

In *Chapter 3*, *Core Microsoft 365 Components*, we discussed the different platforms that can provide collaboration between coworkers:

- **Exchange Online** provides email communication, a calendar, contacts, and tabs.

- **SharePoint Online** provides a single repository of sorts in which members can store, share, and edit files, data, and news.

- **Teams** provides a hub for people to chat and video conference while incorporating SharePoint Online, **OneDrive for Business**, and other apps within a single interface.

These core technologies provide a basis for collaboration and productivity. We've mentioned these foundational services of Microsoft 365 several times.

These apps and services may either work on top of the core Microsoft 365 technologies, such as SharePoint Online or Teams, or complement collaboration by providing different functions. In this section, we will cover the other collaboration products that also come with Microsoft 365 as part of the suite. The MS-900 exam will contain scenarios where you need to identify the correct service to meet an organization's needs.

The following table provides a list of additional Microsoft 365 services and one-line descriptions for each:

Service	Description
Delve	Manage your Microsoft 365 profile and discover and manage personal insights and relevant data based on who you work with and what you work on.
Bookings	Allow customers to schedule meetings and book appointments with people in the organization.
Excel	This is a powerful spreadsheet program that's used to discover and connect to data and model, analyze, and visualize insights.
Lists	Create or manage tasks lists through Teams, SharePoint Online, or the app.
Forms	Build simple surveys, quizzes, and polls to easily share with others and see the results in real time.
Kaizala	This is a phone number-based secure mobile chat app for work.
Microsoft Viva (formerly known as MyAnalytics)	This helps you build better work and productivity habits using analytics and insights from Microsoft 365. MyAnalytics is being rebranded as Microsoft Viva Insights.
OneDrive	Store, access, and share files in one place from multiple devices.
OneNote	This is a digital notebook for capturing and organizing notes across all devices.
Outlook	This provides email and a calendar in one rich and familiar Outlook experience.
Tasks by Planner and To Do (formerly known as Planner)	Easily create and manage simple plans, organize and assign tasks, share files, and get progress updates from other teammates.
Power Apps	Build and publish modules, rich forms, and web apps with various data sources with little to no code.
Power Automate (formerly Microsoft Flow)	Seamlessly integrate apps and services to automate time-consuming and repetitive tasks.
Power BI	Create coherent, interactive, and engaging dashboards from various data sources and easily share insights.

Service	Description
Power Virtual Agents	Build and publish no-code chatbots to address routine questions at scale.
PowerPoint	This is a powerful presentation platform for delivering clear and engaging displays during meetings and proposals.
Stream	This is a secure workplace video platform for managing video content such as recorded training, announcements, or meetings and sharing it within the organization.
Sway	This is a digital storytelling platform for creating and sharing interactive reports, presentations, and personal stories.
To Do (combined now with Planner)	Create task lists to manage, prioritize, and complete.
Whiteboard	This is a freeform canvas that you can use to ideate and collaborate. It is designed for pen, touch, and keyboard.
Word	This is a document platform for word processing, editing, and sharing.
Yammer	This is an enterprise social network platform for connecting with coworkers and classmates, sharing information, and organizing projects.

Table 7.1 – Microsoft 365 services

Each of these services is designed to seamlessly integrate with the Microsoft 365 platform. They can operate individually or be integrated into SharePoint Online, Teams, or both to help with collaboration and productivity.

> **Familiarity with Terminology**
>
> Make sure that you know each app and the collaboration and productivity features it provides to an organization for the exam.

However, there are additional apps and services native to Microsoft 365 that come with the core services and offer more features – services such as **Stream, Tasks by Planner and To Do, Forms, Yammer,** and **Power Platform.** You'll need to know about these different services so that you can address any other collaboration needs within your organization and pass the MS-900 exam.

We'll take a look at some of the apps in a little more detail next.

Task by Planner and To Do

Task by Planner and To Do (formerly known as Planner) can be used to create simple projects or plans and allows for participants to assign and manage tasks. Planner can be integrated into Teams, as shown in the following screenshot:

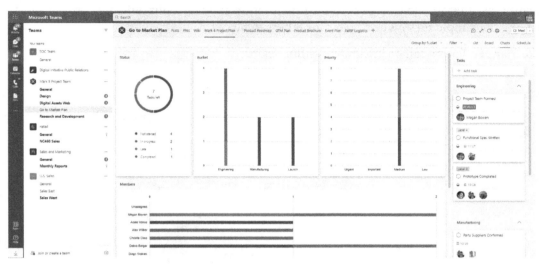

Figure 7.1 – Planner in Teams

Planner can also be accessed directly through a browser, as shown in the following screenshot:

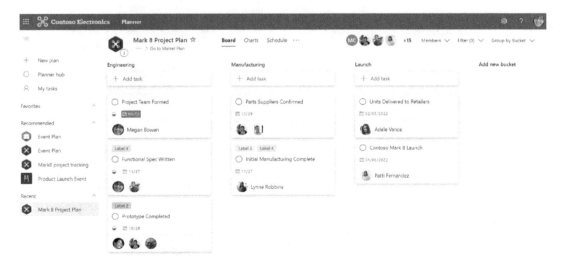

Figure 7.2 – Tasks by Planner on the web

Planner can be incorporated into a Team to start a list of tasks, due dates, and assignments. The app provides different views to help you organize tasks and plans.

Forms

Forms is another way to engage both the organization and the community by creating and sending out simple surveys and forms for others to fill out.

Like Planner, Forms can be integrated within Teams:

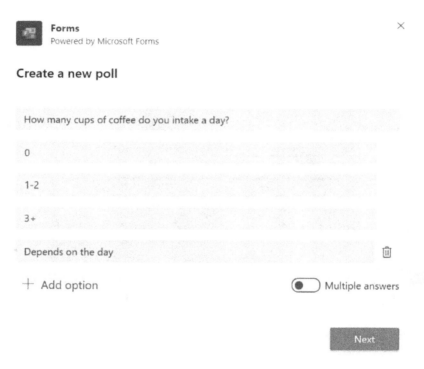

Figure 7.3 – Creating a form

Forms can be used directly inside the Teams client. Forms also has a web interface, as shown in the following screenshot:

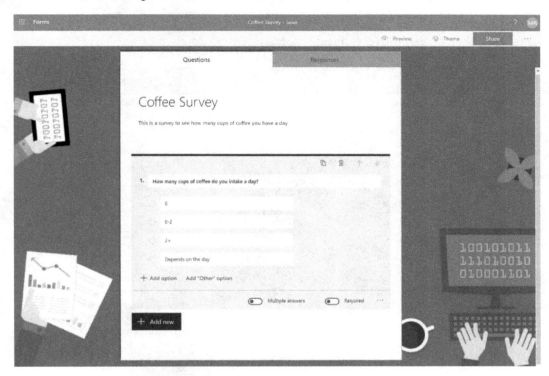

Figure 7.4 – Forms in web view

You can create a form and then send or share it with others. As responses start coming in, you can track and export them to Excel for further analysis. You can also view them without having to leave the Teams interface.

Stream

Microsoft Stream is an enterprise video hosting platform. It can be used to host and share videos, including live events and training content.

Stream, like other Microsoft 365 applications, has a powerful web interface:

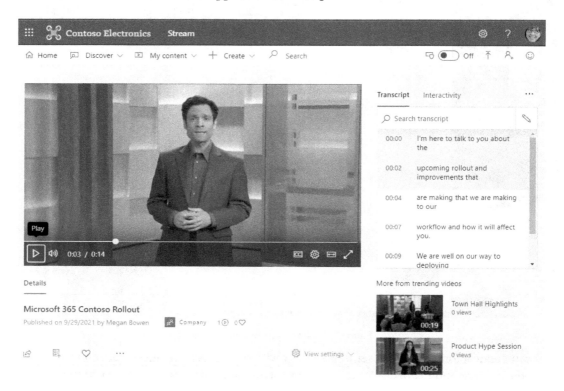

Figure 7.5 – Stream in web view

It can also be embedded inside other collaborative tools such as SharePoint Online, as shown here:

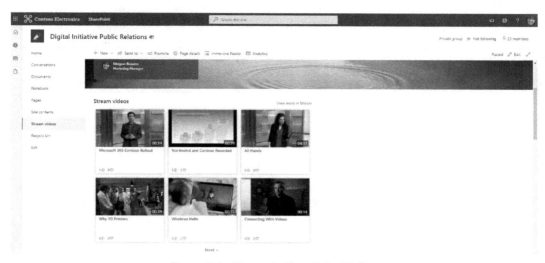

Figure 7.6 – Stream in SharePoint Online

Stream videos and channels can also be added to Microsoft Teams channels.

> **Upcoming Changes to Stream**
>
> Microsoft announced that Stream will be transitioned to a SharePoint-based technology starting sometime in 2021. The current version of Stream will be renamed **Stream (Classic)**, while the new version will be named **Stream (On SharePoint)**.

Yammer

Yammer is a social networking platform that's integrated into Microsoft 365. Yammer has a feed-style interface and is organized by creating groups. Yammer can be used to post announcements, host live events, take polls, follow conversations, and participate in chats. It supports images, file attachments, GIFs, and @ mentions, like other popular social networking platforms.

Yammer can be used to replace the SharePoint Online newsfeed or can be configured as a part of the web interface on a modern SharePoint page, as shown in the following screenshot:

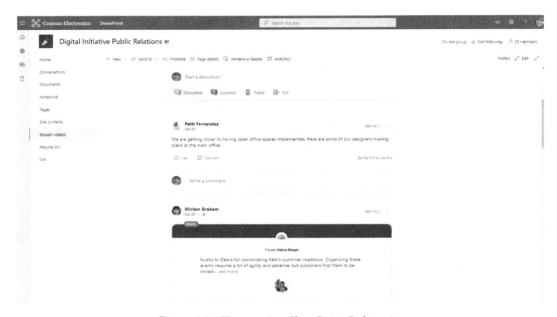

Figure 7.7 – Yammer in a SharePoint Online site

As you can see, these applications have a lot of integrations with other components in Microsoft 365. This application integration allows you to move between applications and draw the user's attention to certain pieces of content, regardless of which user interface experience they're using. For example, you can mention or tag a user in Teams and they'll get an activity notification in Teams, as well as one in Outlook. If you mention or tag a user in Yammer, they'll get notifications in Yammer and Outlook. You can use Teams to bring together Stream, video channels, or Yammer group content, making users aware of updates in a single user interface instead of relying on a user being logged into the site or application you're commenting on.

Power Platform

Microsoft's Power Platform is made up of four powerful technologies: Power BI, Power Apps, Power Automate, and Power Virtual Agents. All these technologies, along with seamless integration with other third-party apps and Microsoft's Microsoft 365 Apps, Dynamics 365, and Azure, can create some powerful end-to-end business solutions.

All Power Platform apps are available in the Teams app store, and you can pin them to the left handrail to access them quickly. The following screenshot depicts Power Virtual Agents in Microsoft Teams:

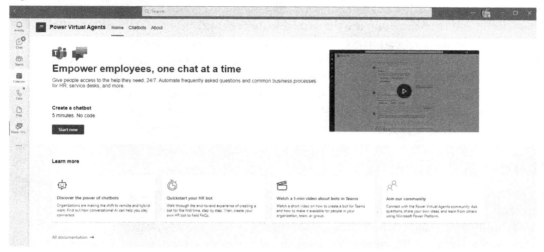

Figure 7.8 – Power Virtual Agents in Teams

Power Virtual Agents can be pinned on the left handrail. This is the landing page for Power Virtual Agents. From Teams, you can click **Start now** to begin building a chatbot.

Another avenue is to access it in the web view, as shown in the following screenshot:

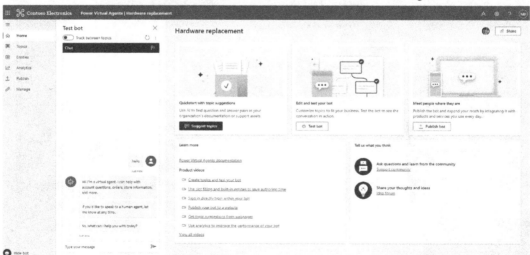

Figure 7.9 – Power Virtual Agents on the web

You can build a chatbot through a browser as well.

Let's look at an example of using the Power Platform to streamline a process is. Let's say your IT team wants to modernize hardware device requests. You can create a power virtual agent that will handle one of the most frequently asked questions, *"where do I request a new device?"*. The bot can answer by pointing the end user to a Power App, in which the end user can compare the available devices and choose the hardware that best fits their needs. That can trigger Power Automate to start the replacement process, maybe with a third-party app such as Salesforce, and alert the end user's manager of a laptop replacement request for awareness. At the end of the month, the IT team can access Power BI to understand device-related trends. For example, which device model has been requested the most in the past 3 months? This can help the business make smarter decisions on which model they need to order more or less of.

Third-party apps

Non-Microsoft apps can also be integrated into your ecosystem. Azure, Dynamics 365, and Microsoft 365 Apps can all integrate with third-party apps very seamlessly. For example, you can add an external application such as Salesforce or ServiceNow to your Teams environment and make it available for users in your organization that rely on it daily.

For example, you might have an IT team that manages support tickets with ServiceNow. You can add **Now Virtual Agent**, ServiceNow's bot, to your Teams view:

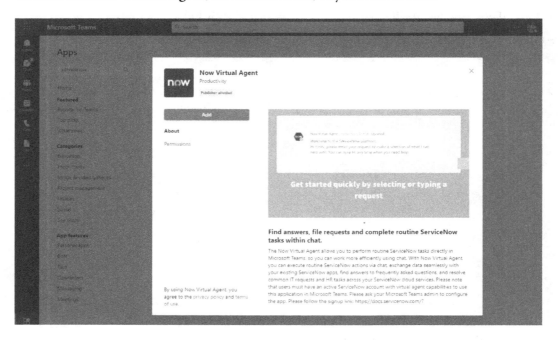

Figure 7.10 – ServiceNow in Teams

This way, you can remain in Teams while answering all the tickets from ServiceNow using **Now Virtual Agent** to help boost productivity and collaboration.

In the next section, we will cover how the enterprise mobility concepts surrounding device and application management help secure these services.

Understanding enterprise mobility and device and application management

Smartphones are essentially pocket-sized portable personal computers. Workers use their phones to check their emails, join meetings, make calls, view and share documents, and more. More than ever, workers need flexible work hours and the ability to work remotely. Workers in the field can have more flexible and powerful options at their disposal.

Organizations need to find a way to balance performing such activities and enabling productivity without increasing risks such as accidental data leakage. Additionally, work responsibilities might require users to be able to access their work data or applications from a remote location using potentially insecure or non-managed devices. Administrators need to manage the assets of the organization and allow collaboration and productivity in the most secure way possible.

For some, the immediate response to some of these scenarios might be to block users from accessing data entirely. However, as the workforce changes, other organizations will adapt and find ways to empower their teams to get more done in non-traditional, flexible ways. The organizations that do this will have a competitive advantage over those that don't.

In the next three sections, we'll discuss enterprise mobility features, device management, and application management to help address these needs.

Enterprise Mobility and Security

Enterprise Mobility and Security is a modern mobility management and security platform that helps businesses secure their organizations. Enterprise Mobility and Security commonly refers to the use of mobile devices, such as smartphones and tablets, and computing devices such as Windows and Mac laptops for business purposes. The concept of enterprise mobility and security also frequently encompasses **Bring-Your-Own-Device (BYOD)** scenarios, where the workforce uses personal devices for business purposes securely.

Enterprise Mobility and Security empowers end users to work in new and flexible ways. Mobile devices such as laptops, tablets, and smartphones have access to work data through the browser and/or apps. This section will go into detail about apps for iOS and Android devices.

Microsoft has released mobile versions of its popular collaboration and productivity tools on both the Android and iOS platforms.

The following is a screenshot of the App Store for iPads and iPhones (`https://apps.apple.com/us/developer/microsoft-corporation/id298856275`):

Figure 7.11 – Apple store

A similar experience is available for Android devices through the Google Play Store (`https://play.google.com/store/apps/developer?id=Microsoft+Corporation`), as shown in the following screenshot:

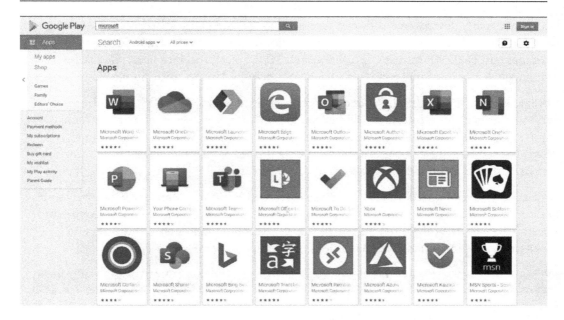

Figure 7.12 – Google Play Store

To use any of these apps, follow these steps:

1. Visit the Apple App Store or Google Play Store on your device.

2. Locate an app and download it.

3. Launch the app on your device.

4. Sign in to the app with your Office 365 username and password.

Now that you've seen the tools that are available for collaboration on mobile platforms, we'll move on to device management.

Device management

Administrators can use **Intune** (part of the Enterprise Mobility and Security suite) to manage a company or personal device – any device that has access to corporate data. We covered Intune earlier in *Chapter 3, Core Microsoft 365 Components*, but in this section, we will deep dive into some scenarios and capabilities for device management.

Users have many devices that they can access, edit, or share company data, files, and other resources with. To protect these, most organizations choose some form of **Mobile Device Management** (**MDM**). Intune is a full-featured MDM platform. Intune can be used to set or manage *device* configurations for macOS, Windows, iOS, and Android devices.

For example, on any of the supported platforms (Windows, macOS, iOS, or Android), administrators can use Intune's MDM capability to configure device restrictions such as requiring a minimum password length or disabling the device camera. Intune can also be used to remotely reset, delete, or wipe all data on lost or stolen devices, prohibiting malicious parties from obtaining access to corporate assets.

Policies can be configured directly from the Microsoft Endpoint Manager portal by going to `https://endpoint.microsoft.com`. In the following example, we've configured a policy that sets the minimum password length to eight alphanumeric characters and wipes the device if an incorrect passcode is entered five times:

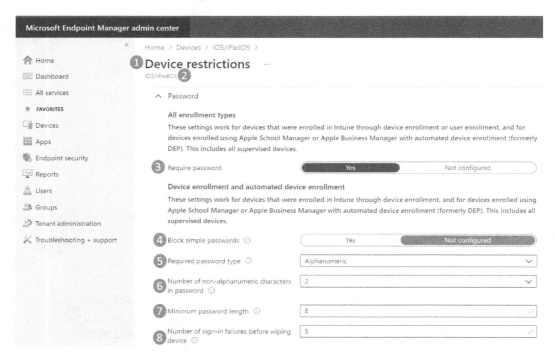

Figure 7.13 – Device configuration

Let's examine the policy profile in a little more detail. Each of the numbered configuration items in the preceding screenshot is referenced in the following list:

1. **Profile type**: Select which type of configuration this profile manages. Profile types include device features, restrictions, and email. For a complete list of profile types, see https://docs.microsoft.com/en-us/intune/configuration/ device-profilesOne.

2. **Platform**: Identify which platform these policies configure. In this case, the policy targets iOS devices. To configure additional platforms, you must create another profile.

3. **Password**: This toggle controls whether a password will be required to unlock the device. In this case, a password is required.

4. **Simple passwords**: This toggle controls whether simple passwords (passcodes such as 1234 or 0000) are blocked.

5. **Required password type**: An alphanumeric password is selected, though other options such as **Numeric only** are available.

6. **Number of non-alphanumeric characters in password**: Two non-alphanumeric characters are required.

7. **Minimum password length**: The minimum length has been set to eight characters, though it can go up to 14.

8. **Number of sign-in failures before wiping device**: The user has five tries before the device is wiped and all their data is erased. This is equivalent to performing a hard reset on the device.

For more information on other device configurations, please see https://docs. microsoft.com/en-us/intune/configuration/device-profiles.

By setting this simple password requirement profile, any user with an enrolled iOS/iPad device accessing corporate data would have to adhere to these rules. This way, access to company data is permitted once these password configurations have been set.

To use device profiles, devices must be **enrolled** in Intune. Device enrollment involves allowing an organization to control settings on the device. Many users – especially those in BYOD scenarios – might be wary of this configuration or see it as an intrusion.

Fortunately, Intune can manage security at an even more granular level, which we will cover in the next section.

Application management

Intune also provides **Mobile Application Management** (**MAM**) capabilities. Like MDM, MAM controls certain aspects of the user experience when connecting to organizational data. While MDM manages the *device* level, MAM manages the *application* level.

As we've discussed throughout this book, Microsoft 365 relies heavily on the concept of identity-driven security. All Office 365 applications can be accessed by signing into them, essentially securing them as containers. Intune can differentiate which data belongs to a profile that's signed in as a managed identity and which data is not (whether it's a managed identity from another tenant or a consumer identity).

This allows administrators to set requirements and configurations so that a user can safely use managed apps on an unmanaged (or managed) mobile device. MAM can not only be used to set security requirements – it can also deploy, publish, monitor, and update apps on a device.

To best illustrate MAM's capabilities, let's look at an example of a user who frequently uses the Teams app to stay up to date with team activities and participate in chats and meetings from their personal, non-managed iOS device. This user utilizes their iOS device to access both organizational data and their data.

The following screenshot depicts access requirements for the Microsoft Teams:

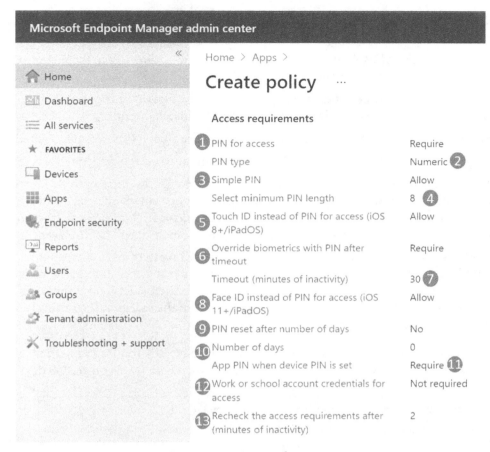

Figure 7.14 – App configuration

Let's walk through the configuration. The policies numbered in the preceding screenshot are explained as follows:

1. **Pin for access**: Requires a PIN for access to the Teams app.

2. **Pin type**: Requires the PIN to be numeric. The other type is a *passcode*, which requires at least one alphabetic character.

3. **Simple PIN**: This allows users to use simple PINs, such as 1234 or 0000.

4. **Select minimum PIN length**: Requires the PIN to be at least eight characters.

5. **Touch ID instead of PIN for access (iOS 8+/ iPadOS)**: Allows Touch ID biometric input in place of a PIN for supported devices.

6. **Override Touch ID with PIN after timeout**: If configured, it requires a PIN after inactivity.

7. **Timeout (minutes of inactivity)**: Specify the period of inactivity that constitutes a timeout (30 minutes, in this case).

8. **Face ID instead of PIN for access (iOS 11+ / iPadOS)**: Allows Face ID biometric input in place of a PIN for supported devices.

9. **PIN reset after number of days**: Forces the PIN to be reset after the specified number of days. Alternatively, select **No** to disable this requirement.

10. **Number of days**: Specifies the number of days before an app PIN reset is required.

11. **App PIN when device PIN is set**: Requires PIN input when the device's PIN is set.

12. **Work or school account credentials for access**: Select the **Require** option to force the user to sign in with their work or school account instead of entering a PIN for access. If you set this option to **Require** and biometric or PIN prompts are turned on, multiple prompts (corporate as well as PIN or biometric) will be displayed.

13. **Recheck the access requirements after (minutes of inactivity)**: Configures the length of inactivity (in minutes) before the app requires the user to re-authenticate or meet the access requirements. This setting is shared across all Intune-managed PIN-enabled applications from the same publisher. In the example, the setting has been configured for *2 minutes*.

This policy requires the end user to input a simple eight-digit PIN (or use biometrics such as Face or Touch ID) every time a user wants to access Microsoft Teams on an iOS device.

Microsoft Mobile Application Management Deep Dive

For more information on overall MAM capabilities, please see `https://docs.microsoft.com/en-us/intune/apps/app-management`. For more information on the iOS-specific settings shown earlier, refer to `https://docs.microsoft.com/en-us/intune/apps/app-protection-policy-settings-ios`.

Intune MAM can publish, update, and monitor mobile apps. MAM can also support custom apps and third-party apps that have incorporated the Intune SDK components, such as Salesforce. MAM can only target and remove a company-related app on a device instead of wiping the whole device, as well as control data movement between managed applications (an example of this might be prohibiting data from a managed identity in a Microsoft Word profile app from being copied to an insecure or unmanaged application, such as iMessage or SMS messages).

As you've seen, you can use both MDM and MAM to ensure users are securely accessing organizational data.

Summary

In this chapter, we identified some of the other collaboration tools that come with the Microsoft 365 platform, such as Forms, Planner, Yammer, and Power Platform. These services can drive additional productivity gains inside an organization.

We also explored what enterprise mobility means in terms of organizational productivity, as well as some scenarios where Microsoft Intune can help secure mobile device experiences. Emphasizing the security features and capabilities will be important as organizations look toward moving more workloads to cloud services.

In the next chapter, we will discuss Microsoft 365 Analytics and how it can give users valuable insights into their daily habits.

Questions

Answer the following questions to test your knowledge of this chapter. You can find the answers in *Chapter 18, Assessments*:

1. Enterprise mobility is _____.

    A.   Only for Windows and Mac computers.

    B.   A business approach that allows users to accomplish their jobs from anywhere.

    C.   Insecure and should be avoided at all costs.

    D.   A legacy mindset does not apply to the Microsoft 365 platform.

2. You need to enable your users to create and manage projects using the Microsoft 365 suite. Which application is best suited to accomplish this task?

    A.   Microsoft Outlook

    B.   SharePoint Online

    C.   Planner

    D.   Stream

3. You are the administrator of your organization. The marketing team needs to create a survey that they can send to external respondents. Which Microsoft 365 application is best suited to accomplish this task?

    A.   Planner

    B.   To Do

    C.   Forms

    D.   Surveys

4. You are hosting a live event. After the live event, users who were unable to attend wanted to view the recording. Which application is best suited to accomplish this task?

    A.   Stream

    B.   Planner

    C.   Forms

    D.   Azure Active Directory

5. MAM requires Intune device enrollment.

    A.   True

    B.   False

6. MDM requires Intune device enrollment.

    A.   True

    B.   False

7. You need to create a profile for every _____ you wish to manage when configuring MDM.

    A.   Platform

    B.   Brand

    C.   Laptop

    D.   Application

8. Microsoft Enterprise Mobility and Security features rely on _____-driven security.

    A.   Application

    B.   Software

    C.   Identity

    D.   Platform

9. Users can connect their Microsoft mobile applications to their organization's process by doing what?

    A.   Installing a certificate on their device.

    B.   Signing into the productivity applications using their Microsoft 365 identity.

    C.   Configuring their Apple ID or Google ID so that it matches their Microsoft 365 identity.

    D.   Configuring Azure Active Directory Identity Protection.

10. You need to enable an internal social networking platform to allow users to communicate informally. Which Microsoft 365 application is best suited to accomplish this?

    A.   Stream

    B.   Forms

    C.   Planner

    D.   Yammer

11. _____ allows you to use biometrics instead of a PIN. Choose two.

    A.   Microsoft **Mobile Device Management (MDM)**

    B.   Azure Device Registration

    C.   Microsoft **Mobile Application Management (MAM)**

    D.   Intune Device Registration

8
Microsoft 365 Analytics

Analytics is an important aspect of every corporate deployment. Among other benefits, it helps organizations understand how services have been deployed and how users are consuming those services. Analytics should be able to reveal complex insights, but they should also be accessible enough to allow organizations to answer important questions right away, such as who is using what, what features or services are the most popular, or which services are not being used at all. Ideally, an analytics solution should also be extensible or accessible using programmatic methods or interfaces such as APIs, which allow data to easily be imported into other applications.

Microsoft 365 Analytics provides this feature set. Besides service usage, these reports can be used to better understand current employee working habits. This will enable report viewers, from IT or **Adoption and Change Management** (**ACM**) teams, to be able to leverage continuously updated company usage data to build on their adoption strategy. This can help organizations promote desired work habits or tools, which are in line with an organization's productivity strategy.

In this chapter, you will learn about the different reports that are available in Microsoft 365 that present this information. These tools and reports are as follows:

- Learning about Activity reports
- Understanding Microsoft 365 Usage Analytics
- Exploring MyAnalytics and Viva Insights
- Examining Workplace Analytics

Learning about Activity reports

Activity reports in Microsoft 365 provide administrators and report viewers with the required data to understand how core components of Microsoft 365 are being used across the organization. To access Activity reports, users should have at least one of the following built-in administrator roles:

- Global admins
- Exchange admins
- SharePoint admins
- Skype for Business admins
- Global reader (with no user details)
- Usage Summary Reports reader (with no user details)
- Reports reader
- Teams Administrator
- Teams Communications Administrator

> **Note**
> More information about the different administrator roles is available at
> `https://docs.microsoft.com/en-us/office365/admin/`
> `add-users/about-admin-roles?view=o365-worldwide.`

Activity reports present data about specific activities being executed by users in services, as well as the device profile that is being used to access them. It provides the following reports:

- Microsoft browser usage
- Email activity
- Mailbox usage
- Office activations
- Active users
- Email apps usage
- Forms activity
- Dynamics 365 Customer Voice activity
- Microsoft 365 groups
- OneDrive for Business user activity
- OneDrive for Business usage
- Microsoft 365 Apps usage
- SharePoint site usage
- SharePoint activity
- Skype for Business Online activity
- Skype for Business Online conference organized activity
- Skype for Business Online conference participant activity
- Skype for Business Online peer-to-peer activity
- Yammer activity
- Yammer device usage
- Yammer groups activity report
- Microsoft Teams user activity
- Microsoft Teams device usage

The **Activity reports** screen displays an overview of some of the popular service-based reports, as shown in the following screenshot:

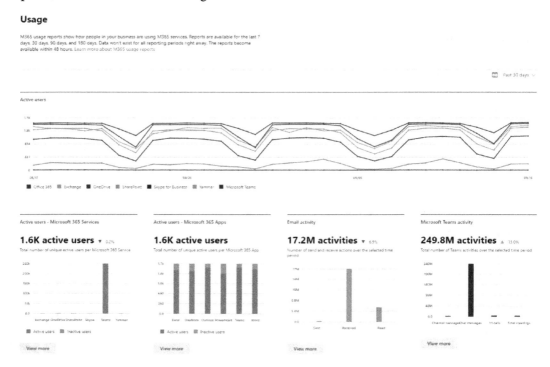

Figure 8.1 – Activity reports

To access these reports, follow these steps:

1. Navigate to the Microsoft 365 admin center (`https://admin.microsoft.com`).

2.   Select **Reports | Usage**:

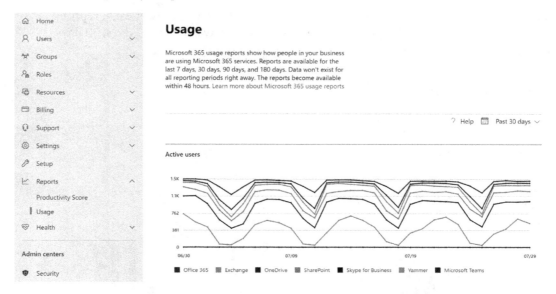

Figure 8.2 – Microsoft 365 Admin center usage report

> **Reports in Depth**
>
> If you hover your mouse over any of the report's charts, you can view a callout
> with a summary of the data being presented for that particular day.

To access detailed information about each of the available reports, you must scroll
through the page. Once you find the report you are interested in reviewing, click on **View
more**. With the desired report open, you can follow the steps in the next section to begin
manipulating and exporting reports data.

Exporting reports

Activity reports are updated automatically, and, within the chart view of each, report viewers can filter historical report data. Report ranges are available for 7 days, 30 days, 90 days, and 180 days, as shown in the following screenshot:

Figure 8.3 – Office 365 usage report with active users view

Below each report, report viewers also have a detailed table view of the numerical data presented in the charts. To download and export a report's data, follow these steps:

1. Log into the Microsoft 365 admin center (`https://admin.microsoft.com`).

2. Select **Reports | Usage**.

3. Click on **View more** on the report that you wish to download the underlying data for:

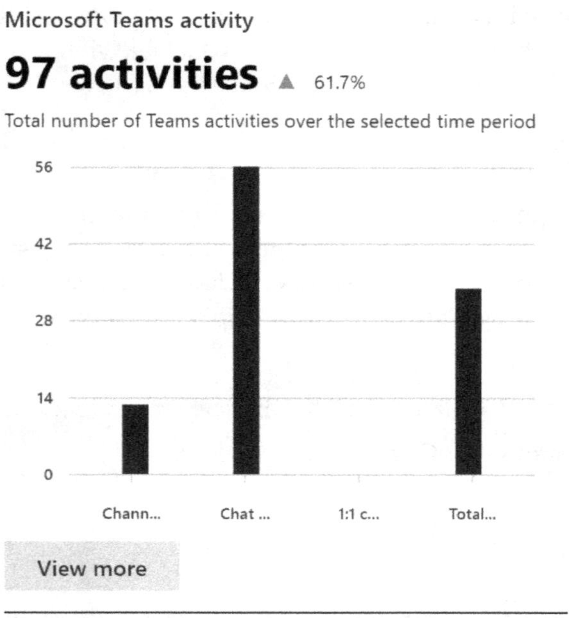
Microsoft Teams activity
97 activities ▲ 61.7%
Total number of Teams activities over the selected time period
56
42
28
14
0
Chann...
Chat ...
1:1 c...
Total...
View more

Figure 8.4 – Selecting View more to drill down into the underlying data

Select the **Export** link on the right-hand side of the page to download a CSV file containing the data presented in the graph:

Licensed Activity
Export
Licensed users
Number of activities by type for licensed users
12
9
6
3
0
06/30
07/09
07/19
07/29
Channel messages
Chat messages
1:1 calls
Total meetings

Figure 8.5 – Exporting the report data

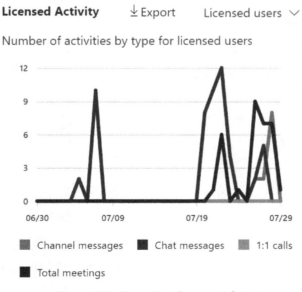

Once you have downloaded the data, you can analyze it with other tools, such as Excel or Power BI. Besides the chart view, each report shows a table view, which details what actions were taken by which users, which adds up to the chart view.

Anonymizing data

Many organizations, due to regulatory obligations, don't want report readers to be able to display actual users or their display names when they're reviewing statistical data about an organization. This data can sometimes be classified as **Personally Identifiable Information** (**PII**), depending on the locality. Administrators can anonymize the report by performing the following steps:

1. Log into the Microsoft 365 admin center (`https://admin.microsoft.com`).

2. Expand **Settings** and select **Org settings**.

3. Select **Reports**:

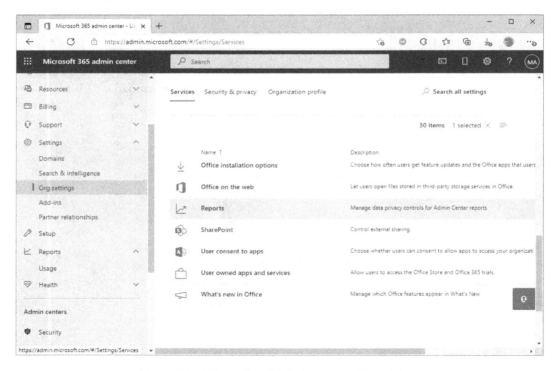

Figure 8.6 – Microsoft 365 Admin center – Org settings

4. Clear the checkbox for **Display concealed user, group, and site names in all reports**:

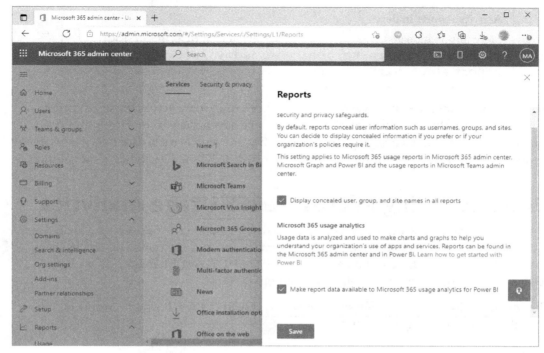

Figure 8.7 – Options to remove identifying information

5.   Click **Save**.

Anonymization will be enabled for Activity reports. When you download any reports where a username or display name is typically shown, it will be replaced with a randomized character string, as shown in the following screenshot:

Username	Is licensed	Last activity date (UTC) ↓	Channel messages	Chat messages	1:1 calls
AB8BF4F3C6A4413D4200F8D	√	Thursday, July 29, 2021	12	14	0
104EE39116FF687CC2409A81§	√	Wednesday, July 28, 2021	0	0	0
A0AC08CFD598A26AFDEBE6I	√	Tuesday, July 27, 2021	0	35	0
5C360CFA0B97DEA63D4743£	√	Saturday, July 24, 2021	0	4	0
AB55F9E1CEA7C27118503013	√	Monday, May 31, 2021	0	0	0
4E306F0EFD2E9DACEF411734	√	Tuesday, May 25, 2021	0	0	0
45F5E1901F9B7D5DF0E54C99	√	Tuesday, May 25, 2021	0	0	0

↓ Export   20 items

Figure 8.8 – Activity reports with anonymized usernames

> **Activity reports in depth**
>
> More information about Activity reports can be found at `https://docs.microsoft.com/en-us/office365/admin/activity-reports/activity-reports?view=o365-worldwide`.

Activity reports are the easiest way to view a service's usage data across the organization as it is available automatically to all the users with the appropriate roles. However, sometimes, organizations need to customize reports or even have a broader view of usage across the organization. For those use cases, Microsoft 365 Usage Analytics is the solution.

Understanding Microsoft 365 Usage Analytics

Some organizations may need a more customized or granular view of usage and analytics data. Microsoft 365 Usage Analytics enables users to view and customize reports by using up to 12 months of data. Report data can be published in Power BI, making it available to be shared with other users across the organization.

The Microsoft 365 Usage Analytics dashboard, as shown in the following screenshot, has several tiles showing usage snapshots:

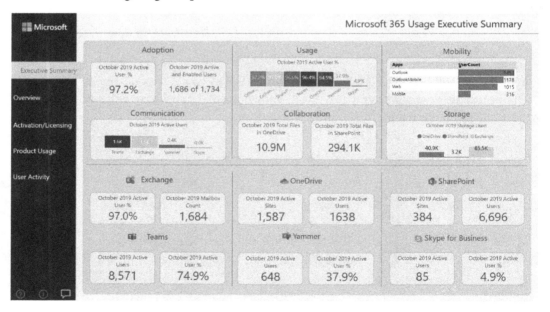

Figure 8.9 – Usage Analytics

Microsoft 365 Usage Analytics is not enabled by default and requires a Power BI Pro license. Usage Analytics can be activated by administrators by performing the following steps:

1. Navigate to the Microsoft 365 admin center (`https://admin.microsoft.com`).

2. Select **Reports | Usage**.

3. Scroll to the bottom of the page and select **Get started** from the **Microsoft 365 usage analytics** card, as shown in the following screenshot:

Microsoft 365 usage analytics

Get the most from your subscription. Analyze and explore usage data in Power BI. Click below to opt in to Microsoft 365 Usage Analytics.

Get started

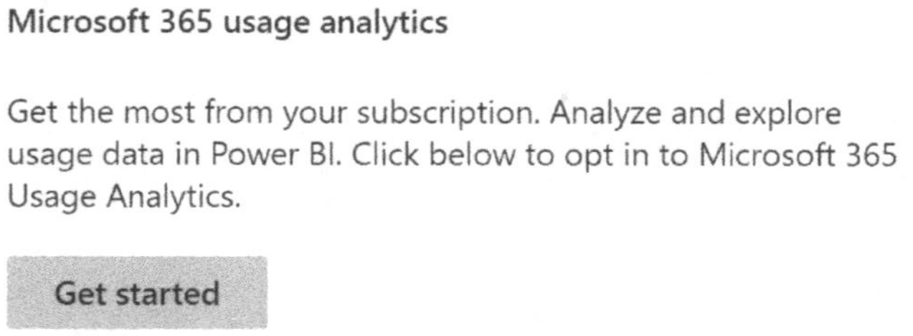

Figure 8.10 – Getting started with Microsoft 365 usage analytics

4. Check the **Make organizational usage data available to Microsoft 365 usage analytics for Power BI** checkbox and click **Save**.

5. Click **Close**.

6. Once the data has been made available to Microsoft 365 Usage Analytics, wait a few moments, take note of the tenant ID, and click on **Go to Power BI**, as shown in the following screenshot:

Microsoft 365 usage analytics

Get the most from your subscription. Analyze and explore usage data in Power BI.

How do I use Microsoft 365 usage analytics?

⊘ Your data is now available. Use tenant ID   ✕
in Power BI to
instantiate Microsoft 365 usage analytics. Please
choose "oAuth2" as your authentication method.

Go to Power BI

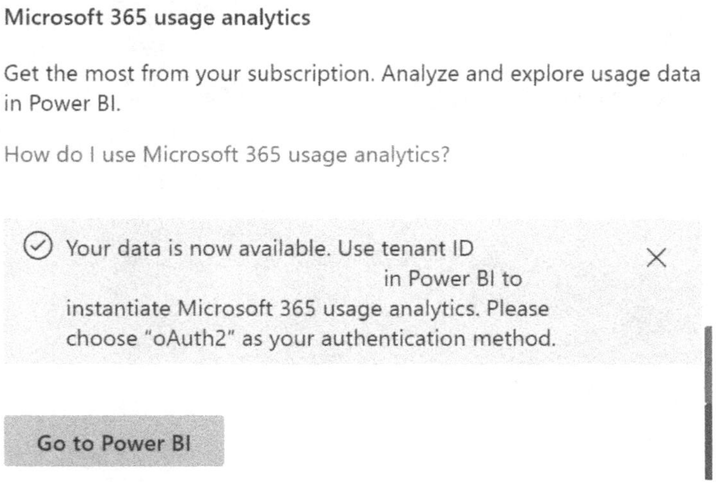

Figure 8.11 – Launching Power BI

7. Select **Get Data** at the bottom-left portion of the page and select **Get** under the **Services** tile to open a dialog.

8. Search for Microsoft 365, click on the **Microsoft 365 Usage Analytics** card, and click **Get It Now**:

Figure 8.12 – Acquiring the Microsoft 365 Usage Analytics app

9. Once the app has been added, launch it and select **Connect your data**.

10. Insert your tenant ID, which you copied previously, and sign in using the **OAuth2** authentication method, as shown in the following screenshot:

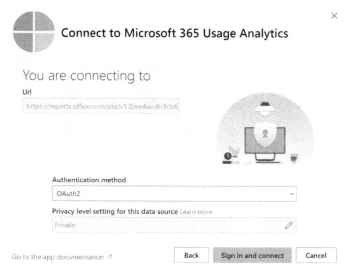

Figure 8.13 – Configuring OAuth2 for Microsoft Usage Analytics

11. The app will be installed, as shown in the following gallery screenshot:

Figure 8.14 – Usage Analytics has been installed

12. Click on the tile to launch the app, shown in the following screenshot:

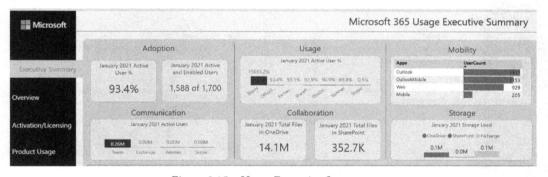

Figure 8.15 – Usage Executive Summary

Microsoft 365 Usage Analytics can also be customized, allowing organizations to integrate existing company information with their service's usage data, which can be accomplished by doing the following:

- Creating reports directly in the browser
- Creating reports from scratch with Power BI Desktop
- Editing the Microsoft 365 Usage Analytics Power BI template file

In addition to the usage reports targeted toward business owners or administrators, which have already been introduced in this chapter, some reports can help individual users understand and shape how they work, which we will cover next.

Exploring MyAnalytics and Viva Insights

Almost every person approaches their work differently. Without dedicating time to taking measurements and understanding how you work, it may not be obvious how you're spending your time. **MyAnalytics** solves this by providing users with a personal view of their working habits, broken into measurable areas, such as the following:

- **Focus**: Time for individual work

- **Wellbeing**: Time disconnected from work

- **Network**: Relationship with people in your network

- **Collaboration**: Time spent in meetings and calls

The following screenshot illustrates an example of a MyAnalytics personal view:

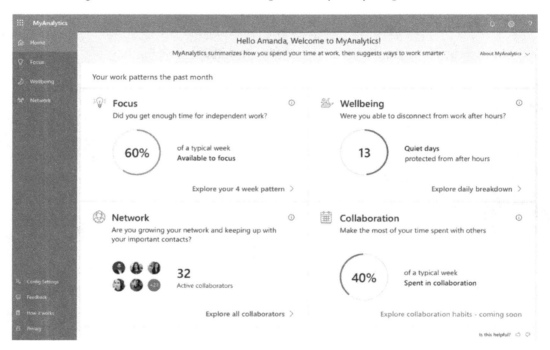

Figure 8.16 – MyAnalytics personal view

In addition to details about how users have spent their time and their connections, MyAnalytics provides suggestions for users to help them improve their collaboration, network, and focus time. The MyAnalytics dashboard can be accessed from the following URL: `https://myanalytics.microsoft.com`. There is also an Outlook add-in, called **Insights**, that you can use to share insights about working habits, as well as messages being sent or received, as shown in the following screenshot:

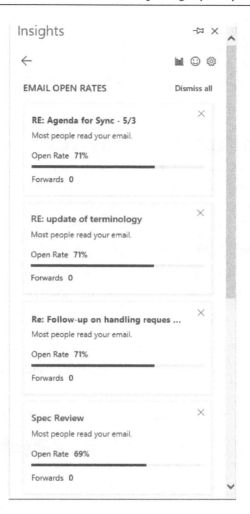

Figure 8.17 – Insights in MyAnalytics

MyAnalytics and Microsoft Viva Insights

More information about MyAnalytics, including its add-ins, is available
at `https://docs.microsoft.com/en-us/Workplace-Analytics/myanalytics/use/mya-elements`.

At the time of writing (August 2021), Microsoft has announced that MyAnalytics is becoming part of Microsoft Viva – more specifically, Viva Insights – which builds on top of existing features, whereas adding new capabilities, which, although not covered in detail in this book, are part of recommended reading at `https://docs.microsoft.com/en-us/insights/viva-teams-app`.

Understanding how and who we can work with is one of the first steps to start improving our working habits. MyAnalytics users can see their data and receive suggestions about how to improve to be more productive across different measures. When it comes to organizational insights, Workplace Analytics is the tool we should leverage. We will cover this next.

Examining Workplace Analytics

Whereas MyAnalytics is the best tool individuals can leverage to obtain insights on their day-to-day actions, Workplace Analytics provides insights at the organization level. With Workplace Analytics, organizations can review their overall company collaboration and time spent culture by exploring stats such as the following:

- **Week in the life**: Weekly collaboration

- **Meetings Overview**: Meetings norms within the organization

- **Management and coaching**: Collaboration between managers and employees

- **Internal networks**: Network connections between organization employees

- **External collaboration**: Organization employees' connections with external users

- **Teams collaboration**: How employees use Teams for communication and collaboration

The following screenshot illustrates an example of the **Week in the life** view:

Figure 8.18 – Workplace Analytics

In addition to details about how people are collaborating, Workplace Analytics helps drive these insights into actions through plans. **Plans** allows organizations to define actions to drive better work habits. To support analysts through the process of identifying opportunities for improvements, Analytics has an **Opportunities** view:

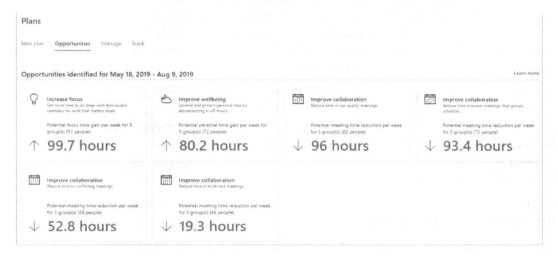

Figure 8.19 – Workplace Analytics – Opportunities

Getting Started with Workplace Analytics

More information about Workplace Analytics, including its plans, is available at https://docs.microsoft.com/en-us/workplace-analytics/overview/get-started.

At the time of writing (August 2021), Microsoft has announced that Workplace Analytics is becoming part of Microsoft Viva – more specifically, Viva Insights – which builds on top of existing features, whereas adding new capabilities, which, although not covered in detail in this book, are part of the recommended reading at https://docs.microsoft.com/en-us/insights/viva-teams-app.

Understanding how organization employees spend their time and who they collaborate with is something leaders are interested in having access to, both to foster an organization's culture as well as understand what can be improved, and where to invest time into existing opportunities.

Summary

Microsoft 365 provides organizations with different data views and analyses that can be used to support their adoption strategy for services. In addition to the reports presented in this chapter, Microsoft 365 includes other admin centers, such as SharePoint, Teams, and Security & Compliance, where information related to the usage of those services can be found, including scores that can help organizations understand how their productivity, compliance, and security practices are configured across the organizations as part of Productivity, Compliance, and Secure Score.

In this chapter, we learned about how report viewers can answer important questions regarding their service usage through Activity reports and how Microsoft 365 Usage Analytics reports allow organizations to explore their own users' interactions. In addition to this, we covered how MyAnalytics enables users to understand how they work to improve their working habits, and how Workplace Analytics provides collaboration and time spent insights across the organization.

As you've seen, Microsoft 365 provides several analytics tools to help organizations realize the most from their investments.

In the next chapter, we will introduce security and compliance concepts with Microsoft 365 and what tools organizations have available to them to increase their security stance.

Questions

Use the following questions to test your knowledge of this chapter. You can find the answers in *Chapter 18, Assessment*:

1. You are a Microsoft 365 administrator for your organization. As part of a business initiative, you have been asked for both aggregate data and detailed dashboards of where your organization stands concerning Microsoft 365 adoption. What two tools would be most helpful in providing this data?

    A. Microsoft 365 Activity reports

    B. Azure audit logs

    C. Security & Compliance Center audit logs

    D. Microsoft 365 Usage Analytics

    E. Power BI

    F. Excel

    G. SharePoint Site Collection Reports

2. You want to enable users to review their work habit analytics. Which service should you direct them to?

   A.   Microsoft 365 Activity reports

   B.   MyAnalytics

   C.   Microsoft 365 Usage Analytics

   D.   Power BI

3. Identify four reporting areas for MyAnalytics.

   A.   Focus

   B.   Security

   C.   Wellbeing

   D.   Network

   E.   Collaboration

   F.   Teamwork

4. Microsoft 365 Usage Analytics can be imported into which two tools or services?

   A.   Power BI

   B.   Power BI Desktop

   C.   Power BI Network

   D.   Power BI Enterprise

5. To connect Microsoft 365 Usage Analytics to Power BI, what data must you provide?

   A.   Activity report ID

   B.   Tenant ID

   C.   Power BI Template ID

   D.   Global Administrator Object ID

6. Microsoft 365 Activity reports are accessed through which interface?

   A.   Security & Compliance Center

   B.   Microsoft 365 Admin Center

   C.   Report Center

   D.   SharePoint Admin Center

7. To reduce exposure for personally identifiable information, administrators can enable what feature for Microsoft 365 Activity reports?

    A.   Randomization

    B.   Anonymization

    C.   Exfiltration

    D.   Obfuscation

8. MyAnalytics is becoming part of which Microsoft 365 feature?

    A.   Viva

    B.   SharePoint

    C.   Power BI

    D.   Kaizala

9. Workplace Analytics can be used to secretly monitor employees working from home.

    A.   True

    B.   False

10. _____ helps organization analysts identify areas of workplace habit improvement.

    A.   MyAnalytics Desktop

    B.   Plans

    C.   Insights

    D.   Opportunities

Section 3: Understanding Security, Compliance, Privacy, and Trust in Microsoft 365

In this section, you'll learn how the Microsoft 365 platform allows organizations to secure their infrastructure and provides roadmaps to track and achieve compliance with international regulations and standards such as GDPR and NIST 800-53.

This section comprises the following chapters:

- *Chapter 9, Understanding Security and Compliance Concepts with Microsoft 365*
- *Chapter 10, Understanding Identity Protection and Management*
- *Chapter 11, Endpoint and Security Management*
- *Chapter 12, Exploring the Service Trust Portal, Compliance Manager, and the Microsoft 365 Security Center*

9
Understanding Security and Compliance Concepts with Microsoft 365

Data security and compliance with regulatory acts are important for nearly every organization. From privacy legislation (such as the **European Union's (EU's) General Data Protection Regulation (GDPR)** or the **United States' (US) Health Insurance Portability and Accountability Act (HIPAA)** to financial regulations (the **Sarbanes-Oxley (SOX) Act)** to industry compliance (**Payment Card Industry Data Security Standard (PCI DSS)**), organizations need to be mindful of how data is stored and transmitted.

With the rise of cybersecurity breaches and attacks, there is an urgent need to understand the proper configurations of available services and features. As we mentioned in *Chapter 7, Understanding Collaboration and Mobility with Microsoft 365*, cloud services have changed the way organizations plan and deploy technology and secure data.

A clear understanding of Microsoft 365's out-of-the-box security and compliance-related features and services is the key to successfully deploying cloud services.

In this chapter, we will cover the key security pillars of protection and introduce Secure Score, a tool that can help companies increase their security posture.

In this chapter, we will explore the following security and compliance concepts:

- Identity
- Documents
- Network
- Devices
- Secure Score

We'll also look at a tool Microsoft provides that can be used to evaluate a tenant's security posture—Secure Score. Let's get started!

Identity

Cloud services pose new security and access challenges. Traditionally, users do the following:

- Only access the organization's resources inside the organization's network perimeter
- Only access the organization's services that are hosted on the organization's hardware

With cloud services, enterprise mobility, **bring-your-own-device** (**BYOD**) objectives, and the consumerization of **information technology** (**IT**), organizations are unable to think of security and access in the traditional way. Users are accessing a variety of services from a multitude of vendors from both company-owned and personal devices. Identity is the new security perimeter for companies since it is the ultimate key to access.

From a cloud service perspective, identity defines who users are, what permissions they have, and what they can do with these permissions. With that, organizations need to plan how to protect users wherever they are.

As we have discussed throughout this book, Microsoft 365 already includes a directory service called **Azure Active Directory** (**AAD**). AAD stores the identity information for your Microsoft 365 tenant. AAD has several features that can be planned and deployed to further improve an organization's security stance, such as the following:

- Users and attributes
- Groups

- Permissions
- Audit logs
- Credential management

Let's look at each in more detail.

Users and attributes

AAD allows organizations to manage their users and attributes. The entire user life cycle, including a user's creation, license assignment, and deletion, can be managed directly from the cloud admin centers, or, if you prefer, you could manage users from PowerShell or Microsoft Graph. Moreover, if an organization already has a directory in place, such as **Active Directory (AD)**, it can also synchronize it with AAD in order to replicate users, attributes, groups, and even password hashes.

> **Note**
>
> Microsoft Graph is a *unified programmability model* that ties in services such as Office 365, Dynamics 365, Azure, AAD, and more. For more information, please go to `https://docs.microsoft.com/en-us/graph/overview`.

A view of the list of users in a tenant, along with their currently assigned licenses from the Microsoft 365 admin center, can be seen in the following screenshot:

Figure 9.1 – Microsoft 365 admin center active users

From this view, administrators can view users and their assigned licenses. If a user does not have a license assigned, the **Licenses** column will show **Unlicensed**. Active users can either be *cloud-only users* or users in your AD that have been synchronized to Microsoft 365.

> **Important Note**
> Different cloud identity models, features, and scenarios will be covered in more detail in the next chapter.

In addition, AAD enables the management of users' attributes, such as **Display Name**, **User Principal Name** (which is how users are identified during the login process), **Job Title**, **Office Location**, **Usage Location**, **Sign-In Status** (**Allowed** or **Blocked**), and **Manager**. These users and attributes are made available across the entire Microsoft 365 platform.

For every user in the organization, administrators can view their current attributes, as shown in the following screenshot:

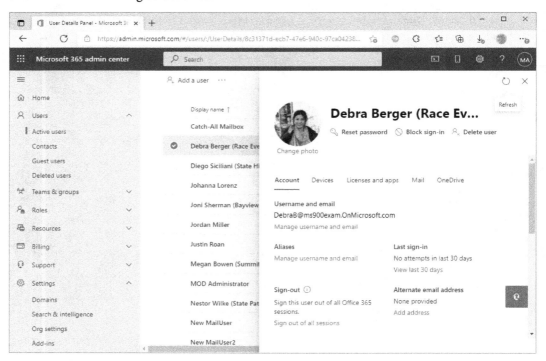

Figure 9.2 – User attribute details

Next, we'll look at the concept of groups.

Groups

Microsoft 365 supports different types of groups that can be used across services for security permissions assignment, email distribution, team collaboration, and more. The different types of groups that are available in Microsoft 365, along with their recommended usage scenarios, are listed here:

- **Distribution list groups**: Used for sending emails to a group of users.

- **Security groups**: Used for granting permissions to SharePoint resources such as site administration.

- **Mail-enabled security groups**: Similar to security groups, but also allows emails to be sent to members, like in a distribution group.

- **Microsoft 365 Groups**: A new security construct that has both security and collaboration features. These groups were previously known as Microsoft 365 Groups and Modern Groups.

> **Important Note**
>
> A comparison list of the group types is available at the following documentation: `https://docs.microsoft.com/en-us/office365/admin/create-groups/compare-groups?view=o365-worldwide`.

Through the admin center as well as PowerShell or Microsoft Graph, administrators can view current groups along with their group types, as shown in the following screenshot:

Figure 9.3 – View of Microsoft 365 admin center groups

In addition, when creating a new group, the administrator can select the group type, as shown in the following screenshot:

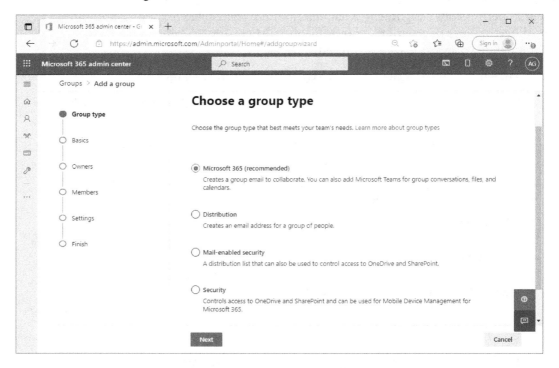

Figure 9.4 – Group creation in the Microsoft 365 admin center

In the preceding screenshot, a Microsoft 365 group has been selected. As we've discussed throughout this book, Microsoft 365 groups are tightly integrated with many Microsoft 365 services, including Teams, Planner, SharePoint, and Yammer.

Depending on the organizational business and security requirements, Microsoft 365 groups can be configured to allow members to invite external users. When a Microsoft 365 group is created, the service automatically assigns and provides access to several resources across the suite, such as the following:

- Shared mailbox for group emails
- SharePoint team site for document and content sharing
- Planner plan for task collaboration
- Teams team as the collaboration hub, if created in Microsoft Teams
- Yammer group for social networking, if created in Yammer
- Power BI workspace

Microsoft 365 groups have a wide variety of features available, such as the following:

- Group naming policies, to help ensure naming standards across groups
- Group expiration, to ensure old or unused groups are retired
- Dynamic membership, which is used to keep the group membership updated automatically
- External users
- Group writeback from AAD back to AD, allowing the group to show up in an on-premises **global address list (GAL)**

Each of these features should be carefully evaluated to make sure the best options are selected for the organization's needs.

Permissions

Permissions allow organizations to provide certain individuals with elevated access so that they can perform specific operations in the service. A common strategy that's shared across different Microsoft 365 admin centers is the concept of **role-based access control (RBAC)**. RBAC will allow, under the minimum level of permissions needed, users (categorized by roles) to execute their tasks and only their tasks.

Microsoft 365 has a granular permissions model that allows organizations to have multiple administrators whose administrative abilities can be scoped to certain groups of tasks. Some of the roles that are available in Microsoft 365 are outlined here:

- **Global admin**: The most permissive role with the rights to access and modify all configurations in all the admin centers. Can also reset the passwords of all users and add and manage domains.
- **Billing admin**: Makes purchases, manages subscriptions and service requests, and monitors the health service.
- **Helpdesk admin**: Can reset passwords for non-admin users, help users sign out, manage service requests, and monitor service health.
- **License admin**: Can assign and remove user licenses and usage location.
- **Reports reader**: Access reports dashboard, Power BI adoption content packs, sign-in reports, and the Microsoft Graph reporting **application programming interface (API)**.

- **User admin**: Reset user passwords, manage users and groups, manage service requests, and monitor service health.

- **Groups admin**: Creates and manages groups, including group naming and expiration policies.

- **Password admin**: Resets passwords for all non-administrative users.

- **Exchange admin**: Full access to the **Exchange Online** (**EXO**) admin center, manages Microsoft 365 groups and service requests, and monitors service health.

- **SharePoint admin**: Full access to the **SharePoint Online** (**SPO**) admin center, manages Microsoft 365 groups and service requests, and monitors service health.

- **Teams administrator**: Full access to the Teams admin center, manages Microsoft 365 groups and service requests, and monitors service health.

- **Teams communication admin**: Assigns telephone numbers, creates and manages voice and meeting policies, and reads call analytics.

- **Teams device admin**: Configures and manages devices used for Microsoft Teams services, such as Teams Rooms, Teams displays, and phones.

> **Important Note**
>
> **Microsoft 365 security roles deep dive**: While it's not important to know all of the roles for the *MS-900* exam, it's important to be familiar with a few core roles (global admin, billing admin, user admin, password admin, license admin) and the overall concepts of role-based administration. You can see a more complete list here: `https://docs.microsoft.com/en-us/ office365/admin/add-users/about-admin-roles`.

To assign a role to a user in the Microsoft 365 admin center, an administrator with proper permissions can edit a user's properties and assign an administrator role under **Manage admin roles**, as shown in the following screenshot:

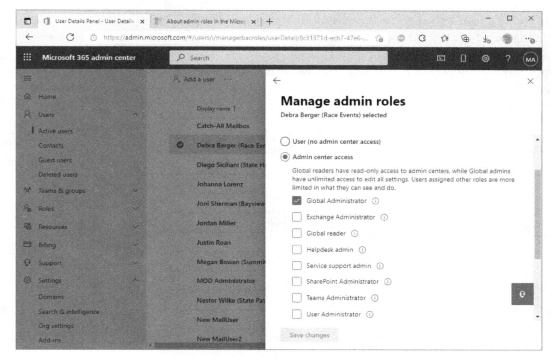

Figure 9.5 – Assigning an admin role

Additionally, more granular roles can be assigned in the AAD **Roles and administrators** blade, which is available in the Azure portal (`https://aad.portal.azure.com`), as shown in the following screenshot:

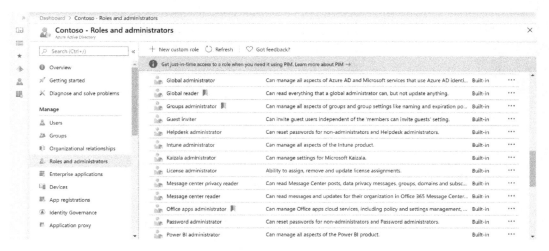

Figure 9.6 – AAD Roles and administrators blade

As part of a least-privilege model, organizations can also use **Privileged Identity Management (PIM)**. PIM allows designated users to be granted elevated permissions for a period of time. PIM can be configured with a series of workflows to ensure proper approval is granted before assigning the role permissions. With this feature, organizations are able to significantly limit the number of fully privileged accounts in their environment, reducing their attack surface.

AAD PIM is configured through the Azure portal (navigate to `https://portal.azure.com` and search for `Privileged Identity`), as shown in the following screenshot:

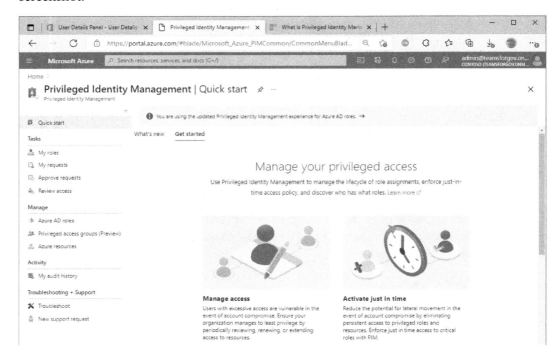

Figure 9.7 – PIM

Organizations should follow best practices when considering their permission, role, and administration strategies. Some recommendations include the following:

- Have no more than four global admins and no less than two.
- Whenever possible, assign the *least permissive* role to administrators.
- Require **multi-factor authentication** (**MFA**) from all admins and end users.

We'll look at more recommendations later in this chapter.

Audit logs

Successful operations and governance strategies rely partially on being able to audit actions taken in the service. Microsoft 365 allows administrators to review activities that are performed either by users or administrators through the audit logs. Audit logs are available in the Microsoft 365 compliance center, which is located at `https://compliance.microsoft.com/auditlogsearch`.

Some audited actions include the following:

- File and page operations
- Sharing and access request activities
- Exchange mailbox activity
- User administration activity
- Role administration activity
- **eDiscovery** tasks
- Microsoft Teams operations
- Exchange admin operations

For a complete list of all currently audited activities, please check out the following documentation: `https://docs.microsoft.com/en-us/office365/securitycompliance/search-the-audit-log-in-security-and-compliance`.

Previously, audit logging was disabled by default. In new organizations, Microsoft has automatically enabled it; however, it can still be disabled manually via an administrator.

You should check to ensure that auditing is turned on. Administrators can enable this by opening the Microsoft 365 compliance center and clicking on **Start recording user and admin activity**, as shown in the following screenshot:

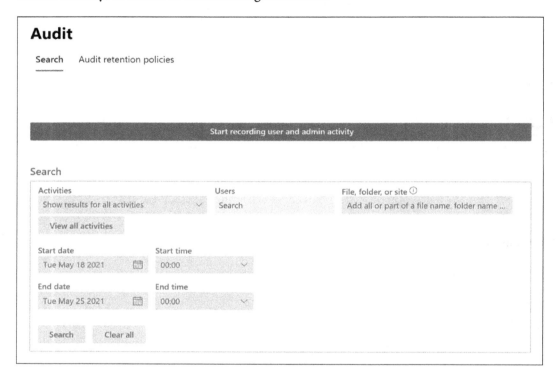

Figure 9.8 – Enabling auditing

When viewing audit logs, administrators can filter audit logs according to the following options:

- **Activities**
- **Start date**
- **End date**
- **Users**
- **File, folder, or site**

Currently, Microsoft 365 audit logs are retained in the service for 90 days for users with a Microsoft 365 **Enterprise 3 (E3)** license, or for 1 year for users with a Microsoft 365 **Enterprise 5 (E5)** license. If an organization wants to retain data for a longer period of time, it will need to plan and deploy a solution to capture that data, such as Azure Sentinel, Log Analytics, or an on-premises **Security Information and Event Management (SIEM)** product. This can be accomplished through PowerShell or with the Office 365 Management Activity API.

To export a list of audit log entries, an administrator can open the audited data and click on **Export results**, as shown in the following screenshot:

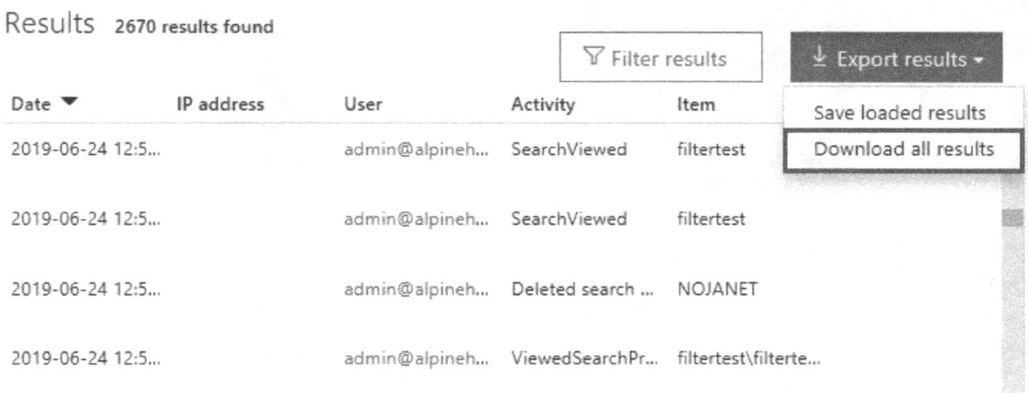

Figure 9.9 – Exporting audit search results

A report will be made available to an administrator in **comma-separated values (CSV)** format.

Next, we'll look at the features of audit retention policies.

Audit retention policies

As mentioned in the previous section, audit logs have a default retention period: users with E3 licenses are enabled for 90-day retention, and users with E5 licenses are enabled for up to 1 year's retention.

With the Microsoft 365 compliance center, you can create retention policies to govern how long audit data is preserved. In addition to the default policy terms, you can purchase and apply licenses for 10 years of additional audit log retention.

Audit retention policies can be scoped to users and record types, as shown in the following screenshot:

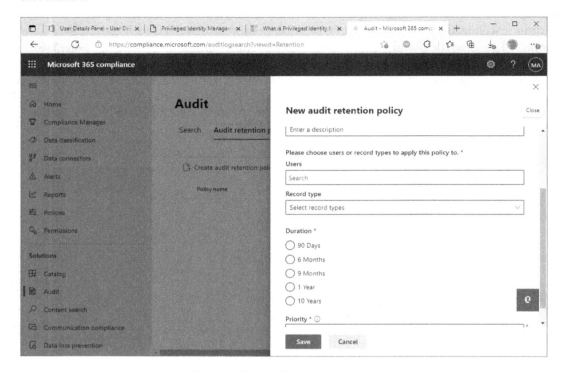

Figure 9.10 – Audit retention policy

A tenant can have up to 50 audit retention policies.

Alerts

Another common scenario is to alert an operations team whenever a specific activity occurs. An example would include any one of the following:

- Notifying a user who shared a document externally
- Blocking unauthorized administrators
- Blocking a potentially compromised account that is performing a suspicious activity

To do that, administrators can leverage **activity alerts**, which allows them to create rules based on conditions comprised of the following:

- Activities to be performed by one or more users
- Users who are under investigation

Whenever a user does anything that trips an alert, an email will be sent to the recipient configured in the alert, notifying them about the flagged activity. From here, the administrator can open the audit log search in the Microsoft 365 compliance center to review and investigate user activities.

The following screenshot shows an example of a notification email:

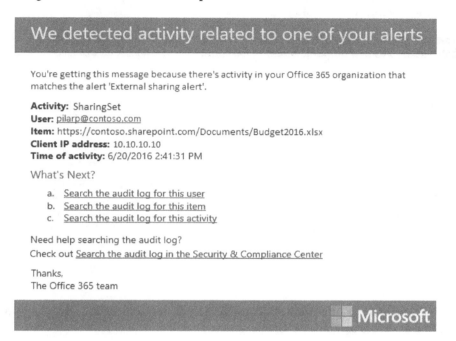

Figure 9.11 – Activity alert email

Administrators can automate activities that will be performed in the service whenever a set of actions occur. To accomplish this, they can leverage **Cloud App Security (CAS)**. CAS allows administrators to create policies to perform actions such as the following:

- Suspending a user

- Requiring a user to sign in again

- Notifying a user

> **Important Note**
> CAS policies, including activity, file, and anomaly detection, are out of the scope of this book. However, you can learn more about CAS here: `https://docs.microsoft.com/en-us/cloud-app-security/what-is-cloud-app-security`.

So, for example, a user triggers a specific activity alert that warrants that user to be suspended. Instead of an administrator performing the suspension manually, CAS can execute a workflow to automatically take action.

Administrators can also review alerts in the CAS portal (`https://portal.cloudappsecurity.com`) that were triggered and take action where appropriate, as shown in the following screenshot:

Figure 9.12 – CAS alerts

There are multiple ways to filter the results, such as by resolution status, category, and severity. Administrators can also export the results.

Credential management

Credentials confirm a user's identity during the sign-in process. Besides a password, AAD supports different types of authentication challenges. AAD already includes a password policy that can be adjusted to fit a company's requirements and can synchronize password requirements from an on-premises AD as well. An organization may also be interested in a self-service password reset for its end users.

Password policy

A password policy can define a password's minimum length, when and if the password expires, and password strength. The password expiration policy, located in the Microsoft 365 admin center under **Settings | Org settings | Security & privacy**, determines the **Days before passwords expire** and **Days before a user is notified about expiration settings,** as shown in the following screenshot:

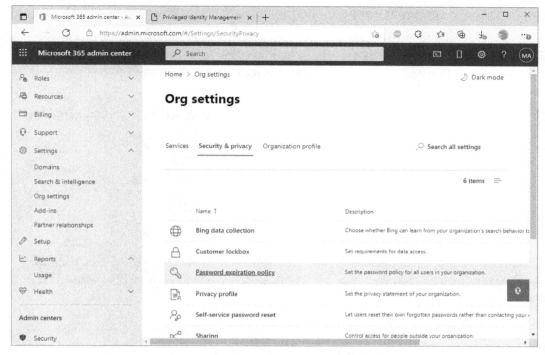

Figure 9.13 – Password expiration policy

The number of days before a password expires can range from 14 to 730 days, and the number of days before a user is notified can range from 1 to 30 days.

When an organization decides to sync user passwords from an on-premises AD to AAD, *existing local password policies* will govern the minimum requirements, such as the following:

- Length
- History
- Expiration time
- Complexity

Setting a simple password policy can help reduce user confusion and helpdesk support tickets within an organization.

Self-service password reset

Another common request from organizations regarding credential management is to allow users to reset their own passwords without needing to open a support ticket. AAD provides a feature called **self-service password reset** that can allow users to confirm their identities and reset their passwords.

The AAD self-service password reset confirmation is validated based on a combination of the following methods:

- Mobile phone
- Office phone
- Security questions
- Email

In addition, if configured, passwords that have been reset in AAD can be written back to a local AD (`https://portal.azure.com` | **Azure Active Directory** | **Password reset**), as shown in the following screenshot:

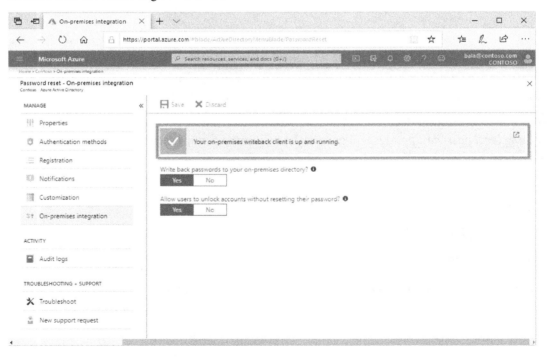

Figure 9.14 – Azure self-service password reset

More information on Azure password management and policies is available at `https://docs.microsoft.com/en-us/office365/admin/misc/password-policy-recommendations`.

Password writeback is recommended to ensure users maintain the same password on-premises that they do in AAD.

Next, we will explore security and compliance concepts for documents within an organization.

Documents

Document authoring, storage, and sharing are the key components of every organization's collaboration strategy. Here, administrators need to implement policies such as the following:

- Where users will be able to store files
- How and where users will be able to access files
- How the files can be shared inside and, if enabled, outside the organization
- How long documents will be retained for
- How auditors can understand who accessed or deleted a document or find documents that contain specific information
- How documents can be classified and protected

This section will explore the following concepts:

- Document storage
- Sharing
- Auditing
- Retention
- eDiscovery
- Classification and protection

Let's explore each of these.

Document storage

Although documents can be accessed from almost all the services of the suite, Microsoft 365 has three primary interfaces, listed next, where users can store, share, and collaborate on files. Both locations are automatically covered under the organization security and compliance requirements:

- **OneDrive for Business (ODFB)**: Personal documents

- **SPO sites**: Team, group, or department documents

- **Teams**: Team, group, or department documents

The underlying storage component for all of the interfaces is SPO. Documents stored in SPO (or any service that leverages SharePoint) are automatically indexed, support custom metadata, have versioning enabled, and can be synchronized between desktop and mobile devices.

The following table depicts the main differences between OneDrive, SPO, and Teams for document storage:

Feature	ODFB	SPO or Teams
Storage space	Per user and varies according to the plan, ranging from 2 **gigabytes** (**GB**) to unlimited storage. An administrator can increase the limit up to 5 **terabytes** (**TB**) of storage, but beyond that would require a service ticket up to 25 TB. Beyond 25 TB would require more storage.	Per tenant. Every user license will add to the tenant pooled storage, and administrators will be able to decide whether sites will have a manually set amount of storage or whether the site storage will be consumed automatically out of the tenant pooled storage.
Ownership	Per user. Each user is accountable for managing what to do with the files in their personal storage.	Per group or user. It is a good practice to assign SharePoint site permissions to a security group or Microsoft 365 group, rather than individual users, but it is up to each user with the appropriate permissions to decide how to manage the storage space.

Teams integration	Yes. Users can access their personal storage inside the Files left-rail icon in Microsoft Teams. In addition, inside individual or group chat conversations, files that have been shared are automatically uploaded to the OneDrive site of the user sharing the file.	Yes. Each team automatically has a SharePoint site, which is where Teams channel files are stored and can be accessed or edited by users.
Sync client	Yes. Users can synchronize and access a local copy of their personal ODFB with the sync client.	Yes. Users can decide which SPO libraries they will choose to synchronize locally, and they can have more than one library synced at the same time. Users can also decide which folders of these libraries will be synced.
Mobile client	Yes (ODFB mobile app)	Yes (ODFB, SharePoint, and Teams mobile apps)
File storage limit (at the time of writing)	250 GB	250 GB
Sharing	Managed by the user, who is the owner of personal storage. Global sharing controls can be configured by administrators to prevent external sharing.	Managed by the SharePoint site, which includes its members, owners, and visitors. If a site is connected to a Microsoft Teams team, user permissions to access files are managed inside Teams itself. In addition, users with appropriate permissions can also choose to share individual files or folders, without sharing the entire site. Global sharing controls can be configured by administrators to prevent external sharing.
Audit logs	Yes. Auditors can review sharing and file activities on OneDrive.	Yes. Auditors can review sharing and file activities on SPO sites.

Table 9.1 – Storage locations, features, and capabilities

We'll explore sharing in the next section.

Sharing

Among the benefits of storing documents in OneDrive, SharePoint, or Teams is the ability to share files without needing to send a copy to each recipient. Efficient file sharing is also important because it allows organizations to manage access to content. Documents sent as email attachments may be outside the management or oversight of security, compliance, or business administrators. When shared inside the framework of ODFB, SharePoint, or Teams, files are kept in place and can be configured so that users cannot send them to another party.

Sharing can be done by almost all clients. Supported clients include the following:

- Mobile app
- Web client
- Desktop sync client
- Outlook client
- Teams client

Outlook sharing is particularly interesting because it allows users to attach files to email messages as "cloud attachments," thus automatically sharing those files out of their OneDrive personal storage. End users can even configure the permissions the recipients can have for these files, as shown in the following screenshot:

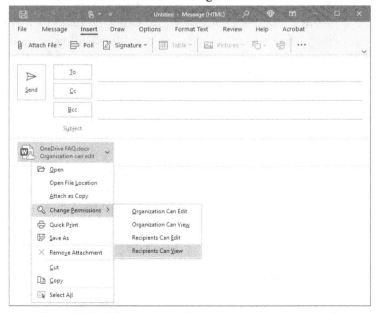

Figure 9.15 – Managing attachment permissions in Outlook

In addition, owners or users with the appropriate permissions can review and even revoke permissions that have been assigned to others at any time through the SharePoint or OneDrive **user interface (UI)** by selecting the file, clicking on **Details**, and selecting **Manage access**. An example of managing permissions is shown in the following screenshot:

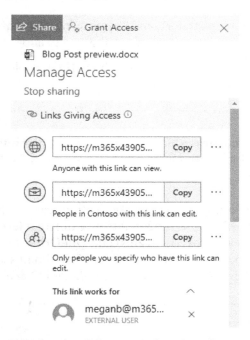

Figure 9.16 – OneDrive permissions management

If you click **Stop sharing**, the link to the document becomes invalid to external users. External users, as we discussed previously, are users that are outside the boundary of the tenant.

Sharing admin controls

Administrators can govern how sharing will be configured for the organization, under the following categories:

- **Anyone**: Users can create links to files that can be shared with people without requiring any type of authentication.

- **New and existing external users**: Users can invite existing or external users that aren't enrolled in their organization directory.

- **Existing external users**: Users can only invite external users who have already accepted an invitation.

- **Only people in your organization**: Users can invite internal users only. This means files can't be shared with external users.

OneDrive, SharePoint site administrators, and Teams owners can invite internal and external users (if the overall tenant settings are configured to allow it).

However, if needed, organizations can leverage a **Guest Inviter** role, granting non-administrators the ability to invite guests.

> **Important Note**
> Organizations can also restrict which domains users can share with. By defining allow or block lists, administrators can allow or prohibit sharing with specific domains.

While many settings can be configured globally, exceptions can still be made for groups of individuals. Sharing controls can be modified to give different levels of permissiveness between **SharePoint** (which also governs Teams) and **OneDrive**, though the OneDrive setting may never be more permissive than the overall SharePoint setting. Sharing controls are managed in the SharePoint admin center under **Policies | Sharing**, as shown in the following screenshot:

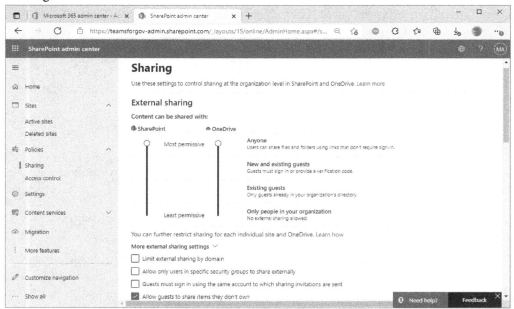

Figure 9.17 – SharePoint and OneDrive sharing controls

Several best practices can be considered to protect an organization while allowing guests to collaborate with it. Among them are the following:

- Defining group and team classifications (such as **Internal Only**, **Confidential**, and so on) and limiting which groups are eligible for guest access

- Defining authentication requirements for guests, such as MFA

- Forcing guests to accept terms of use

- Frequently reviewing guest access to enforce that only allowed users are guests (such as with **access reviews**)

- Defining client access requirements for guests

- Frequently reviewing activities in the audit log search

Security, compliance, and governance conversations should include a proposed strategy on guest access.

More information on configuring guest access for Microsoft Teams can be found here: `https://docs.microsoft.com/en-us/microsoftteams/guest-access`.

Auditing

Auditing determines which actions were performed by which identity, and at what time those actions were performed. As we described earlier, Microsoft 365 allows administrators to audit actions that are performed in the service regarding file sharing and collaboration, syncing, and deletion and access. The main auditing activities for files are listed as follows:

- Accessed file
- Copied file
- Deleted file
- Deleted file from the recycle bin
- Deleted file from the second-stage recycle bin
- Downloaded file
- Moved file
- Uploaded file

In addition, sharing is also part of the audited log activities, and the main sharing audited activities are listed as follows:

- Created access request
- Created a company shareable link
- Created a sharing invitation
- Shared file, folder, or site
- Used a company shareable link
- Withdrew sharing invitation

A view of the audited sharing activities inside the **Microsoft 365 compliance center** (under **Audit**) can be seen in the following screenshot:

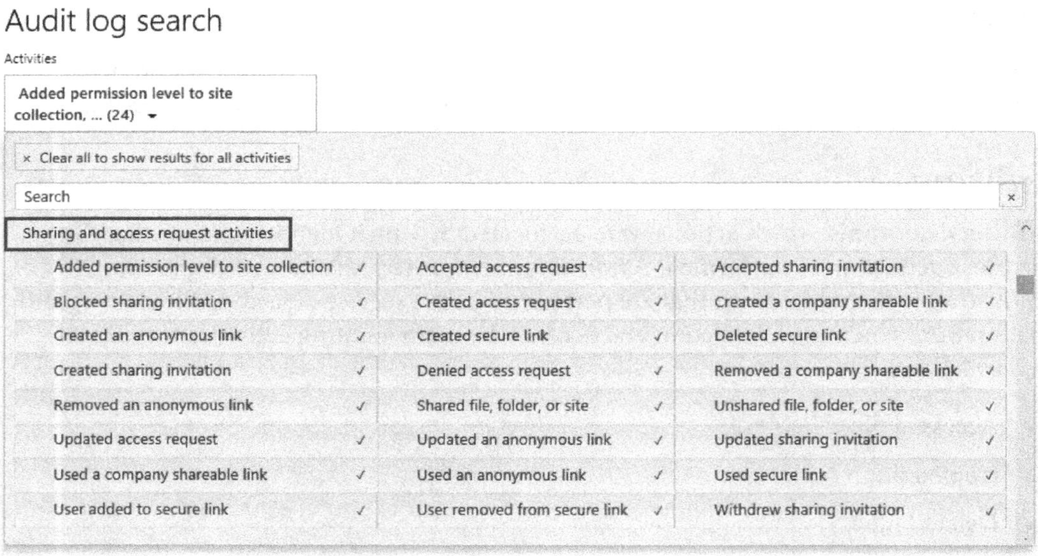

Audit log search

Activities

Added permission level to site collection, ... (24) ▾

× Clear all to show results for all activities

Search   ×

Sharing and access request activities

Added permission level to site collection	✓	Accepted access request	✓	Accepted sharing invitation	✓
Blocked sharing invitation	✓	Created access request	✓	Created a company shareable link	✓
Created an anonymous link	✓	Created secure link	✓	Deleted secure link	✓
Created sharing invitation	✓	Denied access request	✓	Removed a company shareable link	✓
Removed an anonymous link	✓	Shared file, folder, or site	✓	Unshared file, folder, or site	✓
Updated access request	✓	Updated an anonymous link	✓	Updated sharing invitation	✓
Used a company shareable link	✓	Used an anonymous link	✓	Used secure link	✓
User added to secure link	✓	User removed from secure link	✓	Withdrew sharing invitation	✓

Figure 9.18 – Audit activities

As we mentioned earlier, administrators should leverage audit logs, along with activity alerts and CAS policies, to understand which actions are being taken by users and administrators regarding files and sharing inside their organization.

Retention

The document life cycle describes what happens to documents as they are acted upon throughout a system. This includes activities such as renaming, deleting, moving to other sites or folders, and being labeled and retired. **Retention** is the process that preserves copies of that document data as it progresses throughout its life cycle. Retention is an important part of helping organizations comply with regulatory obligations and business requirements.

Microsoft 365 includes a default life cycle policy that preserves versions and can keep deleted documents for up to 93 days. Versioning (enabled by default) keeps copies of incrementally changed documents; deleted documents are retained in the recycle bin. If no further actions are taken, documents can be restored or permanently deleted, within 93 days, across the two-stage recycle bin that's available in OneDrive and SharePoint.

If retention policies have been configured, deleted documents are moved to a secured location called the **Preservation Hold Library**. At the end of the retention period, they are permanently deleted. Retention policies can also control the deletion of documents, ensuring that organizations can comply with requirements to preserve data for—or delete data after—a certain period of time.

An example of how documents move through the various life cycles can be seen in the following diagram, either for data that has been preserved through a retention policy (arrow **1**) or data that goes through the normal two-stage deletion process (arrow **2**):

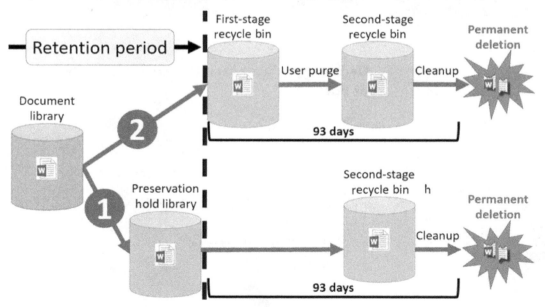

Figure 9.19 – Documents moving through SharePoint storage life cycle

Retention policies can also be configured with a feature called a *preservation lock*, which prevents data being protected by a retention policy from having its retention controls altered to a shorter or less restrictive period of time. This control is typically used for organizations that need to comply with **Security and Exchange Commission (SEC)** *Rule 17a-4*, which stipulates the regulatory standards. Enabling a preservation lock on a retention policy restricts the following actions:

- The retention period of the policy can't be decreased, though it may be increased or extended.

- Users can't be removed from the policy, though they may be added.

- The retention policy cannot be deleted.

Retention policies can be applied to storage locations in order to delete or retain information, based on a set of conditions. These policies allow administrators to select where policies will be applied and specify how content will be managed for each location. Retention policies can be configured to preserve data for a minimum amount of time, and then either take no action or delete it at the end of the retention period.

The following screenshot shows the available delete actions in a retention policy:

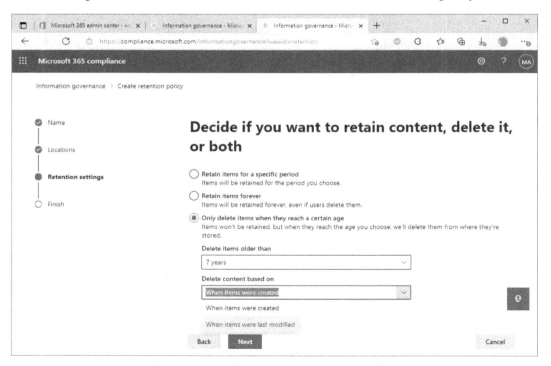

Figure 9.20 – Delete actions in a retention policy

If the policy in *Figure 9.20* is applied to Document A, Document A will be deleted 7 years after it was created, if it hasn't already been deleted. If the content was deleted, it will not be discoverable.

However, if you configure a policy as displayed in the following screenshot, the behavior is different:

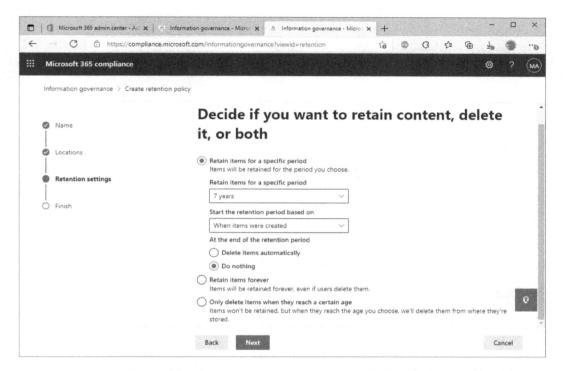

Figure 9.21 – Retention policy to preserve content for 7 years

For this policy, Document A will be retained for 7 years. If a user attempts to delete the document, it will be moved to the Preservation Hold Library and retained for the remainder of the retention policy. At any time between when it was created and when the retention policy allows the document to be purged, the document will be discoverable. After 7 years, it will be deleted.

eDiscovery

By default, every document stored in OneDrive and SharePoint is indexed. Content stored in Teams (messages and files), as well as email content, is also indexed, making it available for search.

eDiscovery searches can be launched inside the **Microsoft 365 compliance center** under the **eDiscovery** node. A search can be configured to locate data based on certain conditions, such as the following:

- Attachment names
- Importance
- Has attachments or not
- Date when the message was sent or received
- Size
- Subject
- Authors
- File types
- Created on
- Created by
- Modified on
- Modified by
- Detected language
- Path
- Size
- Title

Administrators can configure which users will be able to search for content inside their organizations by defining a set of permissions. There are two main permission roles related to eDiscovery, as follows:

- **eDiscovery managers**: Search for content inside their organization and preview or export search results. However, eDiscovery managers can only access and manage cases they have created.

- **eDiscovery administrators**: In addition to being able to perform the same search tasks as eDiscovery managers, eDiscovery administrators can also access and manage any search case that's created in their organization.

The eDiscovery process consists of a set of activities that can be performed, such as the following:

- Creating a case and assigning users to work on the case
- Optionally placing content to be searched on hold so that any changes that are made won't interfere with the search results
- Defining locations to be searched
- Creating one or more queries to find the desired information
- Reviewing result statistics
- Exporting search results for further analysis

> **Important Note**
>
> Microsoft 365 eDiscovery supports **Keyword Query Language** (**KQL**) for creating searches. You can learn more about structuring KQL queries here: `https://docs.microsoft.com/en-us/microsoft-365/compliance/keyword-queries-and-search-conditions`.

All the activities that are performed during an eDiscovery investigation are audited and can be reviewed and exported. eDiscovery activities, as with other auditable activities in Microsoft 365, can also be configured to trigger alerts.

In addition to the core eDiscovery features for search, hold, and export, organizations can also leverage Advanced eDiscovery. Advanced eDiscovery is a technology-assisted review platform, designed to use a combination of **machine learning** (**ML**) and human training to teach the engine what is responsive to a particular query. It's generally recommended for large datasets that need a minimum of 10,000 items to perform many of the advanced functions. Advanced eDiscovery enhances native case and content searches with the following capabilities:

- Advanced data preparation, which removes duplicates, similar documents, and categorizes information according to themes
- Trains data based on relevance to the case so that reviewers can analyze the relevant data and decide on the right amount of data to be reviewed
- Exports relevant case data for further review

Advanced eDiscovery is outside the scope of the *MS-900* exam, but more information on the capabilities of the platform is available at `https://docs.microsoft.com/en-us/microsoft-365/compliance/office-365-advanced-ediscovery`.

Classification and protection

Microsoft 365 allows users and administrators to classify and protect documents stored in OneDrive, SharePoint, or locally, as well as email messages, using the **Azure Information Protection** (**AIP**) service.

Administrators create classification labels and configure the actions available to users of the label—for example, a label can be configured to allow or deny the ability to take screenshots, copy content, or print it. Labels can be used to prevent people from modifying the recipients of a message or forwarding it to others.

Once the labels have been configured and published, users can apply them to protect documents, files, and emails.

Administrators can also audit and control how classification and encryption technologies are used across the organization. Content can be classified using a number of methods, including the following:

- Outlook

- Office applications such as Word or Excel

- EXO transport rules, which modify specific message properties throughout its transport

- Security & Compliance Center **data loss prevention** (**DLP**) rules

- Windows Explorer using the AIP unified labeling client

After classification has been applied, the email message or document will display its tag, and users, if authorized to open the file, will be able to review which actions they are allowed to take on that information, as shown in the following screenshot:

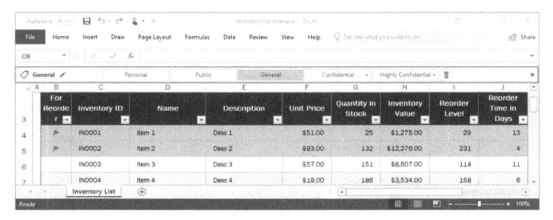

Figure 9.22 – Classification label

AIP is part of both Microsoft 365 E3 and Microsoft 365 E5. In Microsoft 365 E3, users must perform data classification manually. With Microsoft 365 E5, administrators can configure classification so that it happens automatically, such as when an application detects sensitive content such as credit card or social security numbers.

Next, we'll turn our attention to security and compliance concepts for networking.

Network

Microsoft 365 services are generally accessed over the public internet. In this section, we'll discuss how users will access the Microsoft 365 service and how data will flow to, and be stored in, the service.

Administrators need to understand the following concepts when considering Microsoft 365 in terms of networking:

- Connectivity
- Encryption
- Performance

In the upcoming sections, we'll look at these in a detailed manner.

Connectivity

As a cloud service, Microsoft 365 components are not available on the internal network. Network administrators must allow internal users to access the internet endpoints for the Microsoft 365 service, which may mean configuring existing appliances such as firewalls and proxy devices.

Endpoints, which can be **Internet Protocol (IP)** addresses or **Uniform Resource Locators (URLs)**, are classified into three categories, as follows:

- **Optimize**: Required for connectivity to services and represents over 75% of the consumed bandwidth
- **Allow**: Required for connectivity, but not as sensitive to latency as **Optimize** endpoints
- **Default**: Endpoints that can be treated as normal internet traffic

Organizations should plan for network best practices when planning their Microsoft 365 deployment. Among the recommended practices are the following:

- Differentiating Microsoft 365 traffic from normal internet traffic

- Egressing network connections locally so that users will be routed as quickly as possible to the Microsoft network

- Bypassing proxies to reduce the amount of time needed for data to arrive at Office 365 services

Microsoft 365 administrators and network administrators should work together to plan a network connectivity strategy. To help plan effectively, Microsoft provides a web service for obtaining the IP addresses and URLs that are used in the service.

> **Important Note**
> More information about the Office 365 IP Address and URL web service is available in the following documentation: `https://docs.microsoft.com/en-us/microsoft-365/enterprise/microsoft-365-ip-web-service?view=o365-worldwide`.

Microsoft typically recommends bypassing proxy devices for network traffic destined for Microsoft 365.

Encryption

Encryption is a mechanism that's used to protect information from unauthorized access. Microsoft 365 implements several encryption technologies across the platform. Encryption is enforced for data in two core states, outlined as follows:

- **At rest**: Data that is stored in the service. This includes files and documents uploaded to OneDrive, SharePoint, and Teams, as well as email content. Data at rest is protected through the use of BitLocker, **Distributed Key Manager** (**DKM**), and Customer Key for Microsoft 365. Depending on the service, data may also be stored in blob storage, with each chunk being encrypted using the **key store**.

- **In transit**: Refers to data that is being transferred between clients and services, as well as between different endpoints within the service and data centers. Data in transit is protected via **Transport Layer Security** (**TLS**) and **IP Security** (**IPsec**). TLS is typically used to secure application-layer traffic between clients and services, while IPsec is used to secure the underlying physical or logical networking connections.

In addition to the built-in encryption technologies, customers can also apply unique content encryption to files and email messages using the AIP client. Not only does AIP provide data classification services, as we described earlier, but it can also be used to encrypt content at the file or document level.

The following diagram depicts how AIP encryption works:

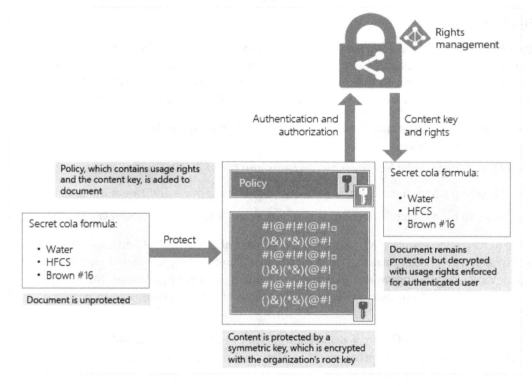

Figure 9.23 – AIP and Azure Rights Management (Azure RMS)

Customers in highly regulated industries may be required to control the encryption keys that are used in the service. To accomplish this, organizations may use the **Customer Key** service, which allows them to manage the key life cycle and can be used to encrypt data in the following services:

- EXO, including Skype for Business Online and Microsoft Teams data stored in user mailboxes
- Files stored in OneDrive and SPO

Setting up the Customer Key service requires additional Azure services, such as Key Vault, as well as further considerations that are out of the scope of this book. You can learn more about Customer Key here: `https://docs.microsoft.com/en-us/microsoft-365/compliance/controlling-your-data-using-customer-key`.

Performance

Since Microsoft 365 is a cloud service, organizations should follow best practices during the network planning phase. Customers should ensure adequate network capacity and redundancy are available so that users have consistent, reliable connectivity to the service. Network performance planning should consider the following, among other things:

- How to make sure that the correct ports, IP addresses, and URLs are allowed for Office 365 services
- How to reduce the latency between users and the Office 365 network
- How to prepare the customer network so that it supports additional internet traffic
- How to plan Office 365 features so that they use a local cache whenever possible

As we described previously, Microsoft provides a list of URLs and IP addresses that are used by its services. Organizations should use this data to configure their networking and edge devices. Depending on the security requirements and configurations, the network should be prepared to update devices, should Microsoft add or remove endpoints and services.

To reduce the amount of latency, organizations should consider Office 365 network best practices, such as bypassing proxies and local network egress (as opposed to backhauled connections to a central office) so that information arrives at the Office 365 network through the shortest path.

To help measure the latency, organizations can use tools such as **PsPing** or **tracetcp** against Office 365 services such as the following:

- `outlook.office365.com`
- `<tenant>.sharepoint.com`
- `portal.microsoftonline.com`

There are also calculators and tools available to help measure latency, such as the Network Onboarding Tool and the Network Assessment Tool, that help organizations understand where improvements need to be made, as shown in the following screenshot:

Figure 9.24 – Network Onboarding Tool

Important Note

You can learn more about the Network Onboarding Tool at `https://techcommunity.microsoft.com/t5/Office-365-Networking/Updated-Office-365-Network-Onboarding-Tool-POC-with-new-network/m-p/711130`.

Also, to prepare the network for additional Office 365 traffic, customers that have currently been deployed with on-premises systems should plan to accommodate the network traffic that's necessary to communicate with Microsoft 365 services. Another planning tool, known as the Network Planner for Microsoft Teams (available in the Teams admin center at `https://admin.teams.microsoft.com`), can be used to estimate how much traffic the Teams workload will contribute to their overall internet bandwidth. The Network Planner for Microsoft Teams tool can be seen in the following screenshot:

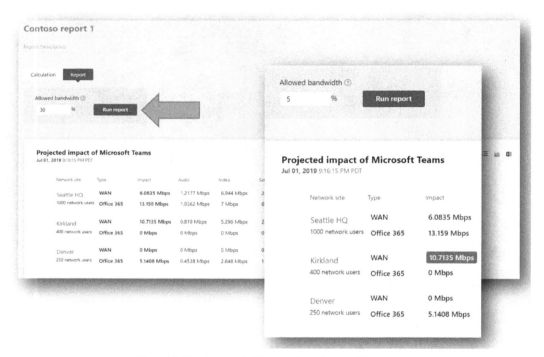

Figure 9.25 – Network Planner for Microsoft Teams

Organizations that are deploying services such as Microsoft Teams for phone systems, audio conferencing, and video or Microsoft Stream for video may also want to consider deploying **Quality of Service** (**QoS**), which allows them to prioritize some types of network traffic over others to provide better real-time communication experiences.

The following diagram shows an example of how an organization might use QoS to shape its traffic:

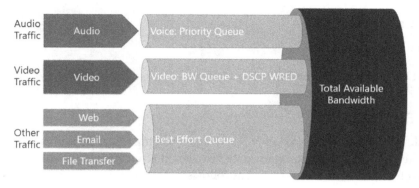

Figure 9.26 – QoS example

In addition to network traffic, companies should understand which features are available in the service clients, which can help reduce the amount of internet traffic that's needed. Some of these features are listed as follows:

- **Outlook cache**: This stores a local copy of the user's email data that can be used offline.

- **OneDrive sync client**: This can keep a local copy of both a user's personal OneDrive storage and their selected SPO libraries.

- **Microsoft 365 apps binaries and servicing updates**: As we discussed in *Chapter 6*, *Deploying Microsoft 365 Apps*, for installation update distribution.

Network planning is an ongoing task that requires, among other things, the engagement and commitment of both the networking and Microsoft 365 administrative teams to ensure the optimal **user experience** (**UX**).

Finally, we will cover security and compliance concepts for devices.

Devices

Devices play an important role during the entire UX with Microsoft 365 because services can be accessed from several clients, such as web, desktop, and mobile devices. Administrators should plan for which devices users will be allowed to access Microsoft 365 services from, if devices will be managed or not, and which protection controls are available in those devices, such as Windows 10 security features.

This section will explore the following concepts for devices:

- Device access
- Device management
- Device protection

We'll look at each of these in the following sections.

Device access

Managing device access for Microsoft 365 is key to ensuring that only known devices can access the service or store company data. Two main strategies can be used to control device access for Microsoft 365, outlined as follows:

- **Network restriction**: Microsoft 365 services can only be accessed from authorized network locations such as inside the organization perimeter, where managed devices reside. This scenario is enforced in the service during the authentication and authorization phase, where users identify themselves and their locations before being granted access to services.

- **Conditional Access**: Services can only be accessed when conditions, such as group membership, device compliance, network region, or MFA, are satisfied.

A network restriction implementation can be implemented with one or more of the following four features:

- **Conditional Access**: As we mentioned previously, Conditional Access can be used to interrogate devices accessing the service for their IP address information and then grant or deny access based on that (among other conditions). Microsoft recommends configuring Conditional Access as the best way to manage device and application access.

- **AD Federation Services (AD FS) claims rules**: In an identity federation scenario, claims are information about users that is exchanged between different **identity providers (IdPs)**, such as between a local AD and AAD. In this case, claims rules allow administrators to configure conditions that must be satisfied to enable the authorization. Organizations frequently use AD FS claims rules to limit access to services based on IP addresses.

> **Important Note**
>
> AD FS claims rules for Office 365 services do not work effectively for geofencing purposes. In most Office 365 application scenarios, users attempt to access the Office 365 service from their device and are redirected to the on-premises environment. The result is that the "client IP address" being presented to AD FS is from Office 365, not the originating client device.

- **EXO client access rules**: Administrators can configure conditions to authorize access to EXO services. Among the services that administrators can configure EXO client access rules for are **the Exchange Admin Center (EAC)**, PowerShell, Exchange ActiveSync, and **Exchange Web Services (EWS)**.

- **ODFB and SPO device access**: Administrators can configure which networks users are authorized to access OneDrive and SharePoint content. This setting also applies to external users and administrator access, so it is recommended to be well planned before the settings are rolled out for users. It affects all services that use SharePoint (such as OneDrive, SPO, and Microsoft Teams). Misconfiguring the allowed networks will prevent users from being able to access the service and will require a phone call to be made to Microsoft Support that they will resolve.

The following screenshot shows the device access configuration options in the SharePoint admin center:

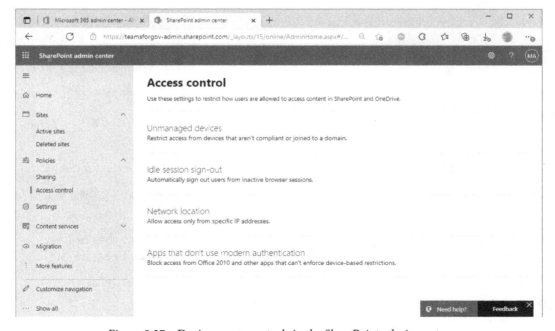

Figure 9.27 – Device access controls in the SharePoint admin center

The most flexible (and preferred) approach for controlling authorized locations is to create Conditional Access policies that, as with the previous options, define conditions and actions.

The following diagram shows the main components of a Conditional Access policy:

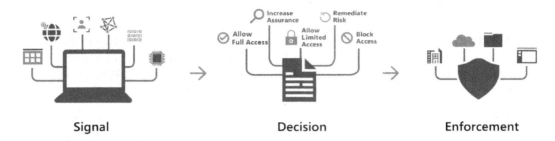

Figure 9.28 – Conditional Access overview

The core conditions for building a Conditional Access policy are set out as follows:

- Users and groups
- Sign-in risk
- Device platform
- Location
- Client apps
- Device state

After being validated, administrators can configure actions such as the following:

- Blocking access
- Granting access, but requiring MFA
- Granting access, but requiring a device to be compliant with Intune requirements
- Enforcing limited session usage, such as preventing users from opening SharePoint documents locally

As part of testing a Conditional Access policy, administrators can simulate a set of conditions, such as user and location, to understand which policy should be set up and what would happen as a result of this policy being implemented.

We'll talk about device management in the next section.

Device management

Microsoft 365 allows administrators to manage devices that are used to connect to services. Administrators can enforce features and stipulations, such as requiring a password to unlock a device, making sure that the device is not rooted or jailbroken, and being able to selectively wipe company data from the device. The following two services can be used to manage devices:

- **Intune**: Intune offers the ability to manage device certificates, Wi-Fi and **virtual private networks** (**VPNs**), and email profiles, deploy apps to users, and manage app protection as well as device compliance, preventing jailbroken/rooted devices from accessing corporate resources, defining password policies, and disabling cameras.

- **Mobile Device Management (MDM) for Office 365**: MDM for Office 365 provides a subset of Intune features, such as preventing the connection of jailbroken or rooted devices, disabling cameras, and defining a password policy.

The following table lists the main differences between MDM for Office and Intune capabilities:

Feature	Intune	MDM for Office 365
Where devices are managed	In the Intune management portal	In the Security & Compliance Center
Supported devices	iOS, macOS, Android, and Windows devices	iOS, Android, and Windows devices
Main capabilities	Requiring a password, defining a number of sign-in failures before the device is wiped, password expiration, jailbreak or rooted detection and corporate wipe, pushing certificates to devices for Wi-Fi networks or VPNs, viewing reports on compliant and not compliant devices, and pushing applications to devices	Requiring a password, defining a number of sign-in failures before the device is wiped, password expiration, and jailbreak or rooted detection and corporate wipe

Table 9.2 – Device management

In addition to MDM scenarios, Intune provides **Mobile Application Management (MAM)** capabilities, allowing controls to be applied to specific applications, such as the following:

- Requiring a **personal identification number** (**PIN**) to open the app

- Encrypting corporate app data

- Data wipe for a full or selective wipe

- Blocking copy and paste between corporate and personal applications

Organizations that already have an MDM solution to manage corporate devices can still use Intune to manage applications with MAM. For more information on MAM, go to `https://docs.microsoft.com/en-us/intune/apps/app-protection-policy`.

Device protection

Windows 10 devices include several security features that administrators should consider during their device planning phase, such as the following:

- **Microsoft Defender antivirus**: Anti-malware that can protect Windows 10 and Windows Server computers (formerly known as Windows Defender Antivirus)

- **Microsoft Defender advanced threat protection** (**ATP**): Advanced protection against threats leveraging behavioral sensors, security analytics across different Microsoft services, and **threat intelligence** (**TI**) by Microsoft hunters and security teams

- **Microsoft Defender Application Guard**: Isolates untrusted sites that are opened in an isolated Hyper-V-enabled container, separate from the host operating system (formerly known as Windows Defender Application Guard)

- **Windows Hello for Business**: Replace passwords with strong **two-factor authentication** (**2FA**) on PCs and mobile devices using a device-specific PIN or biometric credential that can't be captured or replayed on other devices

- **Credential Guard**: The component responsible for isolating secrets that are used throughout the machine to prevent unauthorized access

- **Windows Defender Application Control**: Allows only authorized applications to run in users' machines

- **BitLocker**: Whole-disk encryption, integrated with a device's Trusted Computing Module or Trusted Platform Module chip and the Windows 10 operating system

- **Windows Information Protection (WIP)**: Protects against data leakage separating personal and corporate data (previously known as **Enterprise Data Protection (EDP)**)

Microsoft Defender ATP can also protect Windows 7, Windows 8.1, Windows Server, and macOS. More information about Microsoft Defender ATP can be found here: `https://docs.microsoft.com/en-us/windows/security/threat-protection/microsoft-defender-atp/microsoft-defender-advanced-threat-protection`.

More information about Windows 10 security features can be found in the following documentation: `https://docs.microsoft.com/en-us/microsoft-365/enterprise/windows10-enable-security-features`.

Secure Score

Microsoft 365 has several security features that can be configured in different ways, depending on an organization's requirements. However, many organizations aren't aware of all of the settings, the order in which to address them, or how they might impact the UX.

Additionally, organizations are faced with the following questions:

- How can they understand the current security best practices?

- How does their current deployment compare to the best practices?

Secure Score is a service included with Microsoft 365 that contains a list of dozens of security-focused features (each with a point value), compares an organization's current settings against the Microsoft-recommended best practices, and assigns the tenant a score. It allows organizations to understand their current security posture and understand which actions need to be taken to improve their current score. Microsoft Secure Score can be accessed through the Microsoft 365 Defender portal at `https://security.microsoft.com` and can be seen in the following screenshot:

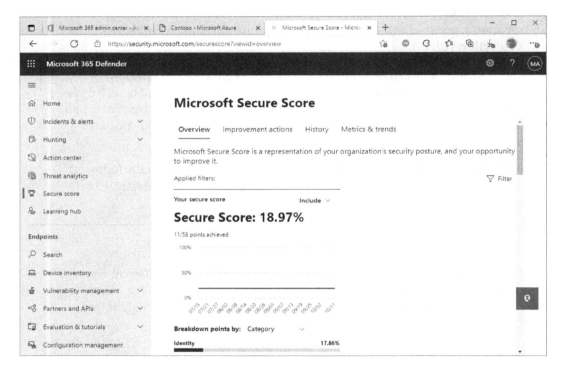

Figure 9.29 – Microsoft Secure Score

Actions settings are organized according to the following categories:

- **Identity**
- **Data**
- **Device**
- **Apps**

The following screenshot shows various improvement actions, sorted by category:

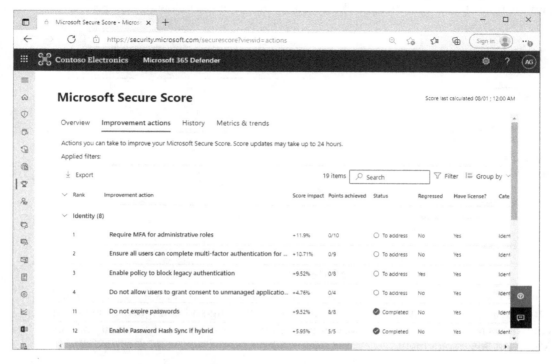

Figure 9.30 – Microsoft Secure Score improvement actions

For each improvement action, administrators can review a description, which attacks or risks it mitigates, related compliance controls, and how its implementation will impact users. The score is recalculated (typically after 48 hours) and the updated score is shown on the dashboard. The Secure Score console provides links to the admin centers where actions need to be taken. The Secure Score console also includes an acknowledgment toggle that lets organizations indicate whether they have implemented an action in a third-party system that isn't tracked by Secure Score, allowing them to maintain an accurate score for their environment.

As organizations make changes over time, they can see the history of actions they've taken and the impact their modifications have had, as shown in the following screenshot:

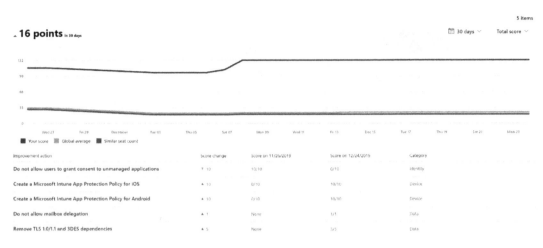

Figure 9.31 – Secure Score history

Microsoft recommends reviewing Secure Score controls and reports frequently to make sure you are implementing current best practices, enabling and configuring new security controls as features become available, and continuously improving the security of your Microsoft 365 deployment.

Summary

Microsoft 365 was built with security features in mind. Administrators should take some time to understand the wide range of features and controls that are available to them for delegating and administering the security aspects of tenants.

In this chapter, you learned about the security concepts and controls for managing identity, documents, networking, and devices. In addition, we discussed managing access to resources through credentials, network perimeter controls, and Conditional Access. Finally, we discussed the benefit and visibility that Secure Score brings to an organization and how it can be used to continuously improve and monitor an organization's security stance.

In the next chapter, we will cover identity protection and management.

Questions

Answer the following questions to test your knowledge of this chapter. You can find the answers in *Chapter 18, Assessments*:

1. Identify two features or capabilities of Secure Score.

    A. Recommend security configurations for Microsoft 365 services.

    B. Track user security policies.

    C. Provide configuration steps for security recommendations or links to configuration controls.

    D. Administer user risk policies.

2. Identify two features of Intune MAM.

    A. Define application-based security policies.

    B. Wipe managed device.

    C. Wipe the managed application profile.

    D. Require device PIN.

3. Where is Intune managed?

    A. Microsoft 365 admin center

    B. Azure portal

    C. Security & Compliance Center

    D. Intune Control Panel

4. Where is Microsoft MDM managed?

    A. Microsoft 365 admin center

    B. Azure portal

    C. Microsoft Endpoint Manager admin center

    D. Intune Control Panel

5. Identify the four types of groups available in Microsoft 365.

    A. Microsoft 365 Groups

    B. Security groups

    C. Mail-enabled security groups

    D. Domain local groups

E. Distribution lists

F. Global groups

G. Universal groups

H. Local groups

6. eDiscovery managers can see what?

A. All cases

B. Only cases that they created or that are assigned to them

7. eDiscovery administrators can see what?

A. All cases

B. Only cases that they created or that are assigned to them

8. Secure Score actions are grouped into which four categories?

A. Identity

B. Network

C. Data

D. Windows

E. Azure

F. Device

G. Apps

H. MFA

9. You are the SharePoint administrator for your organization. You need to allow OneDrive users to share documents with external users who have already been added to your organization's AAD tenant. Which option should you choose?

A. Anyone

B. New and existing external users

C. Existing external users

D. Only people in your organization

10. Identify the two true statements about OneDrive sharing controls.

A. They can have the same level of permissiveness as SharePoint sharing controls.

B. They can be more permissive than SharePoint sharing controls.

C.   They can be less permissive than SharePoint sharing controls.

D.   They must be the same as the SharePoint sharing controls.

11. Which three terms apply to the SPO document life cycle?

A.   Two-stage recycle bin

B.   AAD recycle bin

C.   Preservation Hold Library

D.   Versioning

12. When deploying AAD Connect **password hash synchronization (PHS)**, what happens to the AAD password policy?

A.   Nothing.

B.   The AAD password policy wins.

C.   The on-premises AD password control settings are synchronized to AAD.

D.   Organizations must choose which password policy controls to deploy.

13. You are a security manager for your organization. You need to configure document classification. Which tool should you use?

A.   Classification explorer

B.   AIP

C.   Azure Identity Protection

D.   Exchange DLP policies

14. In which two ways does Microsoft 365 encrypt data?

A.   At rest

B.   At bay

C.   In utero

D.   In transit

15. Microsoft recommends customers configure _____ so that password changes in Azure are updated in the on-premises AD.

A.   Password change management

B.   Password writeback

C.   Exchange hybrid writeback

D.   PIM

16. Microsoft Defender ATP can protect macOS-based computers.

A.   True

B.   False

17. You are the compliance administrator for your organization and need to perform a search for users who have accessed certain SharePoint sites. Which tool should you use?

A.   Microsoft 365 admin center

B.   Audit log search in the compliance center

C.   SharePoint Report Server

D.   SharePoint admin center

18. _____ can be used to govern the life cycle and retention of audit logs.

A.   Azure Sentinel

B.   DLP

C.   Label policies

D.   Audit retention policies

19. _____ security principles are an understanding that threats can come from inside or outside an organization's network.

A.   User

B.   Network

C.   Zero-trust

D.   Implied trust

E.   Explicit trust

10
Understanding Identity Protection and Management

In the previous chapter, we saw the importance of protecting the identity of users, as users can potentially access cloud services from anywhere with an internet connection.

Traditionally, identity has been managed internally with directory services such as **Microsoft Azure Active Directory** (**Azure AD**). When incorporating cloud services into your organization's infrastructure and service portfolio, you'll need to understand how to provide access to those cloud resources. Ideally, you'll want to use a **single sign-on** (**SSO**) capability that enables users to authenticate with a single identity across multiple platforms and services.

In this chapter, we're going to talk about the kinds of identity models available, their applications, and some of the ways to protect identity. We will cover the following topics:

- Understanding identity models
- Introduction to multi-factor authentication (MFA)
- Access reviews

While basic features are available to all Azure AD plans, there are additional security features that are available to customers who subscribe to **Enterprise Mobility + Security (EMS)** plans, which include premium versions of Azure AD.

Let's dig in!

Understanding identity models

When describing how users access a service, the identity and authentication processes are the key concepts to understand. In this section, we're going to discuss three core identity models (as well as some sub-features of each) and how they work in the context of **Microsoft 365**. The three models are as follows:

- Cloud identity
- Hybrid or synchronized identity
- Federated identity

Let's look at each in detail.

Cloud identity

Cloud identity is the simplest form of identity. It's the same form of identity you typically use when you sign up for other consumer cloud services or access retail and personal banking sites.

With regards to Microsoft 365 and cloud identity, the identity is stored and completely managed inside of Azure AD and Microsoft 365. You can manage this identity through the **Microsoft 365 Admin Center** (`https://admin.microsoft.com`), through the **Azure Portal** (`https://aad.portal.azure.com`), or by scripting with **PowerShell** or **Microsoft Graph**.

When a user authenticates to the service, they are providing an identity that has been created in the service. This user identity is separate from any other identity they may have (such as the username and password they use to log in to their computer or other services).

Hybrid identity

Hybrid identity (or **synchronized identity**) refers to the integration of an on-premises **identity provider** (**IdP**) with a cloud IdP. Changes made in one environment (typically, the on-premises environment) are synchronized with and made available in the cloud environment.

To utilize a hybrid or synchronized identity in your Microsoft 365 deployment, you should install and configure a directory synchronization service to copy your identities from an on-premises directory to Azure AD. Microsoft has a free software appliance, **Azure Active Directory Connect (AAD Connect)**, that performs this function.

There are also third-party vendors that provide similar solutions, though they are outside the scope of the MS-900 exam and may not support all of the identity protection features of the Microsoft 365 platform.

The concept of synchronized identity has three core sub-configuration concepts:

- Synchronized identity with cloud authentication
- Synchronized identity with pass-through authentication
- Federated identity

All of these configurations include the optional ability to synchronize user password data.

Linking On-Premises and Cloud Identities

Objects synchronized with Azure AD are linked to their on-premises account by way of a property called the `ImmutableID`. The `ImmutableID` value in Azure AD as a `base64` conversion of an object's on-premises Azure AD `objectGuid` value. You can obtain the `ImmutableID` value for any on-premises directory object with the following PowerShell command, where `sAMAccountName` is the pre-**Windows 2000** account name for an identity whose `ImmutableID` value you wish to compute:

```
$ImmutableID = [system.
convert]::ToBase64String((Get-AdUser
sAMAccountName).objectGuid.ToByteArray())
```

Let's say you have a user object whose GUID value is `c0587102-28af-4546-983b-cd9f59fcc4d2`. After running that value through the conversion, the resulting value to be stored in `$ImmutableID` is the `base64` string value `AnFYwK8oRkWYO82fWfzE0g==`.

To get a better understanding of what each identity model does, let's dig into them deeper.

Synchronized identity with cloud authentication

With a synchronized identity model, you are essentially configuring your organization's directory objects to be replicated in Azure AD. This includes a number of properties (first and last names, email addresses, office information, manager reporting configurations, physical addresses, and phone numbers, among others). You have the option to configure this *with* or *without* password hashes.

> **Azure AD Attributes Deep Dive**
>
> For an exhaustive list of the attributes synchronized to Azure AD, see `https://docs.microsoft.com/en-us/azure/active-directory/hybrid/reference-connect-sync-attributes-synchronized`.

Password hash synchronization enables an Azure AD user to use the same password as the corresponding on-premises account. If you choose to synchronize identity *with password hashes* (the default configuration), then a hash of the user's on-premises password is computed and synchronized to Azure AD. Authentication will be performed by Azure AD using the synchronized credential when a user attempts to access resources. In order to synchronize password hashes, the account specified in the AAD Connect setup must have two specific Azure AD rights granted (**Replicating Directory Changes** and **Replicating Directory Changes All**). These rights can be delegated manually (using a tool such as the AAD Connect **Advanced Permissions** tool at `http://aka.ms/aadpermissions`) or by making the synchronization service account a member of either Domain Admins or Enterprise Admins groups. While the default synchronization time for AAD Connect is every 30 minutes, password changes on-premises are processed and synchronized to Azure AD immediately as a separate process.

> **Password Hash Synchronization Deep Dive**
>
> For a deeper understanding of how the AAD Connect password hash synchronization works, see `https://docs.microsoft.com/en-us/azure/active-directory/hybrid/whatis-phs`.

If you choose to synchronize identity *without* password hashes, then all of the same account details are synchronized *except* the password. Users have to maintain the password separately. This option is commonly configured if you are going to configure a federation service outside of AAD Connect, though you are not required to do so. Authentication will be performed by Azure AD using the synchronized user identity with a cloud password (if no federated authentication has been configured), or the request will be redirected to the federated IDP if the federation has been configured.

Password hash synchronization doesn't rely on any on-premises infrastructure to validate passwords or authentication attempts. If the on-premises environment is unavailable, then users will still be able to log in to Azure AD-protected resources since the authentication attempt is processed against the service.

With or without password hash synchronization, users are able to change their passwords independently in Office 365. If you deploy password hash synchronization, Microsoft recommends you also deploy **password writeback** or **self-service password reset (SSPR)** so that when a user changes their password in Office 365, it's synchronized back to the on-premises Active Directory environment.

Synchronized identity with pass-through authentication

Pass-through authentication is an authentication method that, like standard synchronized identity, replicates account information to Azure AD. However, with the default pass-through authentication configuration, no password hashes are synchronized. Instead, password validation happens in the on-premises environment.

After this option is configured, AAD Connect Setup installs an authentication agent on the AAD Connect server that maintains a persistent outbound connection to Azure AD. Azure AD authentication agents register with the Azure AD service. Since pass-through authentication relies on an on-premises infrastructure to validate login requests, it is recommended that you install multiple pass-through authentication agents for redundancy. The Azure AD authentication agent's service communication is secured with public-key cryptography. Each agent has its own public and private key, which are used in the authentication process.

When a user attempts to sign in to a resource protected by Azure AD authentication, the sign-in process encrypts the user's identity with the public keys of all the registered Azure AD authentication agents and places this request in a queue. Through the persistent connection maintained by the AAD Connect authentication agent, an on-premises agent picks up the request in the queue, decrypts it with its private key, and then validates the credentials against the on-premises Active Directory environment. The response (success, failure, password expired, or locked out) is returned to the Azure AD service to complete the sign-in process.

Azure AD pass-through authentication only requires outbound connectivity on port 443 from the AAD Connect server (and any additional servers where redundant pass-through authentication agents have been configured).

Pass-Through Authentication Deep Dive

You can learn more about pass-through authentication at `https://docs.microsoft.com/en-us/azure/active-directory/hybrid/how-to-connect-pta-how-it-works`.

Now, let's get a move on and explore federated identity in the next section.

Federated identity

In a similar way to the Azure AD pass-through authentication, **federated identity** processes the identity validation in the on-premises environment. Federated identity requires directory objects to be synchronized to Azure AD.

AAD Connect provides a mechanism to configure federated identity directly for both **Active Directory Federation Services (AD FS)** and **PingFederate**, a third-party federation IdP, from the setup wizard shown in the following screenshot:

Figure 10.1 – The AAD Connect setup User sign-in page

When federation is configured for an environment, authentication attempts are redirected from the Azure AD login portal to a web server hosting the federated IdP service endpoint. When a user is redirected to the IdP service endpoint, they enter their credentials if necessary and the on-premises federation service authenticates the user against the on-premises directory.

When determining which identity model fits your organization's needs, you can refer to the following table:

Requirement	Potential identity and authentication models	Notes
Simplest identity	Cloud identity	Requires no on-premises infrastructure, but also provides no integration with on-premises applications or domain features.
On-premises credential verification	Pass-through authentication, federated identity	Both pass-through authentication and federated identity provide the ability to verify user credentials on-premises. Cloud identity and password hash synchronization perform identity verification in the cloud.
Easy integration with conditional access	Cloud identity, pass-through authentication, password hash synchronization	Of the identity models presented, federated identity and third-party IdPs may prove the most difficult to integrate with conditional access.
Integration with a third-party IdP	Only third-party IdPs	Third-party IdPs frequently require their solution componetns to be used end-to-end, so AAD Connect or other Microsoft-provided identity management services typically won't be deployed.
Leaked credential detection	Password hash synchronization, pass-through authentication or federated identity with password hash synchronization enabled and Azure AD Premium P2 license	Azure AD Premium P2 licensing is required in conjunction with an identity and authentication model that includes password hash synchronization.

Table 10.1 – Identity model feature matrix

Once you have chosen an identity and an authentication model, you should think about securing the identity in question. One of the tools available to all users of the Microsoft 365 platform is MFA, which we'll discuss next.

Introduction to multi-factor authentication (MFA)

For most authentication or login attempts, users provide login credentials (usually a username and a password). The methods of authenticating a user's identity typically fall into one of the following three categories:

- **Something the user knows**: A password is the most common example of this method.

- **Something the user has**: This can be some kind of login device, such as a smart card or token, or it can be a text or phone call to a phone number previously registered with the system that the user is attempting to access.

- **Something the user is**: With this method, the user must supply some sort of biometric input, such as a fingerprint, iris scan, or voice passcode.

There are a lot of scenarios, however, where a simple username and password may not be enough to secure valuable resources. In such cases, organizations may wish to further challenge a user during the login process to verify their identity. MFA provides this ability by introducing one or more challenges to the user during the authentication process.

Azure AD has a native MFA service that can be used to further protect users and administrators and can be easily enabled. Today, the following options can be used to further authenticate users with Azure AD MFA:

- SMS or text message

- Phone call

- One-time passcode on a hardware or software token

- Confirmation prompt on a registered authentication app

Azure AD MFA has several features, such as self-service secure registration or the ability for users to bypass MFA if they are connecting from secure, known networks. More in-depth information about the configuration capabilities of Azure AD MFA, including steps to configure third-party tokens for verification, can be found at `https://docs.microsoft.com/en-us/azure/active-directory/authentication/concept-mfa-howitworks`.

Azure AD provides several different identity and authentication models, as well as security controls, to provide a strong level of protection for your organization. Implementing conditional access and Azure AD MFA can help organizations verify that users who are presenting credentials and attempting to obtain access to resources are authorized to do so and are using compliant devices.

MFA is available via several mechanisms in Microsoft 365. All plans are eligible for basic MFA using a feature known as **security defaults**. The basic MFA option does not provide much granularity, and it has fewer authentication options than the features offered through the Azure AD Premium P1 or P2 licenses.

The following table lists the capabilities and features of security defaults and **Conditional Access** (available as part of an Azure AD Premium license):

Feature	Security defaults	Azure AD Premium Conditional Access
MFA notification through Azure Authenticator app	X	X
Verification code from mobile app or hardware token	X	X
Text message to a phone		X
Call to a phone		X
App passwords		X
Business scenario-based authentication		X
MFA based on risk conditions (available only with Azure AD Premium P2)		X

Table 10.2 – Azure AD MFA features

Next, let's discuss the access reviews feature of Azure AD Premium.

Access reviews

Access reviews are an Azure AD Premium feature. They allow organizations to evaluate access to specific resources or group memberships on either an ad-hoc or scheduled basis. For example, you may want to use access reviews to periodically audit the membership of the Microsoft Teams Administrators group.

Access reviews can be delegated to specific administrators, business owners, or even end users who can self-attest their need to continue to maintain access to a resource. Access reviews also allow administrators to configure automation actions, such as removing users from privileged groups if it is determined that they no longer need that access.

Summary

As you've seen, there is a multitude of configuration options available to help organizations of all sizes meet their identity, authentication, and security needs.

In this chapter, we discussed the differences between cloud, synchronized, and federated identity, as well as the security controls available with EMS, such as conditional access and access reviews. We learned which identity model can be used to help meet specific requirements – for example, if your organization needs on-premises identity authentication to comply with your security needs, you'll now know that you should choose between pass-through authentication and federated identity.

In the next chapter, we're going to look at technologies that enable endpoint security control and management.

Questions

Use the following questions to test your knowledge of this chapter. You can find the answers in *Chapter 18, Assessments*:

1. You are the compliance officer for your organization. You need to implement a policy to schedule the periodic verification of Azure AD group memberships. Which tool should you use?

    A.   Conditional Access

    B.   Access reviews

    C.   Privileged identity management

    D.   Privileged authorization management

2. You need to configure an authentication method where users are authenticated on-premises. Which option should you choose?

    A.   Cloud identity

    B.   Password hash synchronization

    C.   Azure AD Federation Services

    D.   Enterprise Mobility + Security

3. You need to configure an authentication method where the password validation for authentication happens on-premises. Which two methods meet this requirement?

   A.   Password hash synchronization

   B.   Pass-through authentication

   C.   Azure AD Federation Services

   D.   Cloud identity

4. You need to configure an authentication method that does not depend on the availability of the on-premises infrastructure. Which two methods should you choose?

   A.   Password hash synchronization

   B.   Pass-through authentication

   C.   Azure AD Federation Services

   D.   Cloud identity

5. Identify three verification methods for Azure MFA:

   A.   SMS or text message

   B.   Desktop popup

   C.   Phone call

   D.   One-time passcode

6. Which of the following are the three main things that are required to authenticate a user?

   A.   Something a user knows

   B.   Something a user has

   C.   Something a user is

   D.   Something a user does

7. Directory synchronization to Azure AD is configured with which tool?

   A.   Azure AD Health Service

   B.   Azure AD Federation Services

   C.   Azure ExpressRoute

   D.   AAD Connect

8. You are the security administrator for your organization. You are concerned that your users may become targets of phishing attacks and you want to help secure their identities in the event that user passwords become compromised. Which product, feature, or service should you configure?

   A. Access reviews

   B. AAD Connect

   C. PingFederate

   D. Azure AD Federation Services

   E. MFA

   F. Password write-back

   G. Hybrid identity

9. The Azure AD object GUID is stored as what property in Azure AD?

   A. Master ID

   B. Master Object Account SID

   C. Synchronized ID

   D. Immutable ID

10. Which identity model is not connected to any on-premises directory or external authentication system?

   A. Federated identity

   B. Cloud identity

   C. Hybrid identity

   D. Synchronized identity

11
Endpoint and Security Management

At the core of Microsoft 365 is the concept of identity-based security management. One of the benefits of using Microsoft 365 is that it includes a directory service, **Azure Active Directory (AAD)**, which can be used to define an organization's cloud service security baseline.

Identity and security administrators alike should understand the main security features that can be integrated between their new and existing solutions. In the case of Microsoft 365, this will likely mean integrating an existing AD on-premises deployment with Azure AD.

In this chapter, we'll highlight some of the basic security features present in both AD (part of an organization's on-premises identity infrastructure) and AAD. Specifically, we'll cover the following topics:

- Understanding directory-based security features
- Addressing common threats with AAD
- Understanding BYOD

By the end of this chapter, you should have an understanding of how some AD security features, such as Group Policy and password management, can be used in conjunction with AAD to mitigate threat risks.

Understanding directory-based security features

Both AD and AAD have several identity and security features built in to help prevent or mitigate threats. In this section, we'll look at some core security features of AD, as well as features available with both AAD Premium Plan 1 and AAD Premium Plan 2, that can be used to help protect organizations.

Active Directory

AD is an on-premises identity store service. It's used to authenticate and authorize computers and internal applications. The core functional container for a security boundary in AD is called a **domain**. A domain contains all of an organization's related security principals, groups, and other objects. Domains are grouped into *trees*, which are logical collections of related objects from either a security or organizational perspective. At the top level, *forests* are made up of one or more trees. The domains in a tree share a contiguous namespace. Each tree in a forest has a namespace, as shown in the following diagram:

Forest
(one or more domain trees that do *not*
form a contiguous namespace)

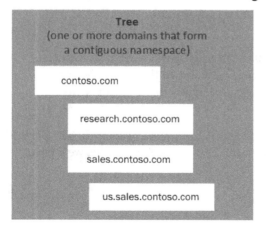
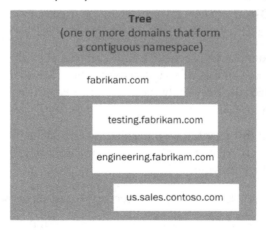

Figure 11.1 – High-level architecture of Active Directory forest and tree namespaces

AD has the following features that can be used to define a security strategy:

- **Group Policy**: While not solely a security feature, Group Policy is used to administratively manage the configuration of policies and features throughout an AD environment. From a security perspective, Group Policy can be used to manage what software can run (through software restriction policies), password policies, and what application or operating system features are available for users.

- **Logon hours**: The logon hours feature is used to define at what days and times a given user can authenticate against AD. This can be used to limit access to certain hours of the day (such as hourly employees who should only be logging in during normal business hours). Administrators can use Group Policy to enforce behaviors such as automatically logging users out of their machines when their logon hours expire.

- **Logon workstations**: While logon hours control at what *time* a user can log into an environment, the logon workstations feature determines which *devices* an account is allowed to use.

- **Logon banner**: The logon banner is a pop-up dialog box that appears when a user attempts to log on to a device. Many organizations use this dialog box to display an acceptable use policy.

- **Resource permissions**: AD allows administrators to apply permissions to file shares, printers, or individual files to manage the access that a user might have over a resource.

- **Role-based access**: AD comes with several built-in roles, such as Account Operators and Print Operators, that can be used to delegate well-defined permission scopes over objects in an environment.

- **Password management**: Administrators can enforce a set of minimum requirements (such as length, history, and special characters) that should be applied to passwords.

Using a combination of written policy and technology enforcement, organizations can use AD to secure their on-premises organizations.

From a cloud perspective, though, organizations must use an AAD identity to manage access control. While we'll look at all of the Azure AD SKUs that are available, for the purposes of the MS-900 exam, we'll mainly focus on the two available premium licensing levels: Azure Active Directory Premium Plan 1 and Azure Active Directory Premium Plan 2.

Azure AD Free

Azure AD Free comes with all Office 365 subscriptions. It focuses on providing an identity store, though it does grant the ability to enable basic **multi-factor authentication** (**MFA**) using the Azure phone authentication app. Azure AD Free for Global Admins expands with the ability to use phone calls and SMS text messages as a second factor for authentication, as well as remembering MFA for trusted devices.

AAD Premium Plan 1

AAD Premium Plan 1 (commonly referred to as **AAD Premium P1**) is the first AAD premium tier. As you've already learned, Azure AD Premium P1 is included in Microsoft 365 E3 as part of Enterprise Mobility + Security E3. It includes several features that can be used as part of an organization's security posture, as detailed here:

- **Conditional Access**: With Conditional Access, administrators can define what conditions must be satisfied to allow or block a user from accessing a specific application. Conditional Access policies can be configured based on the following factors: the user, group membership, IP or geolocation information, device compliance, and the application being used.

- **Custom banned password list**: Administrators can configure a list of banned passwords that shouldn't be allowed in their organization. With configuration, this process can be extended to on-premises AD deployments. The banned password list feature also performs common character substitutions (a and @, o and zero, and so on) when evaluating user passwords. For example, if you put *FABRIKAM* on the banned password list, AAD will also ban *F@BRIK@M*.

- **Self-service password reset** (**SSPR**): Users may forget passwords periodically. The SSPR feature allows them to reset their passwords from anywhere with an internet browser. Password reset is subject to conditions or requirements (such as successfully answering security questions) configured by administrators. After successful validation, user passwords can also be written back to an on-premises identity AD environment.

- **Azure MFA**: MFA prompts users for a second form of identification to confirm their identity when attempting to access a resource. Azure MFA provides administrators with advanced MFA features, such as the ability to configure trusted IP address ranges, custom greetings for phone call authentication, PIN mode, and fraud alerts. Azure MFA can even integrate with on-premises applications and allow organizations to use their compatible tokens for authentication, as opposed to the Azure authenticator phone app.

- **Microsoft Cloud App Discovery**: Frequently, an organization's security team needs to understand what applications are being used across the organization. Sometimes, this leads to the discovery of **shadow IT**, or applications that are being used without the consent of the business. With Microsoft Cloud App Discovery, administrators can import firewalls, and proxy logs can discover application traffic. These logs are analyzed and the discovered applications and the amount of traffic they are generating are made available.

- **Azure Application Proxy**: Many organizations host internal line-of-business applications. These applications sometimes need to be available to users outside of the corporate environment. **Virtual private networks** (**VPNs**) are commonly used to fulfill this need. Azure Application Proxy is another method that can be used to achieve this goal without the complicated configuration of VPN tunnels. One added benefit is that applications configured to use Azure Application Proxy can also take advantage of Azure MFA.

Azure AD Common Features

All AAD tiers have a feature that enables several security configurations and can be used to ensure default levels of protection in organizations. These policies, originally called **baseline policies**, are being deprecated and replaced with a newer feature: **security defaults**. Security defaults will also be available to all tiers. These are binary switches for enabling defaults (such as disabling legacy authentication protocols) tenant-wide. Organizations that wish to use more granular controls must upgrade to Azure AD Premium P1 or P2 to use Conditional Access policies. Azure AD Basic has been phased out and is no longer available for purchase.

As you can see, AAD Premium Plan 1 provides a significant security benefit to organizations. Even more benefits are available in the second tier, which we'll look at next.

AAD Premium Plan 2

AAD Premium 2 (or **AAD P2**) is the highest tier of the AAD service. In addition to the features already included in AAD P1, AAD P2 also provides organizations with the following tools:

- **Identity Protection**: Azure AD Identity Protection is an intelligence service that can understand current signals (data gathered from security and data interactions) and calculate the risk and vulnerabilities of user sessions across the organization. Identity Protection can detect risky behaviors, such as when MFA registration is not configured, or the use of unsanctioned cloud apps unmanaged by **Privileged Identity Management** (**PIM**). Moreover, risk can be detected based on one of the following activities:

  - Users with leaked credentials
  - Sign-ins from anonymous IP addresses
  - Azure AD threat intelligence pattern detections
  - Sign-ins from IP addresses with suspicious activity
  - Sign-ins from unfamiliar locations

  Identity Protection can be used along with Azure AD Conditional Access to enforce MFA or block access whenever an access attempt is identified as a potential risk is detected (referred to as **risk-based Conditional Access policies**). Identity Protection also allows administrators to export risk detection data so that it can be analyzed with third-party tools.

- **PIM**: PIM allows administrators to configure workflows for times when elevated permissions are required to perform a job duty. Once configured, PIM workflows can grant specified permissions for a limited duration of time and then revoke them once the time has expired, thereby helping organizations implement a least-privilege administrative model.

- **Access reviews**: Access reviews allow organizations to recommend and automate permission or group management, such as removing users from groups after periods of activity.

With these tools in place, administrators should find it easier to reduce the attack surface of their organizations. While having access to these tools is important, it's equally important to know how the security features of AAD can help protect organizations. In the next section, we'll outline a few common threats and how AAD can help mitigate them.

Addressing common threats with AAD

Attackers are constantly developing new threats. Microsoft 365 provides organizations with several tools, guidance, and built-in features (such as Secure Score at `https://security.microsoft.com/securescore`) that can be used to improve security.

In this next section, we will explore some examples of common threats and see which Microsoft 365 capabilities can be used to protect against them:

- Compromised accounts
- Compromised devices
- Phishing attempts

First, let's look at compromised user accounts.

Compromised accounts

Credential compromise is one of the most common threats an organization can face. This can happen through any number of mechanisms, such as brute-force password cracking attempts, malware, or social engineering. This can lead to several security issues in the organization, such as the loss of intellectual property or the exposure of customer data.

Microsoft 365 has several features that can be used to protect against compromised accounts, such as the following:

- Enforcing MFA for users
- Detecting risky sign-ins and automating responses, such as prompting for MFA or denying access to resources
- Implementing risk-based Conditional Access
- Enforcing Privileged Access Management to restrict the number of users granted "always-on" administrative access
- Creating activity alerts or Cloud App Security activity policies to detect anomalous activity and act on them
- Creating a Conditional Access policy to enforce which applications users are allowed to access from certain locations on certain devices (such as managed ones), and under which circumstances this is allowed to happen
- Leaked credential reporting

Managing compromised accounts (or preventing them) is key to sustaining a secure computing environment.

Many of these features are referenced and highlighted as part of your organization's **Secure Score**. Secure Score will be examined in more depth in *Chapter 12*, *Exploring the Service Trust Portal, Compliance Manager, and the Microsoft 365 Security Center*.

Compromised machines

Besides protecting against compromised accounts, administrators should plan to implement measures to prevent or address compromised machines. The following Microsoft 365 features can be used:

- Configuring Microsoft 365 Defender policies to further detect anomalies and protect against malicious activity.

- Deploying Microsoft Defender for Identity policies to detect malicious login attempts in AD Domain Services.

- Configuring Windows Defender Credential Guard policies to isolate and protect machine secrets.

- Configuring Windows-controlled folder access to prevent malware from corrupting data.

- Deploying Microsoft Endpoint Manager mobile device and **Mobile Application Management** (**MAM**) policies to protect data on devices.

- Deploying BitLocker for device-level encryption.

A comprehensive device management policy is necessary to prevent damage from compromised machines.

Phishing

Phishing is one of the most common attacks experienced by organizations. With phishing, an attacker is attempting to obtain information from a victim, typically by pretending to be a trusted source (such as a business partner, a well-known brand or organization, a friend, or another employee). Attackers may attempt to compromise users by getting them to click on links pointing to malicious websites or by emailing confidential information. No matter the attack vector, phishing can result in both data and financial loss.

Microsoft 365 provides organizations with several tools to help combat email phishing attempts:

- **Exchange Online Protection (EOP)**: EOP is included with all Microsoft 365 subscriptions and can be used to detect and block spam and virus-infected attachments. EOP uses multiple antivirus engines and is continuously updated with new antivirus signatures. EOP also has protection against anomalous message patterns and includes anti-phishing controls to block suspected attempts. Anti-phishing mechanisms can be configured to detect targeted impersonation attempts.

- **Microsoft Defender for Office 365**: In addition to signature-based malware detection, Defender for Office 365 (formerly known as Office 365 Advanced Threat Protection) includes heuristic technology in the sandbox and allows you to detonate and examine the behavior of message attachments, as well as files stored in SharePoint Online and OneDrive for Business. Defender for Office 365 also maintains a reputation database and checks each link embedded in an email message to see whether the destination website contains known malware or phishing characteristics. Defender for Office 365 can be accessed via the Microsoft 365 Defender portal at `https://security.microsoft.com`.

- **Attack simulation training**: While stopping threats before they reach users is critical, it's also very important to teach users how to respond, should a threat evade detection. Microsoft 365 Defender features an attack simulator, as shown in the following screenshot, that can be used to run phishing campaigns against your users, catalog the results, and help you target training at users and scenarios:

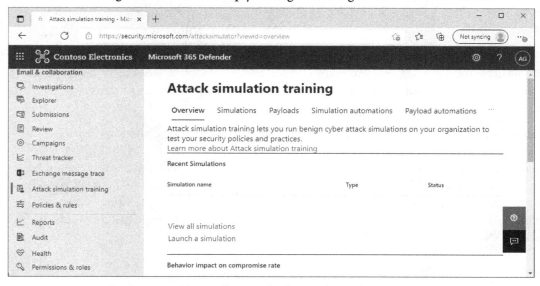

Figure 11.2 – Microsoft 365 Defender attack simulation training

Attack simulation training is part of the Microsoft 365 E5 feature set. The toolset can be accessed at `https://security.microsoft.com/attacksimulator`.

Microsoft 365 has a wide variety of tools to enable organizations to protect themselves against attacks, as well as training users to respond correctly.

Understanding BYOD

Recently, there have been several business, health, and environmental concerns that have caused businesses to consider allowing employees, contractors, or other individuals access to organizational resources with personal devices.

This shift, termed **Bring Your Own Device** (or **BYOD**), provides a lot of flexibility to organizations. It even can be seen as a cost-reduction mechanism (forgoing capital expenditure for devices or even reducing office space). However, it comes with a new set of risks and challenges. Securing organizational data is paramount for security professionals, administrators, and business professionals, and the introduction of personal devices that may be out of date or have been compromised by malware underscores the risk that these devices present.

However, Azure AD Premium features can help mitigate these threats as well.

Mobile device management

The more traditional approach to mobile devices usually involves some sort of device enrollment, where a personal device gets management software installed on it, allowing administrators to limit the types of actions that can be performed or forcing certain types of compliance requirements.

With Microsoft 365 and the features from the Enterprise Mobility + Security suite, which is now part of **Microsoft Endpoint Manager**, organizations have access to this type of control.

You can use device enrollment features, as discussed in *Chapter 5*, *Understanding the Concepts of Modern Management*, to enforce device-level restrictions (even in BYOD scenarios). In this instance, devices such as phones, tablets, or personal computers can be enrolled and managed just like corporate devices. These features include jailbreak/rootkit detection, verifying current updates, and forcing lock screen timeouts. Modern device management through Microsoft Endpoint Manager allows you to wipe lost or stolen devices as well.

Mobile Application Management

However, many users are reluctant to give their organizations full access to their devices. That's where **MAM** comes in. MAM allows organizations to manage the data inside applications rather than administering the device as a whole. This allows more selective management and control, giving users the feeling of privacy and independence while organizations can get the assurance of data control.

MAM is available for applications that support profiles, such as Microsoft Outlook. Management is enforced through **app protection policies**.

Popular controls involve restricting copy/paste activities between managed and unmanaged sessions (for example, prohibiting data from being copied from Microsoft Outlook or Microsoft Word into an SMS message). For more information on MAM features, refer to *Chapter 5, Understanding the Concepts of Modern Management*.

There are several benefits of using app protection policies:

- **Data protection at the application level**: Management is integrated into the Azure identity, so the protection capabilities follow the user identity from device to device. Policies can work against both managed (enrolled) and unmanaged devices.

- **App-layer application protections**: You can use security features such as data sharing controls between apps, preventing corporate or managed data from being saved to personal device locations, or requiring the use of a PIN or biometrics to unlock an application's work or organizational security context.

- **Targeted management of data without device enrollment**: If a user leaves the organization, app protection policies allow you to selectively wipe data from the managed identity of an application while leaving the rest of the application's identities and data intact.

Organizations can also combine MDM and MAM policies. You can learn more about app protection policies at `https://docs.microsoft.com/en-us/mem/intune/apps/app-protection-policy`.

Summary

Both AD and Azure AD Premium provide organization administrators with several security features that can be used to safeguard critical data and systems. As we saw, there are controls available to verify and authenticate access, enforce MFA based on several usage and risk scenarios, and detect anomalous behavior patterns.

You also learned about how additional tools in the Microsoft 365 suite, such as the attack simulator, can be used to help train users to respond appropriately to threats. You should now understand some of the core features of Azure AD Premium (such as Conditional Access) and how they can be used to enhance an organization's security.

In the next chapter, we'll begin examining Service Trust Portal and Compliance Manager, which can be used to help organizations achieve and manage compliance with industry standards.

Questions

Answer the following questions to test your knowledge of this chapter. You can find the answers in *Chapter 18, Assessments*:

1. Conditional Access is a feature of _____.

    A. AAD Premium P1

    B. AD

    C. Cloud App Security

    D. Privileged Identity Management

2. Risk-based Conditional Access is a feature of _____.

    A. AAD Premium P1

    B. AAD Premium P2

    C. AD

    D. Privileged Identity Management

3. A self-service password reset can update on-premises and cloud passwords.

    A. True

    B. False

4. The Office 365 attack simulator is part of _____.

    A. Office 365 E3

    B. Microsoft 365 E3

    C. Office 365 E5

    D. Microsoft 365 E5

5. The feature that allows just-in-time rights management and access rights elevation is which of the following?

   A. Privileged Identity Management

   B. Access reviews

   C. Baseline security policies

   D. Security defaults

   E. Conditional Access

6. You are the security administrator for your organization. You want to automate a process to check on group memberships and remove stale accounts from groups. What tool or feature should you use?

   A. Privileged Identity Management

   B. Access reviews

   C. Baseline security policies

   D. Security defaults

   E. Conditional Access

7. You are a network administrator for your organization. You need to provide secure remote access to internal applications and want to use existing AAD Conditional Access policies. What tool or feature should you use?

   A. Azure Application Proxy

   B. Azure reverse proxy

   C. Azure Proxy authentication service

   D. Azure remote applications

8. Microsoft Cloud App Discovery can be used to do which of the following?

   A. Find new applications compatible with Office 365.

   B. Report on application compatibility.

   C. Provide cloud applications to Windows 10 devices.

   D. Identify *shadow IT.*

9. After a security audit, you discover that several users have poor passwords that include your organization's name. What tool or feature can you use to prevent users from choosing passwords that contain specific words?

    A. Self-service password reset

    B. Custom banned password list

    C. Security defaults

    D. Baseline security policies

10. The service desk manager reports that their team spends a significant amount of time helping users who forgot their passwords. What tool or feature can you implement to help increase your organization's productivity?

    A. Multi-factor authentication

    B. Custom banned password list

    C. Self-service password reset

    D. Identity Protection

11. Your organization wants to enable users to use their own devices (BYOD) to access corporate data resources. Users have expressed privacy concerns with the device enrollment process. What feature or service can you implement to manage the data without requiring device enrollment?

    A. Microsoft mobile device management

    B. Microsoft Endpoint Manager

    C. Mobile Data Management

    D. Mobile data encryption

    E. BitLocker

    F. Mobile Application Management

12. The **Chief Information Security Officer (CISO)** for your organization has requested security training for all users as part of the risk and compliance audit. Part of this security training involves running phishing campaigns against the users. What Microsoft 365 service or feature can be used to accomplish this task?

    A. Microsoft Secure Score

    B. Microsoft compliance score

    C. Microsoft 365 Defender attack simulator

    D. Microsoft 365 phishing simulator

13. Azure AD password hash synchronization honors settings configured in Active Directory logon hours.

    A. True

    B. False

14. Azure AD Pass-through Authentication honors settings configured in Active Directory logon hours.

    A. True

    B. False

12

Exploring the Service Trust Portal, Compliance Manager, and the Microsoft 365 Security Center

Most organizations have an assessment process, both from technical and compliance perspectives, that they must go through before authorizing the acquisition or use of a cloud solution. Some questions may arise during this process, such as the following:

- Is Microsoft 365 safe?
- Where is my data stored?

- Who has access to my data?
- What happens to my data if I decide to leave the service?

Information technology (**IT**) administrators, compliance administrators, legal representatives, and security officers typically have some or all of the responsibility for providing these answers to businesses. It is imperative that everyone has a clear understanding of the principles by which Microsoft operates its data centers.

Furthermore, many organizations (especially in regulated industries) are accountable for maintaining compliance against a broad set of standards and regulations.

In this chapter, you will learn about the following components available in Microsoft 365 that can help you answer these questions and be successful:

- **Service Trust Portal (STP)**
- **Insider Risk Management (IRM)**
- Microsoft 365 Security Center

As you'll see in this chapter, the STP, Compliance Manager, and the Microsoft 365 Security Center will help both the business and operational sides of an organization address common concerns and questions when deciding on a Microsoft 365 strategy.

Let's begin!

STP

Many organizations need to have some level of evidentiary data that confirms **cloud service providers** (**CSPs**) are adhering to agreed-upon standards for security and data handling. The Microsoft STP (`https://servicetrust.microsoft.com`) is where all these critical documents are stored.

The core components of the STP include the following:

- Trust documents
- Compliance Manager

Let's look at each of these briefly. First, we'll examine the trust documents.

Trust documents

There are several documents available in the STP that can enable organizations to better understand how the Microsoft 365 platform is designed and operated. With these documents and white papers, organizations can be confident about how their data is being collected, stored, and used in the service. The following sections will provide an example of how these documents can be used to address some of an organization's most common questions.

The areas we'll look at are the following:

- Tenant isolation in Office 365
- Data residency
- Encryption in the Microsoft cloud
- Audit reports
- Data resiliency in Office 365

Most trust documents can be located inside the STP under **Trust Documents | Data Protection | FAQ & White Papers**.

Let's get started.

Tenant isolation in Office 365

Tenant isolation answers the question, *How is my data separated from other organizations?*

Microsoft 365 enables customers to share physical resources such as computing power and storage in what is called a **multi-tenancy** model. In order to isolate one organization's data from another, several forms of protection are implemented, such as the following:

- Logical isolation through **Azure Active Directory** (**Azure AD**)
- Encryption for data at rest
- Encryption for data in transit

The tenant is a logical security boundary, and all information and data related to that organization are held within that container. You can learn more about how Microsoft's tenant isolation procedures are used to separate organizations' data at `https://docs. microsoft.com/en-us/office365/Enterprise/office-365-tenant- isolation-overview`.

Data residency

Data residency answers the question, *Where is my data stored?*

When an organization signs up for Microsoft 365, they indicate where their primary place of business is. This decision maps their tenant to a region, which in turn is used to define which data centers will be used to store their data. Organizations using sovereign clouds (such as *21Vianet* or *Government Community Cloud*) have very explicitly designated storage regions. For security purposes, Microsoft does not disclose the exact address of its data centers. Customers can, however, leverage public documents to learn where in the Microsoft cloud their data is stored, depending on which type of service they are using.

You can learn more about where data is located by visiting `https://products.office.com/en-us/where-is-your-data-located`.

Encryption in the Microsoft cloud

Microsoft uses several encryption technologies to secure data. Encryption technologies and platforms used include the following:

- BitLocker
- Azure **Storage Service Encryption** (**SSE**)
- **Distributed Key Manager** (**DKM**)
- **Internet Protocol Security** (**IPsec**)
- **Transport Layer Security** (**TLS**)

Depending on the data's activity status (at rest or in transit) and in which service it resides, encryption may be 128-bit or 256-bit **Advanced Encryption Standard** (**AES**). Many Microsoft 365 services also allow customers to manage their own encryption keys, further restricting access to their data.

> **Note**
> You can learn more about the encryption protocols and standards used at `https://docs.microsoft.com/en-us/microsoft-365/compliance/office-365-encryption-risks-and-protections`.

Audit reports

Many organizations adhere to a variety of compliance standards or protocols. Some organizations choose to do this for their own benefit, while others are required to by their customers, constituents, or other statutory obligations.

Whatever the reasons driving compliance, Microsoft 365 provides tools to help organizations achieve and maintain this. One of the benefits of using Microsoft as a CSP is being able to leverage the investments it makes in security and compliance efforts.

When compiling documentation for their own audits, organizations can include attestations and audited control documents as part of their compliance package. Audit reports can be grouped and filtered by technology, industry, and report types, as shown in the following screenshot:

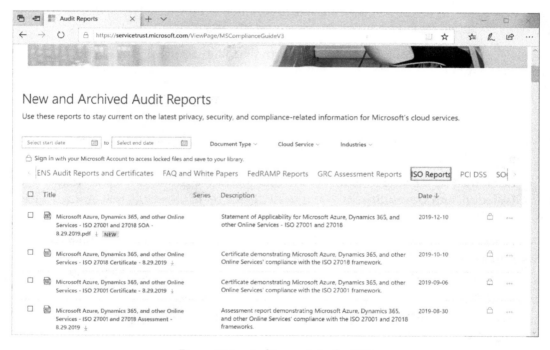

Figure 12.1 – Audit reports in the STP

Audit reports are freely available but do require you to sign in to a Microsoft 365 tenant.

> **Obtaining Audit Reports**
>
> You can view all of the audit reports at `https://servicetrust.microsoft.com/ViewPage/MSComplianceGuideV3`.

These audit reports and trust documents can be used as part of an organization's overall auditing and compliance package. Microsoft provides another service, Compliance Manager, for organizations to track their progress toward completing various compliance goals.

Data resiliency in Office 365

Most organizations have either questions or requirements around retention, backup, compliance, and recoverability. Microsoft addresses these concerns through a framework of data replication, physical backups, and highly available or fault-tolerant designs. Resiliency refers to the concept of being able to continue to provide services, regardless of the types of failures that occur.

Microsoft's goal in Microsoft 365 is designed with the following five data resiliency principles in mind:

- **Critical and non-critical data**: Critical data (such as content) must be preserved at all costs against loss or corruption.

- **Fault domains**: Data must be separated into as many fault zones as possible to provide failure isolation.

- **Data must be monitored to detect whether it fails the Atomicity, Consistency, Isolation, and Durability (ACID) test**: ACID is a set of properties that ensures the validity of a data transaction.

- **Customer data must be protected from corruption**: In order to ensure that data is in a continuously good state, it must be scanned or monitored, repairable, and recoverable. This includes physical and logical monitoring at both the hardware and software layers.

- **Allow customers to be able to recover their own data**: Tools are provided to allow customer autonomy when recovering accidentally deleted data.

Microsoft 365 addresses the potential for data corruption (whether due to hardware or human, application, or operational errors) by replicating data and performing continuous checks on transactions to ensure they are valid. In addition, during the development stages of applications and services, Microsoft conducts thorough code reviews to ensure that all code contributes to the overall efficacy of the system. Application data is monitored and replicated so that transactions can be rolled back to previous good states if necessary.

In addition to corruption, malware and ransomware present challenges to both on-premises and cloud environments. Microsoft 365 uses mechanisms to prevent malware from being introduced through clients or servers, including both heuristic and signature-based detection. Microsoft 365 environments are scanned at regular intervals as well as during times when files are downloaded, opened, or executed. SharePoint Online and OneDrive for Business each include document versioning, which can be used to recover files that may have been encrypted, and Cloud App Security can be used from a customer's perspective to detect anomalous behaviors executed in their environments.

Microsoft 365 also makes use of extensive monitoring with native, third-party, and open source products, using data analytics to predict problems and synthetic transactions to verify that services are responding correctly.

With this understanding of how Microsoft manages its resources, we can move on to how organizations can manage audit and regulatory compliance activities with Compliance Manager.

Compliance Manager

As organizations adopt new services, they need to make sure that doing so enables them to maintain or improve their compliance posture. Compliance Manager enables organizations to review and understand, under a shared responsibility model, which controls are being maintained by the provider (that is, Microsoft) and which controls or actions must be completed by the customer.

A sample of the Compliance Manager (`https://servicetrust.microsoft.com/ComplianceManager/V3`) dashboard is shown in the following screenshot:

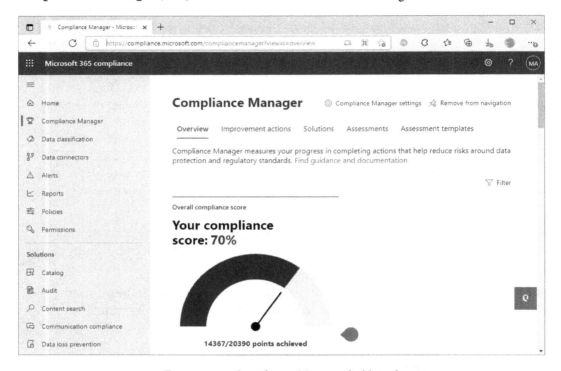

Figure 12.2 – Compliance Manager dashboard

Compliance Manager displays the controls for a given certification and identifies which controls are managed by Microsoft and which controls the customer needs to review to confirm they are being applied in their own organization. For each control, there is a description of what needs to be accomplished that customers can use to help during the assessment process.

Additionally, Compliance Manager allows organizations to upload their own documents in support of their attestation of compliance. As a result of completing their required actions and attestations, organizations will be able to raise their **compliance score**, which is a risk-based score that measures progress in completing actions that help reduce risks.

Compliance Manager has a number of templates, pre-populated with controls that are managed by both Microsoft and the customer. The default templates, included in all subscriptions (as of this writing), are listed as follows:

- **International Organization for Standardization (ISO)** *27001:2013*

- The **European Union (EU) General Data Protection Regulation (GDPR)**

- **National Institute of Standards and Technology (NIST)** *800-53* Revisions 4 and 5
- Microsoft Data Protection Baseline

Additional templates, such as the ones in the following list, are available with specific premium or government subscriptions. Premium templates may be purchased as well:

- ISO *27108:2014*
- ISO *27701:2019*
- NIST *800-171*
- NIST **Cybersecurity Framework (CSF)**
- **Cloud Security Alliance (CSA) Cloud Controls Matrix (CCM)** v3.0.1
- The **Federal Financial Institutions Examination Council (FFIEC)** Information Security booklet
- The **Health Insurance Portability and Accountability Act (HIPAA)** and the **Health Information Technology for Economic and Clinical Health Act (HITECH) Act** (sometimes abbreviated to **HITEC**)
- **Federal Risk and Authorization Management Program (FedRAMP)**
- The **California Consumer Privacy Act (CCPA)**
- The **Information Security Registered Assessors Program (IRAP)/Australian Government Information Security Manual (ISM)**

You can add any of these templates to Compliance Manager, as well as build or import your own templates using Microsoft Excel.

> **Custom Compliance Manager Templates**
>
> Compliance Manager templates are formatted in a Microsoft Excel workbook—not a standard **comma-separated values (CSV)** file. The Excel workbook must have several tabs, including tabs for **Assessment**, **ControlFamily**, **Actions**, and **Owner**. You can learn more about the structure of compliance templates at `https://docs.microsoft.com/en-us/microsoft-365/compliance/working-with-compliance-manager#templates`.

Compliance Manager allows organizations to assign and track compliance-related activities, such as managing evidence or artifacts that can later be provided to auditors. While Compliance Manager does not guarantee that an organization is compliant with a given standard or regulation, it certainly helps in the compliance journey.

To learn more about configuring Compliance Manager templates and controls, see
`https://docs.microsoft.com/en-us/microsoft-365/compliance/`
`compliance-manager-overview`.

Exploring your compliance score

As you learned in the previous section, Compliance Manager is a tool that you can use to track progress against various controls and standards. Your **compliance score** is a dashboard that helps you visualize that progress toward completed recommended improvement actions within the applicable controls.

When you launch Compliance Manager, your score is prominently displayed. An example is shown in the following screenshot:

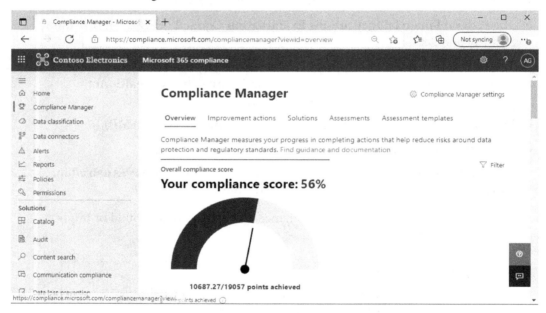

Figure 12.3 – Compliance Manager

At the bottom of the graph depicted in the preceding screenshot, you'll notice your score is represented as a fraction: points achieved/points available.

Your score is made up of three primary parts, as follows:

- **Improvement action score**: Each action is assigned a different value, based on the impact that it has or the potential risk condition that it's addressing. For example, configuring the message quarantine settings in Exchange Online protection is a much lower improvement action score than enabling **multi-factor authentication** (**MFA**).

- **Control score**: The control score is the total of the points earned within a particular control. This score is added to your compliance score when the actions have been implemented successfully and pass the automated testing.

- **Assessment score**: This score is the total of your control scores.

The compliance scores are calculated using the action scores. Each Microsoft action is counted once, as is each technical action that you manage. Each non-technical action (such as a policy or documentation) is counted once per group since these are generally viewed as organization-wide activities that only need to be completed one time.

Your tenant's compliance score is initially calculated using the default Microsoft Data Protection Baseline assessment, which pulls controls and standards from NIST and the CSF, ISO, FedRAMP, and GDPR.

Compliance Manager then automatically recalculates your score based on improvement actions that you perform. Generally, the results of improvement actions are visible in your compliance score the following day.

As we alluded to earlier, actions can be technical and non-technical. Technical actions require configuration of the platform and are scored once per action, regardless of how many groups they belong to. Non-technical actions are managed outside of the Microsoft 365 platform and manually recorded in Compliance Manager. Non-technical actions are classified as either **documentation** or **operational** and are scored at a group level.

Scoring

So, now that you know how the overall score is calculated, let's dig into how actions are assigned scores.

An action's score is based on whether the action is mandatory or discretionary, as well as whether the action is preventative, detective, or corrective. This is described in more detail here:

- **Mandatory**: These are actions that can't be bypassed by the user (either accidentally or intentionally). MFA and system password policies are examples of mandatory actions.

- **Discretionary**: These actions, however, rely on the user following a policy with no technical enforcement. For example, you may implement a policy that instructs each user to swipe a proximity badge to enter a building instead of holding the door open for a group of people.

- **Preventative**: If an action is designed to mitigate a specific risk, it is classified as a preventative action. Implementing an MFA solution is an example of a preventative action designed to minimize the impact of leaked credentials.

- **Detective**: These are monitoring actions designed to identify anomalous behavior. Deploying an application to detect port scanners or regular audits of **electronic discovery (eDiscovery)** logs are actions designed to find potentially malicious behaviors.

- **Corrective**: Corrective actions minimize or repair the damage incurred during an incident. Restoring a system from backups after a breach is an example of a corrective action.

The following table depicts the scores assigned to each category of actions:

Action type	Score
Preventative mandatory	27
Preventative discretionary	9
Detective mandatory	3
Detective discretionary	1
Corrective mandatory	3
Corrective discretionary	1

Table 12.1 – Action types and scores

You can review an individual action's score by selecting **Improvement actions** in Compliance Manager, as shown in the following screenshot:

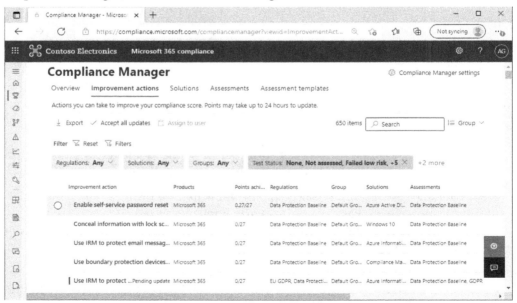

Figure 12.4 – Improvement actions

Next, we'll look at how the new IRM features of Microsoft 365 fit into the compliance story.

IRM

Microsoft 365 contains a set of policy tools to allow organizations to identify risky behaviors and activities as well as act on those alerts. IRM is located inside the Microsoft 365 Compliance portal at `https://compliance.microsoft.com/insiderriskmgmt`. IRM combines components from **data loss prevention** (**DLP**), sensitivity labels, **natural language processing** (**NLP**), sentiment analysis, access-control signals, and triggering events to quickly alert organizations to risks such as potential data theft by a departing employee or sensitive information leaks.

Microsoft 365 IRM is designed to help mitigate various internal risks, such as the following:

- Data theft by a terminated or departing employee

- Intentional or unintentional leaking of sensitive information

- Violations of internal corporate policy, such as offensive language, cyber-bullying, harassment, and threats

These risks (along with others) can be identified and investigated through the IRM process and workflow, as follows:

- **Policies**: IRM policies are used to define in-scope users and risk indicators.

- **Alerts**: Alerts are generated when risk indicators for in-scope users are triggered. These alerts allow administrators to determine the risk status and potentially begin triage actions.

- **Triage**: During triage, analysts review the alerts in detail and decide on the action to take: creating a case to track and work through the alert, adding the alert to an existing case, or dismissing the alert.

- **Investigate**: If analysts create cases or add alerts to existing cases, staff can continue to work and investigate the data in those cases.

- **Action**: Once a case has been investigated, analysts can resolve the case, generate a notice to the employee, or escalate the case for further action and investigation.

Policies are configured via templates in three categories, as shown in the following screenshot:

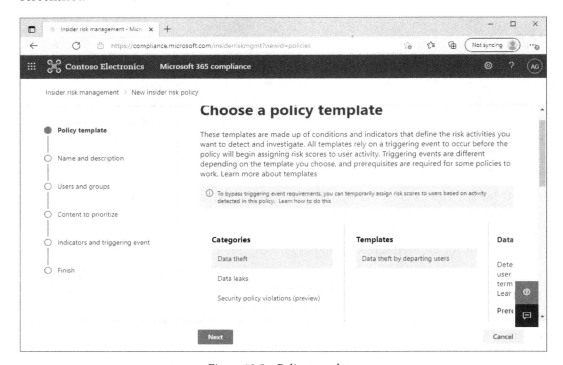

Figure 12.5 – Policy templates

A complete list of categories and templates is listed in the following table:

Category	Template
Data theft	Data theft by departing users
Data leaks	General data leaks
Data leaks	Data leaks by priority users
Data leaks	Data leaks by disgruntled users
Security policy violations	General security policy violations
Security policy violations	Security policy violations by departing users
Security policy violations	Security policy violations by disgruntled users
Security policy violations	Security policy violations by priority users

Table 12.2 – Policy template descriptions

Many IRM scenarios require the configuring of DLP policies as well as identifying groups of users to monitor.

In addition to configuring the policy templates and DLP prerequisites, there are additional data connectors that can be used to import signaling information to help provide more context for risk indicators, as follows:

- **Microsoft 365 Human Resources (HR) connector**: The HR connector can be used to import data from risk management and HR information system platforms. The connector adds indicator data for employment status and dates, termination status, job-level change status, and other HR-related data fields. The connector is required when configuring the following templates:

  - **Data theft by departing users**
  - **Security policy violations by departing users**
  - **Security policy violations by disgruntled users**
  - **Security policy violations by priority users**

- **Physical badging connector**: This connector supports importing data from physical access control systems, including data such as access point **identifiers (IDs)**, time and date values, user IDs, and whether the attempt was successful. In order to correlate access control data with user identities, you'll need to configure the Microsoft 365 HR connector as well.

IRM capabilities can contribute to compliance controls and improve not only your organization's compliance adherence but overall security as well.

IRM Configuration Deep Dive

While deep IRM knowledge isn't necessary for the *MS-900* exam, you can expand your knowledge of the platform by visiting `https://docs.microsoft.com/en-us/microsoft-365/compliance/insider-risk-solution-overview`.

IRM strategies may include configuring not only DLP policies but also things such as Exchange Online Transport Rules or Microsoft Teams Information Barriers to prevent groups of individuals from communicating with each other. All these components work together to mitigate the overall risk and exposure for an organization.

Insider Risk Management requires one of the following subscriptions:

- Microsoft 365 E5 (or comparable) subscription
- Microsoft 365 E3 (or comparable) subscription with the E5 (or comparable) Compliance add-on
- Microsoft 365 E3 (or comparable) subscription with the E5 (or comparable) Insider Risk Management add-on

Finally, we'll examine the Microsoft 365 Security Center and how it can be used to improve both your compliance score and your overall security posture.

Microsoft 365 Security Center

The Microsoft 365 Security Center is a unified portal experience designed to help you investigate and respond to threats across the Microsoft 365 ecosystem. In *Chapter 9, Understanding Security and Compliance Concepts with Microsoft 365*, we introduced the Microsoft 365 Security Center. The Microsoft 365 Security Center, also now known as **Microsoft 365 Defender**, is located at `https://security.microsoft.com`. The Microsoft 365 Security Center pulls together tools and resources from a number of security areas, including threat monitoring and hunting, attack simulation, alerting policies, email message tracing and threat investigation, and auditing, as shown in the following screenshot:

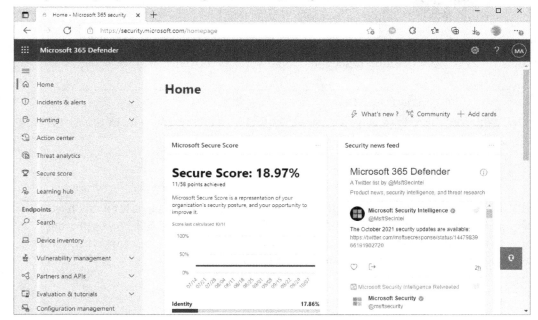

Figure 12.6 – Microsoft 365 Security Center dashboard

Similar to how Compliance Manager can be used to review improvement actions that impact your compliance score, the **Microsoft 365 Security Center** can also be used to review and implement improvement actions that impact your Secure Score, as shown in the following screenshot:

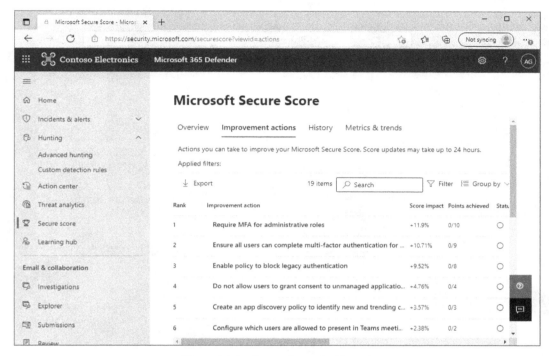

Figure 12.7 – Secure Score dashboard

As previously mentioned, the Microsoft 365 Security Center is also the home of threat analytics, which shows a consolidated view of risks across email and physical devices, as illustrated in the following screenshot:

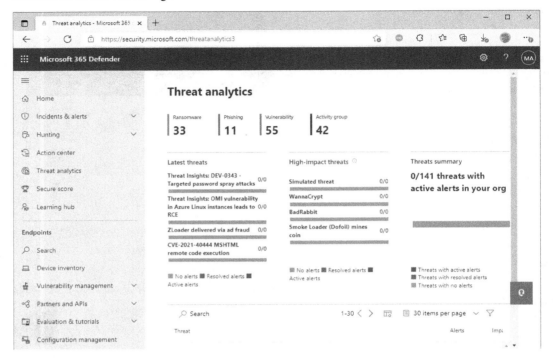

Figure 12.8 – Threat analytics dashboard

You can use the threat analytics and hunting components of the Microsoft 365 Security Center to track possible security risks throughout your organization, as well as create incidents for further review and analysis.

Summary

In this chapter, we discussed both the STP and Compliance Manager. Together, the STP and Compliance Manager can help organizations achieve and maintain compliance with industry-based standards and regulatory controls.

We also covered some of the most common questions organizations have when assessing a cloud service, such as how data is secured, where data is stored, and what data resiliency protection is in place.

Then, we introduced the new IRM features that can be used to help mitigate and manage a variety of risk scenarios, such as data loss from terminated employees or exposure from internal communications. Finally, we reviewed some of the capabilities inside the Microsoft 365 Defender portal, highlighting features such as **Secure Score** and IRM.

In the next chapter, we'll begin reviewing licensing options, including which cloud services may be available on licensing styles or agreements.

Questions

Use the following questions to test your knowledge of this chapter. You can find the answers in *Chapter 18, Assessments*:

1. Which Microsoft 365 tool can organizations use to track their progress against industry compliance standards?

    A.   GDPR Accelerator

    B.   Compliance Accelerator

    C.   Compliance Manager

    D.   Compliance dashboard

2. Identify three encryption technologies or platforms used to secure data in Microsoft 365 from the following:

    A.   BitLocker

    B.   Bootstrapper

    C.   Encryption Manager

    D.   IPsec

    E.   TLS

3. Data residency answers which of the following questions?

    A.   What encryption is used to protect my data?

    B.   Where is my data stored?

    C.   Who has access to my data?

    D.   Which security standards are applied to my data?

4. Tenant isolation refers to which of the following concepts?

   A.   Separation of organizational data in a single-tenant environment

   B.   Separation of organizational data in a multi-tenant environment

   C.   Securing record storage in a third-party system

   D.   GDPR compliance

5. Which two terms apply to how data in Microsoft 365 is encrypted?

   A.   At rest

   B.   In transit

   C.   In potente

   D.   En masse

6. Compliance Manager allows you to import custom templates.

   A.   True

   B.   False

7. GDPR stands for which of the following?

   A.   General Data Privacy Regulation

   B.   General Data Protection Regulation

   C.   General Data Primary Regulation

   D.   General Data Proposed Regulation

8. Compliance Manager contains built-in templates for which three standards?

   A.   NIST *800-53*

   B.   NIST CSF

   C.   Hodge-Simmons

   D.   GDPR

9. Tenant isolation answers which question?

    A. Where is my data stored?

    B. How is my data encrypted?

    C. How does my SP handle my data?

    D. How is my data separated from other organizations?

10. Which three scores make up the compliance score?

    A. Improvement activity score

    B. Improvement action score

    C. Control score

    D. Baseline score

    E. Assessment score

    F. Attainment score

11. The Microsoft 365 Security Center can be used to track your compliance score.

    A. True

    B. False

12. _____ is a set of tools used to mitigate internal scenarios such as data leakage from disgruntled employees.

    A. Internal Risk Management

    B. Insider Risk Management

    C. Internal Risk Mitigation

    D. Insider Risk Mitigation

13. _____ is a tool that allows you to track improvement actions to improve your security posture.

   A.   Secure Score

   B.   Azure Sentinel

   C.   Azure AD Premium

   D.   Advanced Audit

14. What are the five phases of the IRM workflow?

   A.   Assess

   B.   Policies

   C.   Alerts

   D.   Detect

   E.   Respond

   F.   Triage

   G.   Investigate

   H.   Remediate

   I.   Escalate

   J.   Action

Section 4: Understanding Microsoft 365 Pricing and Support

In this section, you'll learn how to acquire Microsoft 365 services, as well as the support and serviceability options and terms. Microsoft provides several options for licensing and support, as well as defined life cycles for every product and service.

This section comprises the following chapters:

13
Licensing in Microsoft 365

As organizations advance through their assessment of Microsoft 365, they will usually discuss it in terms of understanding business value, technical features, requirements, and security and compliance features. Once the business conversations are complete, they will look at acquiring licenses to support their decision. Finally, they'll work through determining the best implementation and deployment options.

In this chapter, we will cover the following topics:

- Microsoft 365 subscription and management options
- Understanding key Microsoft 365 selling points
- Licensing and payment models
- Determining and implementing best practices
- Differences between Azure AD licenses

By the end of this chapter, you should have an understanding of how Microsoft 365 licensing is structured and what decisions you'll need to make when procuring or advising organizations on deciding from available options.

Microsoft 365 subscription and management options

Deciding which Microsoft 365 subscription to acquire is not a simple task. Organizations need to plan and consider various business factors, which will ultimately drive the purchase decision. The following list details some of the common aspects and decision points:

- **Per-user, rather than per device**: For most cloud-based services, organizations should plan on acquiring licensing based on the user rather than device counts. While some industries or roles rely on shared devices or equipment, it will be important to determine which models apply to you. Most organizations will require a mix of individual or user-based licensing, as well as shared or common device licensing. Plan on identifying the numbers of individual users, as well as the numbers of shared devices when estimating costs. While some very specific licensing agreements will allow some organizations (such as education customers) to license Microsoft 365 Apps *only* (not other Microsoft 365 services) on a per-device basis, generally, the Microsoft 365 products and services are licensed per user.

- **Service family**: Depending on your organization's size, type, or region, you may be eligible to acquire different licenses. Some of the service families include Business (maximum of 300 users), Enterprise, Education (only available for educational institutions), Government (only available to public sector organizations), as well as sovereign cloud environments such as Office 365, which are operated by 21Vianet in China or Office 365 Germany.

- **Standalone versus bundle**: If your organization plans to use only one particular piece of Microsoft 365 software or an individual service, you may have the option to acquire plans for standalone services (such as Exchange Online, Microsoft 365 Apps, or SharePoint Online). As you choose services to acquire, however, bundled SKUs frequently provide better value. Most organizations choose to acquire bundles that include several services and provide a cost advantage.

- **Bundle service availability**: Not all services are available in an SKU bundle; bundles may have different levels of service associated with them. It's important to evaluate the exact features that are driving the business decision so that you can purchase them accordingly.

- **Short-term versus long-term**: Even though licenses can be changed, whenever possible, organizations should attempt to predict what their users will need and plan accordingly to avoid surprise reconciliation bills at the end of their billing term.

After deciding on the user and service requirements, organizations can acquire licenses. This license assignment to end users is managed through the **Microsoft 365 admin center**, Azure AD portal, or PowerShell, and an organization can easily review the licenses that are available and have been assigned to users in their tenant, as shown in the following screenshot:

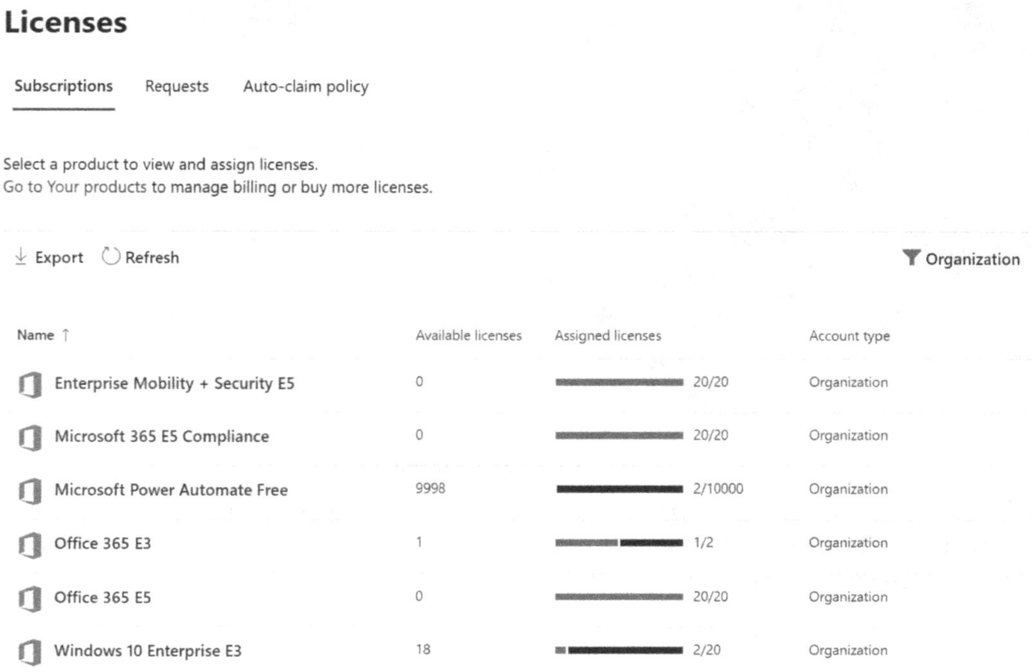

Licenses

Subscriptions   Requests   Auto-claim policy

Select a product to view and assign licenses.
Go to Your products to manage billing or buy more licenses.

↓ Export ○ Refresh   ▼ Organization

Name ↑	Available licenses	Assigned licenses		Account type
Enterprise Mobility + Security E5	0		20/20	Organization
Microsoft 365 E5 Compliance	0		20/20	Organization
Microsoft Power Automate Free	9998		2/10000	Organization
Office 365 E3	1		1/2	Organization
Office 365 E5	0		20/20	Organization
Windows 10 Enterprise E3	18		2/20	Organization

Figure 13.1 – Subscriptions in the Microsoft 365 admin center

By clicking on any of the available licenses, an administrator can review which user they were assigned to. An administrator can then decide if they want to selectively enable or disable one of the component services that's available as part of this license for the selected user, as shown in the following screenshot:

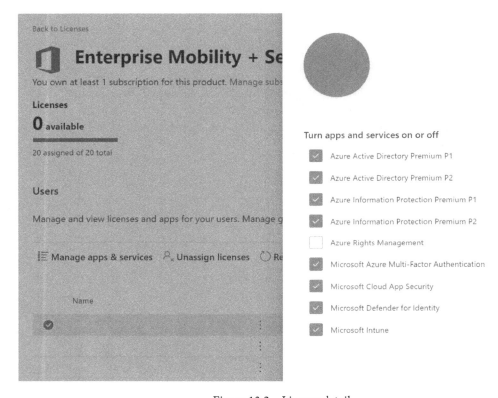

Figure 13.2 – License detail

Under each user's account properties, administrators with proper permissions can also see which licenses have been assigned to particular users, as well as remove or edit these license assignments, as shown in the following screenshot:

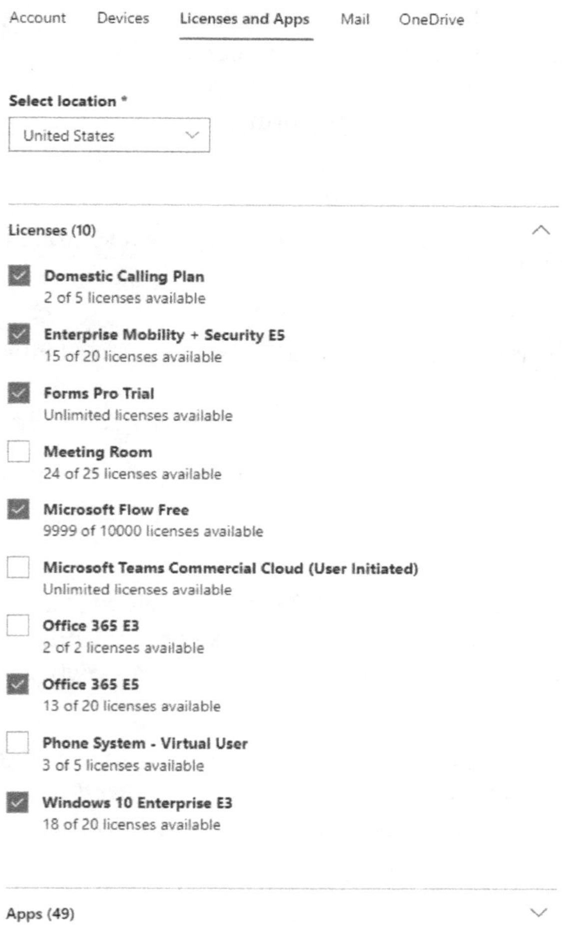

Account   Devices   **Licenses and Apps**   Mail   OneDrive

Select location *

```
United States          ∨
```

Licenses (10)   ∧

☑ **Domestic Calling Plan**
   2 of 5 licenses available

☑ **Enterprise Mobility + Security E5**
   15 of 20 licenses available

☑ **Forms Pro Trial**
   Unlimited licenses available

☐ **Meeting Room**
   24 of 25 licenses available

☑ **Microsoft Flow Free**
   9999 of 10000 licenses available

☐ **Microsoft Teams Commercial Cloud (User Initiated)**
   Unlimited licenses available

☐ **Office 365 E3**
   2 of 2 licenses available

☑ **Office 365 E5**
   13 of 20 licenses available

☐ **Phone System - Virtual User**
   3 of 5 licenses available

☑ **Windows 10 Enterprise E3**
   18 of 20 licenses available

Apps (49)   ∨

Figure 13.3 – User account license detail view

Moreover, license assignments can be automated or made in bulk through Microsoft Graph, PowerShell, or Azure group-based licensing (https://docs.microsoft.com/en-us/azure/active-directory/fundamentals/active-directory-licensing-whatis-azure-portal).

Many applications and services also include the ability to enable or disable features, so it is up to the business and technology teams to discuss what options or features can be managed.

Next, let's look at some of the things that go into the decision-making process, such as working with business stakeholders and requirements gathering. Part of building a Microsoft 365 strategy requires understanding the business requirements, how they map to the key features or selling points in the platform, and what the license procurement requirements are.

Understanding key Microsoft 365 selling points

When making purchasing decisions, some organizations may need different stakeholders' approval before being authorized to acquire a service. This may include needing to document current requirements and why a particular service solves them.

In this section, we'll review some of the key Microsoft 365 selling points.

Productivity

One of the primary design goals of Microsoft 365 is to enable personal and group productivity. This is possible largely due to the integration of the different products and services that comprise the suites, which can be accessed on a variety of devices in a secure and compliant manner.

Under a **Software as a Service** (**SaaS**) model, users have access to a wide variety of applications that are always up to date and managed by Microsoft, which facilitates email, file sharing, chat, meetings, presentation, social networking, storage, business process automation, and low-code development.

Collaboration

People collaborate and work with teams more now than they ever have. Studies performed by organizations such as McKinsey (`https://www.mckinsey.com/industries/technology-media-and-telecommunications/our-insights/the-social-economy`) show that social networking and collaboration lead to increased productivity and output.

In the business landscape, this collaboration happens with both internal and external users, from both a corporate and consumer perspective. Microsoft 365, as a SaaS model, provides services that enable this collaboration in all of these types of scenarios.

For example, organizations can store and share files with users both inside and outside the organization using Microsoft Teams, OneDrive for Business, and SharePoint Online, or by delivering attachments to external individuals using consumer email systems. Other scenarios involve creating and coauthoring files across different Office clients and users or creating a common workspace for groups to collaborate with Microsoft Teams. These collaborative workspaces can reduce context switching while providing access to the relevant tools and experiences for chat, files, meetings, and calls in a single tool.

Security

Microsoft 365 was designed to enable productivity and collaboration while staying secure. Security, one of the pillars of the service, can be seen across the suite, from tenant isolation and data encryption to risk-based conditional access. Microsoft 365 allows organizations to deploy multi-factor authentication services and even extend those to their on-premises applications, in addition to creating and applying data classification tags to documents and messages.

Microsoft 365 also allows organizations to apply data management policies to mobile devices, ensuring that data can't move from managed or privileged applications to unmanaged applications or wipe data in managed devices or applications if users fail to authenticate. These capabilities allow organizations to protect on-premises, cloud, and hybrid environments against attacks such as compromised accounts by detecting unknown activities through several behavioral and heuristic strategies.

In addition, security administrators can access tools such as Secure Score (`https://security.microsoft.com/securescore`) so that they can understand their security posture and evaluate actions they can perform to improve.

Compliance

Microsoft 365 supports organizations throughout their compliance journey. Microsoft is committed to building and maintaining a trusted computing environment and, as such, submits to numerous third-party audits to ensure compliance with industry security standards. Azure and Microsoft 365 services have obtained several industry certifications, such as **Payment Card Industry (PCI)**, **International Standards Organization (ISO) 27001**, **National Institute of Standards and Technology (NIST) 800-53**, **Health Insurance Portability and Accountability Act (HIPAA)**, the **General Data Protection Regulation (GDPR)**, and the **Federal Risk and Authorization Management Program (FedRAMP)**.

Microsoft provides Compliance Manager (`https://servicetrust.microsoft.com/ComplianceManager/v3`), a compliance reporting and management tool, to help organizations track their compliance against various industry standards. Compliance Manager allows administrators to download Microsoft's attestations and compliance certification documents so that they can be included in the organization's documentation. Compliance Manager also catalogs audited controls and allows compliance administrators to track their own organization's compliance actions. The **Compliance Manager** dashboard is shown in the following screenshot:

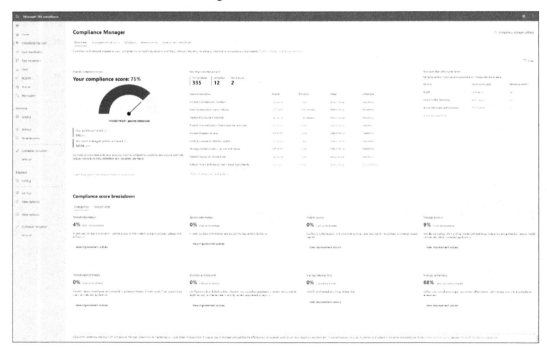

Figure 13.4 – Compliance Manager

From a service perspective, Microsoft 365 provides mechanisms such as the Security & Compliance Center (`https://compliance.microsoft.com`) for administrators to enforce data governance and life cycle policies, encryption, data loss prevention, and eDiscovery case management activities.

While many of the service's features, capabilities, and selling points are available across all service offerings, there are some differences based on which product family an organization purchases. We'll explore some of those differences next.

Licensing and payment models

As you'll see in *Chapter 14, Planning, Predicting, and Comparing Pricing*, there are many different license acquisition and payment models available. Microsoft 365 has these different licensing and payment options so that they are suitable for their wide range of customer requirements. The main licensing service families and SKU bundles, as we discussed earlier in this chapter, are as follows:

- **Microsoft 365 for home**: There are two subscriptions available for personal use: Microsoft 365 Personal and Microsoft 365 Family. The main difference between them is the number of supported users, which corresponds to six in the Family plan versus one in the Personal plan.

- **Microsoft 365 Business**: This bundle is intended for small to medium-sized businesses with up to 300 employees. Microsoft 365 Business offers a compelling mix of features and basic service plans. Microsoft 365 Business does not include advanced compliance features such as retention or the unlimited storage of Microsoft 365 Enterprise plans. It also does not include Windows 10. The available Business plans are Microsoft 365 Business Basic, Microsoft 365 Apps for Business, Microsoft 365 Business Standard, and Microsoft 365 Business Premium. This last one, Microsoft 365 Business Premium, is the only plan that includes Intune and Azure Information Protection.

- **Microsoft 365 Commercial (E-series or F-series)**: These SKU packages are intended for enterprise organizations with variations across the employee usage profile (sometimes referred to as *personas*). Most larger commercial organizations pick a mix of SKUs from this family of services, including SKUs for personas, termed as *information workers* or *knowledge workers*, as well as personas such as *frontline workers* (sometimes referred to as *line workers, front-of-house employees,* or *shift workers*). These SKUs are available worldwide, though some may be reformulated slightly due to encryption and export restrictions or when there are restrictions in place due to sovereign cloud agreements. Microsoft 365 includes Windows, as well as advanced, features. Microsoft 365 E-series plans come with three licensing levels (E1, E3, and E5), with E5 having additional advanced compliance, productivity, and security features available. Some of the key differences between the E and F series are that some E-series plans include 100 GB mailboxes and unlimited OneDrive for Business storage, while F-series plans are limited to 2 GB mailboxes and 1 TB of OneDrive for Business storage.

- **Microsoft 365 A-series**: This set of SKUs is typically used for educational institutions. Educational SKUs exist in the commercial environment and share the same infrastructure but are available at deeply discounted rates to qualifying organizations. Microsoft 365 A-series SKUs are comparable to their E-series counterparts.

- **Microsoft 365 G-series**: The G SKUs are reserved for US government public sector entities, such as federal, state, and local municipality governments or dedicated contractors. These SKUs are not available in commercial or other sovereign clouds. These SKUs are tied to a separate sovereign infrastructure that is wholly inside the United States and is FedRAMP certified. These FedRAMP-certified environments are commonly referred to as **Government Community Cloud (GCC)** Moderate, GCC-High, and GCC-DOD. Organizations that require compliance with IRS Publication 1075 and **Criminal Justice Information Services (CJIS)** typically choose the GCC environments, as do organizations that require United States-based data residency. Like Microsoft 365 E-series, the G-series is also available in two licensing levels (G3 and G5), with a higher level having more advanced productivity, security, and compliance features. G-series SKUs typically don't feature all of the services of commercial SKUs as products must go through additional certification and validation before being offered.

- **Individual licenses**: In addition to the ability to acquire bundled SKU licenses, organizations in any cloud (commercial, public sector, or sovereign) can also acquire individual licenses, either as add-ons to bundles or as standalone products.

Subscription Limitations

It's important to note that you cannot mix SKU service families between the commercial and government ones. If you are purchasing for a government or public sector organization, you should evaluate whether you require compliance with **IRS Publication 1075 (Pub1075)** or CJIS. If you don't require compliance with those services, it may be more beneficial to choose a commercial cloud offering, despite being a public sector organization. Government and public sector organizations are not required to be in a GCC offering, though many choose to be, depending on their reporting, compliance, data residency, or other security requirements.

In addition, some of the different payment models of Microsoft 365 are as follows:

- **Credit card or bank account**: Schedule a recurring credit card charge or bank account draft to pay for services.

- **Invoice**: An organization can receive an invoice with payment terms for Microsoft 365 services.

- **Prepaid product key**: Products and services can be purchased with a pre-paid license key at some retail locations.

> **Payment Detail**
>
> The frequency of these payments can be set to a monthly or yearly basis.
> You can learn more at `https://docs.microsoft.com/en-us/`
> `office365/admin/subscriptions-and-billing/change-`
> `payment-method?view=o365-worldwide`.

As you can see, while there are several decisions to make when choosing the right Microsoft 365 SKU licensing options, your market vertical (small business, enterprise commercial, academic, or public sector) largely defines which family of SKUs you can purchase. We'll look at the exact pricing models more closely in *Chapter 14, Planning, Predicting, and Comparing Pricing.*

In the next section, we'll review some of the best practices for designing a licensing strategy.

Determining and implementing best practices

With several options to choose from, especially from a licensing perspective, companies often have questions about which licenses to acquire. The following is a list of best practices that can help an organization decide how to proceed:

- **Define service and feature requirements**: As we mentioned previously, organizations should evaluate their business requirements and map what services and features that are in the various products map to their business goals and objectives.

- **Define user profiles or personas**: Especially in larger organizations, Microsoft recommends categorizing employees in profiles or *personas* based on their location within the organization (such as C-suite users, frontline workers, or knowledge workers), job roles, or some other business criteria. Once the users have been profiled and organized, identify the particular service and feature requirements that those roles or profiles have and map them to the appropriate features in Microsoft 365. This can be used to drive licensing and SKU assignments. As part of this exercise, organizations should plan for labor force changes (such as seasonal workers).

- **Plan for a baseline**: While different user profiles may allow organizations to choose different products, SKUs, or bundles, it's also important to establish a baseline of required features or services that apply to all users. For example, if you have one requirement that can be fulfilled with Exchange Online Plan 1, but then you have an organizational requirement for retention policies, you'll need to either acquire an archiving add-on or an Exchange Online Plan 2 license to support the business goal.

- **Individual versus bundle**: It may be beneficial to perform an analysis of which features are requirements and can be purchased through bundles or as individual items, as organizations typically don't deploy all the features or products available in a bundle. Frequently, though, if there are two or more required services or features, it's more cost-effective to look at an SKU bundle.

- **Consider add-ons**: Sometimes, though, there are situations where *only* an add-on solves a problem (if a product isn't included in a bundle) or only an add-on service is needed. One example is licensing for Exchange Online shared mailboxes. Organizations are entitled to shared and resource mailboxes *free of charge*. However, the shared or resource mailbox license doesn't support mailbox archiving or retention policies. In this case, if there is a requirement for archiving or retention policies, organizations may want to look at an add-on SKU for Exchange Online Archiving for those mailboxes.

- **Consider the internal deployment roadmap**: If an organization doesn't have plans to deploy a service to all their users at once, they could consider acquiring the service in cycles, ramping up their acquisition as they prepare to onboard more users.

Once the licensing requirements have been worked out, organizations need to decide on their license acquisition plans, as well as their service deployment and implementation plans. Next, we will provide details on the different capabilities available in each Azure AD license option.

Differences between Azure AD licenses

As we've explained so far in this chapter, the choice of which license to acquire is determined by several factors, with one of them being the technical capability of the service. **Azure Active Directory (Azure AD)** is one of them, which requires an understanding of the different capabilities that are available in each plan to decide from before the acquisition.

Now, we will explain what the main service differences between the Azure AD licenses are:

- **Azure Active Directory Free**: Available with a subscription to a commercial service, such as Dynamics or Azure, includes on-premises directory synchronization, reports, and the ability for cloud users to reset their passwords without admin interaction.

- **Azure Active Directory P1**: Available as part of the Microsoft 365 F3 or Microsoft 365 E3 plan or acquired as an add-on for other plans in which it is not available, it includes Azure Active Directory Free features, the ability to create dynamic groups based on a user property, such as a department, conditional access to restrict the access to specific services based on the condition of the user, and the ability for on-premises synchronized users to reset their passwords in the cloud, which are written back to the local directory.

- **Azure Active Directory P2**: Available as part of Microsoft 365 E5 or acquired as an add-on for other plans in which it is not available, it includes Azure Active Directory P1 features, as well as the ability to structure conditional access based on the risk of a user, calculated automatically against several conditions and the Privileged Identity Management service, which allows administrators to configure Just-in-Time access to roles and permissions when needed.

You can learn more about some of the specific features included with Azure Active Directory Premium 1 and Premium 2 by going back to *Chapter 3, Core Microsoft 365 Components*.

Summary

In this chapter, we covered some of the key points an organization should consider when formulating its cloud services purchase plan. A proper Microsoft 365 licensing management plan requires a careful understanding of an organization's requirements and user profiles. In particular, organizations should seek to understand the benefits (directly or indirectly) that a service can provide from productivity, collaboration, security, and compliance perspectives. These benefits are typically articulated to make the case for purchase. This chapter showed you the importance of mapping business requirements to selling points or features in the Microsoft 365 platform to ensure the right services are acquired.

In the next chapter, we'll dive deeper into understanding the purchase and payment subscription models that are available.

Questions

Answer the following questions to test your knowledge of this chapter. You can find the answers in *Chapter 18, Assessments*:

1. You are the IT director for a small commercial organization that contains 220 employees. You are looking for the most cost-effective solution to provide Microsoft 365 services to your users. Which should you choose?

    A.   Microsoft 365 E3

    B.   Microsoft 365 E5

    C.   Microsoft 365 G3

    D.   Microsoft 365 Business Standard

    E.   Microsoft 365 A3

2. When purchasing Enterprise, Government, or Education plans, all the plans must be the same. It is not possible to mix and match E3 and E5 (or G3 and G5) SKUs in the same tenant.

    A.   True

    B.   False

3. You are the IT director for a public sector organization and you require data residency in the United States. What service family should you choose?

    A.   Microsoft 365 Commercial

    B.   Microsoft 365 GCC

    C.   Microsoft 365 Business

    D.   Microsoft 365 Education

4. You are the IT director for a large commercial organization with 15,000 employees worldwide. Which Microsoft 365 product service family should you choose?

    A.   Microsoft 365 Commercial

    B.   Microsoft 365 GCC

    C.   Microsoft 365 Business

    D.   Microsoft 365 Education

5.   Identify three best practices for determining your licensing strategy.

   A.   Plan for a baseline

   B.   Define user profiles or personas

   C.   Define service and feature requirements

   D.   Sign a non-disclosure agreement

6.   Identify two of the key Microsoft 365 selling points.

   A.   Productivity

   B.   Expensive

   C.   Vulnerable

   D.   Compliance

7.   Identify two of the key Microsoft 365 selling points.

   A.   Security

   B.   Collaboration

   C.   Static

   D.   Disconnected

8.   Microsoft 365 is typically licensed _____.

   A.   Per organization

   B.   Per tenant

   C.   Per user

   D.   Per device

9.   Organizations can choose Microsoft GCC if they meet which requirement?

   A.   Public sector

   B.   Compliance

   C.   Educational institution

   D.   Desire

10. Identify three benefits for public sector organizations choosing the GCC sovereign cloud:

   A.   IRS Publication 1070 Compliance

   B.   IRS Publication 1075 Compliance

   C.   **Criminal Justice Information Services (CJIS)** Compliance

   D.   United States Data Residency

11. _____ is a Microsoft-provided tool that customers can use to track compliance against industry standards and controls.

   A.   Compliance Tracker

   B.   License Manager

   C.   Azure Compliance Center

   D.   Compliance Manager

   E.   Azure Security Center

14
Planning, Predicting, and Comparing Pricing

In addition to deciding what features and licenses need to be acquired for an organization's business needs, it's important to decide how best to procure the licenses. While a number of different purchase models exist, a proper agreement should take into consideration the costs over time of a cloud solution when compared to any current or on-premises solution. Different models and purchase arrangements may have additional costs, markups, or discounts, depending on the volume and the acquisition method.

In this chapter, we'll tackle the following:

- Licensing models
- Cost-benefit analysis for on-premises versus the cloud
- Billing options

Let's get going!

Licensing models

At the time of writing, there are two core license acquisition models: **direct licensing** and **indirect licensing**.

Direct licensing refers to when an organization makes a direct purchase, such as through the Microsoft admin center.

Indirect licensing refers to when an organization makes a purchase through a partner or reseller agreement. There are currently six indirect licensing methods available to acquire Microsoft 365, which are as follows:

- **Cloud Solution Provider** (**CSP**): Organizations establish a billing relationship with a provider, who purchases on their behalf and sells the licenses to the customer.

- **Microsoft Open** (**includes Open Value, Open Value Subscription, and Open License**): The Open License program allows customers to buy licensing through a reseller, typically for smaller organizations (more than 5 seats and typically fewer than 500). As of the end of 2021, customers who wish to purchase via Open License will be directed to CSPs. For up-to-date changes to licensing programs, see `https://www.microsoft.com/en-us/licensing`.

- **Enterprise Agreement** (**EA**): A program that is designed for larger organizations (more than 500 users or devices) and can include cloud services and software licenses together.

- **Microsoft Products and Services Agreement** (**MPSA**): A purchasing account structure designed for organizations that use product pools and groupings to determine the price of services. Organizations must have more than 250 users or devices.

- **Services Provider License Agreement** (**SPLA**): A license structure designed for independent software vendors and service providers who want to license and host applications and services for customers.

- **Select Plus**: Select Plus is a purchasing mechanism targeted at large organizations with a number of affiliates who want to purchase as one entity. It is no longer available to commercial customers but is available for public sector customers.

Many Microsoft cloud services are calculated based on the number of users (commonly referred to as *seats*) that will be subscribing to a particular service or plan. Several key characteristics should be assessed when deciding which model is right for your organization:

- The minimum number of seats

- When you can make changes to the number of seats (either additions or removals)

- The cadence of the billing (annual, pay as you go, or some other contract mechanism)
- Which products or services are available under the licensing model
- The duration of the agreement

For the MS-900 exam, we'll highlight the structure and requirements of the **CSP** model.

The CSP program is designed for Microsoft Partners and **Value-Added Resellers (VARs)** as a way to develop long-lasting, holistic partnerships with customers. The CSP program has a wealth of tools available to help partners and VARs provide value to their customers.

When evaluating the CSP program against the aforementioned criteria, we're able to determine the following characteristics:

- A minimum of one seat.
- The number of seats that can be changed on a monthly basis.
- The billing cadence is monthly (sometimes referred to as *pay as you go*).
- All Microsoft Online Services products are available.
- The agreement has a minimum duration of 1 year.

CSP Program Deep Dive

You can find more information about the CSP program licensing models by following this link: `https://partner.microsoft.com/en-us/licensing`. You can also learn more about the other licensing programs, such as EA and Open, at `https://www.microsoft.com/en-us/licensing/licensing-programs/licensing-programs`. It's also important to note that the Select Plus program is no longer accepting new commercial enrollments and is only available for public sector customers.

Licensing and acquisition costs are part of the **Total Cost of Ownership** (**TCO**) of any product or service (whether for on-premises or cloud services). In the next section, we'll examine more closely the case for cloud services by performing a cost-benefit analysis.

Cost-benefit analysis for on-premises versus the cloud

When deciding on a licensing model, many customers ask themselves several questions:

- How much would it cost to proceed with a comparable on-premises solution?
- What is the risk of not doing anything?
- How long will it take to achieve a **Return on Investment (ROI)**?

These types of questions highlight the importance of cost-benefit analysis in an online services solution acquisition.

Organizations should engage in a cost-benefit analysis or produce a business case to ensure they're making a wise business choice. When setting up the analysis, the organization should gather details surrounding the costs and capabilities of their current environment so that they can compare them to the Microsoft 365 solution.

When performing a cost-benefit analysis for a cloud solution, an organization should compare the following benefits of Microsoft 365 against their current infrastructure components or any proposed on-premises infrastructure upgrades:

- Improved security
- Reduced TCO
- End user productivity
- Increased availability and reduced downtime
- Employee savings with new or improved collaboration scenarios
- Employee savings with new or improved mobility scenarios
- Infrastructure maintainability
- Improved compliance
- Travel savings
- Vendor license cost consolidation
- IT administration and deployment savings
- Reduced total cost of risk
- Physical and travel expense cost displacement
- Automation and process improvement savings
- Capital expenditure to operational expenditure cash flow

Out of these, a very important item to highlight is the reduced total cost of risk, which considers how relying on Microsoft 365 to handle all aspects of security needed to run and maintain the service, providing security capabilities such as multi-factor authentication, can significantly reduce the associated usage risk of such solutions.

The following table compares the capabilities of on-premises and cloud deployments:

Capability or Task	On-Premises Deployment	Microsoft 365 Cloud Service Deployment
Infrastructure acquisition and maintenance	Customer-owned and customer-managed.	Microsoft-owned and Microsoft-managed.
Upgrades	Customer's responsibility.	Microsoft's responsibility.
Security	Customer's responsibility.	Microsoft implements security protocols and attestation for engineering and support resources. The customer is responsible for using the tools provided to further secure user identities, applications, and devices.
Compliance	The customer is responsible for developing, deploying, administering, and documenting controls.	Microsoft is responsible for some managed controls. Certification is performed and validated on a regular basis. Microsoft and the customer share responsibility for other controls. The customer is required to follow best practices to implement and document their portion of the controls.
End user productivity	The customer is responsible for measuring productivity with the available tools implemented and maintained locally.	It's the customer's responsibility to manage and report on user adoption with reporting tools provided by Microsoft.

Capability or Task	On-Premises Deployment	Microsoft 365 Cloud Service Deployment
Mobility	Based on versions and applications deployed and managed by the customer and governed by customer networking configuration and capability. It requires the purchase, deployment, configuration, and management of a **Mobile Device Management** (**MDM**) platform.	Available for all apps included in the product suite. An MDM platform is included.
Infrastructure acquisition and maintenance	Customer-owned and customer-managed.	Microsoft-owned and Microsoft-managed.
Upgrades	Customer's responsibility.	Microsoft's responsibility.
Security	Customer's responsibility.	Microsoft implements security protocols and attestation for engineering and support resources. The customer is responsible for using the tools provided to further secure user identities, applications, and devices.
Compliance	The customer is responsible for developing, deploying, administering, and documenting controls.	Microsoft is responsible for some managed controls. Certification is performed and validated on a regular basis. Microsoft and the customer share responsibility for other controls. The customer is required to follow best practices to implement and document their portion of the controls.
End user productivity	The customer is responsible for measuring productivity with the available tools implemented and maintained locally.	It's the customer's responsibility to manage and report on user adoption with reporting tools provided by Microsoft.

Mobility	Based on versions and applications deployed and managed by the customer and governed by customer networking configuration and capability. It requires the purchase, deployment, configuration, and management of an MDM platform.	Available for all apps included in the product suite. An MDM platform is included.

Table 14.1 – Provider responsibility matrix

Organizations should also take advantage of reviewing public case studies and, if possible, study how other companies measured the progress and benefits of a cloud solution. If an organization is engaging with a partner to purchase and deploy services, they may also be able to obtain customer references to get an understanding of a solution's real-world value.

After performing a cost benefit analysis using the tools provided in this section, you can provide your organization with recommendations for adopting services.

Next, we'll look at the various methods to pay for services.

Billing options

Billing or billing cadence has to do with the model with which a license payment is made as well as the frequency of payments. The billing cadence varies depending on the chosen license model.

In direct license models, such as when a customer acquires a solution directly via an online ordering portal, customers can choose to pay by credit card or bank account, by invoice, or by using a prepaid product key. The frequency of these payments can be monthly or annually, and customers can switch their payment methods and frequency over the course of a subscription.

Customers can choose the payment servicing options shown in the following screenshot during the checkout process:

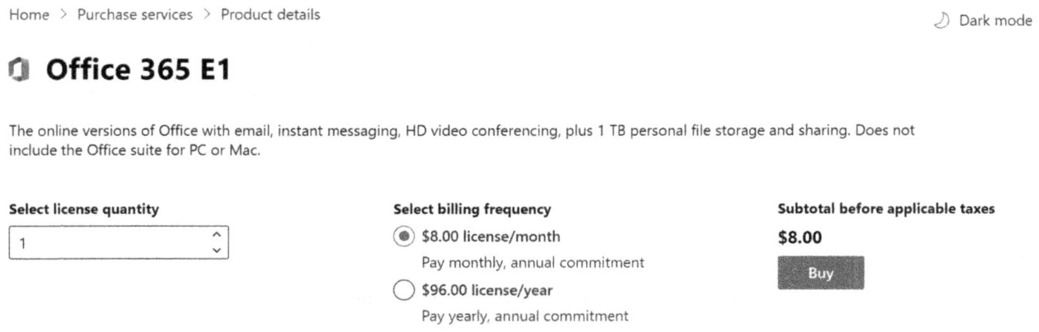

Home > Purchase services > Product details   ☽ Dark mode

🔲 Office 365 E1

The online versions of Office with email, instant messaging, HD video conferencing, plus 1 TB personal file storage and sharing. Does not include the Office suite for PC or Mac.

Select license quantity   **Select billing frequency**   **Subtotal before applicable taxes**

| 1 | ⌃⌄ |

◉ $8.00 license/month   **$8.00**

Pay monthly, annual commitment

○ $96.00 license/year   Buy

Pay yearly, annual commitment

Figure 14.1 – Payment options

> **Payment Options in Microsoft 365**
>
> You can learn more about billing in Microsoft 365 at `https://docs.microsoft.com/en-us/office365/admin/subscriptions-and-billing/subscriptions-and-billing?view=o365-worldwide`.

However, when using an indirect license model, such as CSP, EA, or the Microsoft Products and Services Agreement, purchasing and financing agreements are usually made through a partner or VAR and can have customized terms.

For example, in the CSP license model, the partner receives an invoice from Microsoft for the end customer organization's licenses, and the end customer organization signs a billing or payment agreement with the CSP.

> **How Billing Works with the CSP Program**
>
> You can learn more about billing with the CSP license model at `https://docs.microsoft.com/en-us/partner-center/billing-basics`.

Summary

There are different options from which organizations can choose when deciding on the license model for their agreement so that they can find the one that best suits their needs with regard to billing, duration, seat change requirements, and product availability. As we discussed, one of the main license models available is the CSP model, which is very flexible from both the provider (reseller) and customer perspectives in terms of billing. In addition, we also covered the importance of doing a cost-benefit analysis of the acquisition of a cloud solution, such as Microsoft 365, and we looked at the resources available to help you build it. You should be able to articulate the value and differences of the billing models available in Microsoft 365.

In the next chapter, we're going to look at the types of support and service offerings available with Microsoft 365.

Questions

Use the following questions to test the knowledge you gained in this chapter. You can find the answers in *Chapter 18, Assessments*:

1. Identify four licensing models used to acquire Microsoft licensing.

    A.   Cloud Solution Provider

    B.   Commercial

    C.   Enterprise Agreement

    D.   Enterprise Enrollment

    E.   Microsoft Open

    F.   Service Provider License Agreement

2. Identify four important factors when performing a cost-benefit analysis to acquire a cloud solution.

    A.   Improved security

    B.   Reduced security

    C.   Reduced TCO

    D.   Increased TCO

    E.   Increased end user productivity

    F.   Improved availability

3. Identify four important factors when performing a cost-benefit analysis to acquire a cloud solution.

    A.   Employee savings with new or improved mobility scenarios

    B.   Improved compliance capability

    C.   Reduced compliance capability

    D.   Travel savings

    E.   Reduced downtime

    F.   Increase in physical equipment presence

4. Under a direct license model, which of the following is true of the customer organization?

    A.   Pays Microsoft directly

    B.   Pays a partner or VAR directly

    C.   Is entitled to free licensing

    D.   Has licensing included with hardware purchases

    E.   Can apply for Net 90 terms

5. Under an indirect license model, which of the following is true of the customer organization?

    A.   Pays Microsoft directly

    B.   Pays a partner or VAR directly

    C.   Is entitled to free licensing

    D.   Is not responsible for payment agreements

6. Contoso is a small business that outsources its IT services to Fabrikam. Fabrikam charges Contoso a monthly fee that includes a service desk fee as well as the Microsoft 365 plan licensing. What licensing model is being used?

   A. Microsoft Open

   B. Enterprise Agreement

   C. Retail Solution Provider

   D. Cloud Solution Provider

7. AdventureWorks is an international company with 100,000 users. A Microsoft account executive works directly with the AdventureWorks management to provide a contract for Microsoft 365 services as well as on-premises SQL Server licensing. AdventureWorks pays Microsoft directly. What licensing model is being used?

   A. Microsoft Open

   B. Enterprise Agreement

   C. Retail Solution Provider

   D. Cloud Solution Provider

8. Fabrikam is a Microsoft Partner that provides managed IT services to local small businesses. Fabrikam sells Microsoft 365 services to its customers. Customers acquire the Microsoft 365 services through Fabrikam, and Fabrikam receives invoices from Microsoft for its customers. What licensing model is being used?

   A. Microsoft Open

   B. Enterprise Agreement

   C. Retail Solution Provider

   D. Cloud Solution Provider

15
Support Offerings for Microsoft 365 Services

In this chapter, we're going to take a look at how and when to engage support for your Microsoft 365 environment. It's important to know the boundaries of a service, how to track and interrogate your environment's health, and how to get help when you need it.

There are several resources available to help you understand what is available to you. By the end of this chapter, you should be familiar with the performance and availability you can expect from Microsoft 365, as well as methods for obtaining support.

In this chapter, we'll cover the following topics:

- Understanding Microsoft 365 service-level agreements
- Determining the service health status
- Creating a support request
- Communicating with Microsoft with UserVoice

Let's start!

Understanding Microsoft 365 service-level agreements

Like most service offerings, Microsoft 365 has a **service-level agreement** (**SLA**) attached to it. An SLA is the service provider's commitment to providing a defined level of availability and reliability. In the case of Microsoft 365, the SLA for operation includes 99.9% availability, excluding scheduled downtimes (typically, this is for service upgrades). Microsoft provides a mechanism to recuperate a portion of your bill as service credits, should they fail to meet the SLA.

Microsoft's SLA identifies a few important notes about claims:

- Claims must be submitted to Microsoft's customer support and should include details of the service outage, such as the timeline and duration, the number of users and locations affected, and the steps you took to resolve the issue.

- Claims must be received by the end of the calendar month, following the month where the incident occurred (for example, if the incident occurred on March 15, the claim must be received by April 30).

Microsoft also puts some boundaries and limitations around fulfilling their SLA, such as your organization failing to take necessary actions (for instance, neglecting to disable someone's access or unauthorized access, resulting in you failing to follow good security practices), misuse of the services, loss of network connectivity, or acts outside of your control (such as natural disasters or war).

The SLA guide provides a few key terms and definitions that are used throughout:

Term	Definition
Applicable Monthly Period	If a service credit is owed, this is the number of days during a calendar month that you were a subscriber for a particular service.
Applicable Monthly Service Fees	If a service credit is owed, this value is the total fees that are paid by you for a particular service and are applied to the month in which the service credit is owed.
Downtime	This is defined for each service in the service-specific terms (in the SLA guide for a product or service). Except for Microsoft Azure services, downtime excludes scheduled downtime. Downtime does not include the unavailability of a service due to the limitations described in the service-specific terms.
Error Code	An error code is an indication that a particular service or operation has failed, such as an HTTP 5xx status code.

External Connectivity	External connectivity indicates bidirectional network traffic over supported protocols that can be transmitted to and from a public IP address.
Incident	Incidents refer to one or more events that result in downtime.
Management Portal	A management portal is defined as a Microsoft-provided web interface through which customers may manage the service.
Scheduled Downtime	Scheduled downtime refers to periods of downtime related to network, hardware, or service maintenance or upgrades. Microsoft notifies customers via various mechanisms (such as email, portal alerts, or message center alerts) at least 5 days before a scheduled downtime.
Service Credit	Service Credit refers to applicable monthly service fees that are credited to you following Microsoft's claim approval for a downtime event.
Service Level	A service level is defined as the performance metric(s) that Microsoft agrees to meet in the delivery of a service.
Service Resource	A service resource is an individual resource available within a service.
Success Code	A success code is an indication that an operation has been completed successfully, such as an HTTP 200 result.
Support Window	This defines the time during which a service, service feature, or compatibility with a separate product, service, or feature is supported.
User Minutes	This is calculated by subtracting scheduled downtime from the total number of minutes in a given month and multiplying that by the number of users consuming the service.

Table 15.1 – Terms and definitions

In addition to the general 99.9% uptime that the Microsoft 365 service advertises, Microsoft also provides guidance on how service credits will be apportioned, given the number of outages that occur. This is done on a per-service basis, as shown here:

Monthly Uptime Percentage	Service Credit
< 99.9%	25%
< 99%	50%
< 95%	100%

Table 15.2 – Service credit table

The Microsoft 365 SLA guide is regularly reviewed and updated.

> **Service-Level Agreement Updates**
>
> You can access the detailed SLA guide at `https://www.microsoft.com/licensing/docs/view/Service-Level-Agreements-SLA-for-Online-Services`.

Now that you have an understanding of how Microsoft 365 SLAs are structured and some of the terminology associated with them, we'll look at service health concepts.

Determining the service health status

Microsoft provides several ways you can obtain information about the health of various Microsoft 365 services, including the following resources:

- The Service Health Dashboard
- The Service Status page
- The Microsoft 365 Status Twitter feed

The Service Health Dashboard will have the most comprehensive information regarding service health status and availability and should be the resource you use when determining whether you are experiencing a service outage. However, it doesn't provide any text messaging or other alerting capabilities. The Microsoft 365 Status Twitter feed is a good resource for getting notifications.

We will learn more about these tools and methods next.

The Service Health Dashboard

As stated in the previous section, the Service Health Dashboard should be your first step when determining whether your environment is experiencing issues. The Service Health Dashboard contains the current health status of all Microsoft 365 services. Normally, services will appear as *healthy*, though this status will be updated when a service is experiencing an issue. The Service Health Dashboard will display the most detailed and comprehensive information on any ongoing or resolved issues.

You can access the Service Health Dashboard by performing the following steps:

1. Log into the Microsoft 365 admin center (`https://admin.microsoft.com`) with an account that has either the Global Admin or Service Admin role, expand **Health**, and then select **Service health**:

Service health

All services   Incidents   Advisories   History   Reported issues

View the health status of all services that are available with your current subscriptions.

🗒 Report an issue   ⚙ Preferences

	Service	Health
>	Service	Health
>	Microsoft 365 suite	ⓘ 1 advisory
>	Microsoft Teams	ⓘ 1 advisory
>	SharePoint Online	ⓘ 1 advisory
	Azure Information Protection	✓ Healthy
	Cloud App Security	✓ Healthy
	Dynamics 365 Apps	✓ Healthy
	Exchange Online	✓ Healthy
	Identity Service	✓ Healthy

Figure 15.1 – The Service Health Dashboard

2. For services that display advisories or incidents, you can select the **Advisories** or **Incidents** link next to the service, or expand the **Incidents** or **Advisories** menu option to display the relevant events:

Figure 15.2 – Service advisories

3. You can click on an incident or advisory to review more verbose details, as shown in the following screenshot:

Figure 15.3 – Service incident details

The Service Health Dashboard also allows you to configure preferences to be notified in the case of an incident or advisory that happens for one of the selected services, and you can also report an issue directly from the portal and monitor its progress updates.

The Service Status page

If you are unable to log into the Microsoft 365 admin center, there may be an issue with the admin portal. Microsoft provides a second status page that allows you to check for errors when you're logging into the Microsoft 365 admin center. You can access the **Service Status** page at `https://status.office365.com`. An example of the **Service Status** page is shown in the following screenshot:

Microsoft 365 Service health status

This site is updated when service issues are preventing tenant administrators from accessing Service health in the Microsoft 365 admin center. Alternatively, customers can reference https://www.twitter.com/MSFT365Status for additional insights into widespread, active incidents.

View your Microsoft 365 Service health.

Figure 15.4 – Service health status

If the login services are working correctly, you'll typically see nothing except a link to the Service Health Dashboard, as shown in the preceding screenshot. However, if the login service or admin center portals themselves are experiencing errors, they will be displayed here.

The Microsoft 365 Status Twitter feed

Microsoft also maintains a Twitter feed for the Microsoft 365 service suite. The Microsoft 365 Status Twitter feed includes everything in the Office 365 suite and then adds on Windows and Enterprise Mobility + Security products and services. The Microsoft 365 Status Twitter account is verified (with a blue checkmark) to denote it is an official page, as shown in the following screenshot:

Figure 15.5 – Microsoft 365 Status Twitter profile

You can follow it on Twitter at @MSFT365Status or by navigating to https://twitter.com/msft365status.

If your organization is experiencing issues, you can follow the next section on creating support requests to find help.

In addition to the service health monitoring options presented here, there are other options to access service health data, such as through custom solutions that leverage the Service Communications API, System Center Management Pack for Office 365, and the Microsoft 365 admin app.

Next, we'll look at the process for creating a support request.

Creating a support request

Support requests for Microsoft 365 issues are typically raised through the Microsoft 365 admin center. You can create a support request by performing the following steps:

1. Log into the Microsoft 365 admin center (`https://admin.microsoft.com`) and navigate to **Support** | **New service request**:

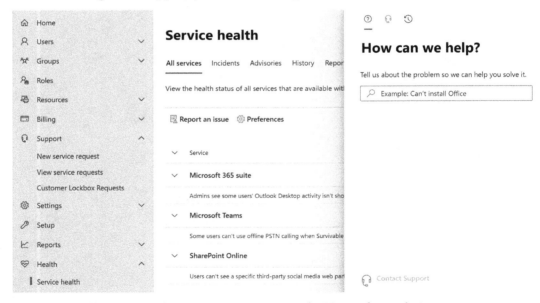

Figure 15.6 – Creating a service request in the Microsoft 365 admin center

2. In the panel that opens, you can type in your questions. If applicable, a list of suggested solutions will be displayed. If no suitable options are displayed, you can select **Contact Support**:

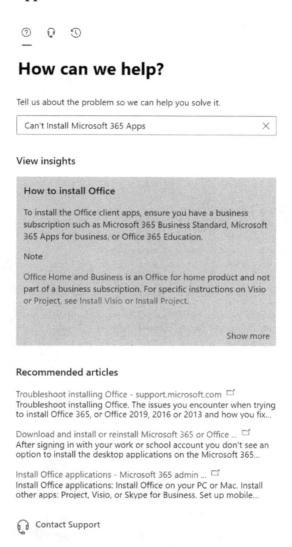

Figure 15.7 – Microsoft 365 service ticket suggestions

3. On the **Contact support** view, you can fill out any required information, select the preferred option to be contacted, and, once ready, click **Contact me**:

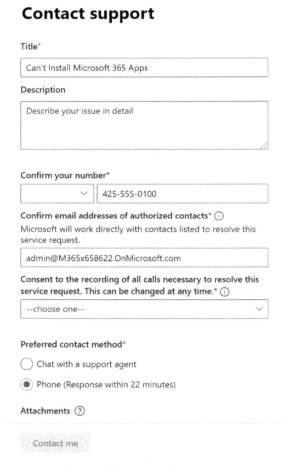

Figure 15.8 – Contacting support

Once a support request has been created, you can select the **Support | View service requests** option in the Microsoft 365 admin center to track the status of your service request or update it with new information:

Figure 15.9 – Service request history

After opening your support ticket, the following Microsoft support matrix details how quickly support personnel will contact you:

Severity Rating	Impact Level	Initial Response Time	Customer Expectations and Notes
Severity A	Critical business impact. Experiencing significant loss or degradation of services, requiring immediate attention. Examples include widespread issues sending or receiving mail, SharePoint sites down, inability to schedule or join meetings, or widespread inability to send or receive instant messages or phone calls.	Microsoft 365 Business Basic, Microsoft 365 Business Standard, Microsoft 365 Business Premium: 24/7 availability, with 1-hour response Microsoft 365 Enterprise, Frontline, Government, and Education plans: 24/7 availability, with 1-hour response Elevated support options available	Severity A is reserved for issues that have a critical business impact, with severe loss and degradation of services for multiple users. Since you have designated that the issue demands an immediate response, you, as a customer, commit to continuous, 24/7 availability to work on the issue every day with the Microsoft team until it's resolved. Should you not be available, Microsoft may, at its discretion, decrease the issue to Severity B. You must also ensure that Microsoft has accurate contact information and that you are available.

Severity Rating	Impact Level	Initial Response Time	Customer Expectations and Notes
Severity B	High business impact. The organization has moderate loss or degradation of services affecting multiple users, but work can continue in a somewhat impaired manner.	Microsoft 365 Business Basic, Microsoft 365 Business Standard, Microsoft 365 Business Premium: Business hours availability, with no response timeline commitment Microsoft 365 Enterprise, Frontline, Government, and Education plans: 24/7 availability, with next-day response timeline commitment Elevated support options available to reduce response time to 2 hours	Severity B issues have a moderate impact on your business with loss and degradation of services, but workarounds are available. If you've submitted an issue as Severity B, you have indicated that the issue demands an urgent response. If you choose 24/7 when you submit the support request, you commit to a continuous, 24/7 operation, every day with the Microsoft team until resolution, similar to Severity A issues. If you open the ticket with a 24/7 expectation but are not available, Microsoft may, at its discretion, lower the issue to Severity C. If you choose business hours-only support when you submit a Severity B incident, Microsoft will contact you during business hours only. You must also ensure that Microsoft has accurate contact information and that you are available.

| Severity C | Medium business impact.

The customer can conduct business with minor disruptions or reductions to services. | Microsoft 365 Business Basic, Microsoft 365 Business Standard, Microsfot 365 Business Premium: Business hours availability, with 1-hour response

Microsoft 365 Enterprise, Frontline, Government, and Education plans: 24/7 availability, with 1-hour response

Elevated support options available to reduce response time to 4 hours | Issues opened as Severity C indicate that the issue has a small impact on your business and may impede the service in a minor way.

For issues that are opened with Severity C, Microsoft will contact you during business hours only.

You must also ensure that Microsoft has accurate contact information and that you are available. |

Table 15.3 – Severity and service response times

Use the preceding table to help determine how to categorize the issues you are facing.

In addition to the support options already mentioned, customers can also purchase paid service and support contracts. This service, called Premier, comes with access to a named support manager (a customer success account manager) that can act on both proactive and reactive issues.

Next, we'll look at feedback mechanisms for Microsoft 365 products and services.

Communicating with Microsoft through UserVoice

When it comes to ideas and opportunities for improvement across the services being used, it is common that organizations might have feedback to share, based on their usage experience. In many cases, the best tool where these new ideas can be submitted is UserVoice. Users can review and search from ideas submitted by others, as well as submitting their own ideas, as shown in the following screenshot:

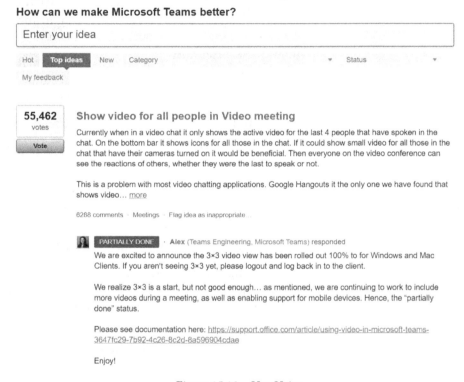

Figure 15.10 – UserVoice

Microsoft engineering reviews ideas submitted for inclusion in the product roadmap.

> **UserVoice Update**
>
> In March 2021, Microsoft confirmed that they are migrating away from UserVoice as a feedback collection mechanism. This is happening on a per-product basis. Announcements will be posted in each product's UserVoice forum as the migration approaches. Questions mentioning UserVoice may still occur on the exam due to the overlap of when the exam content was refreshed and the announcement was made.

Microsoft relies on customer feedback to ensure that they are continuing to develop meaningful products for the marketplace.

Summary

In this chapter, you learned about the Microsoft 365 SLAs, including what it guarantees and what limitations have been put around them. Additionally, you learned how to monitor the various channels that Microsoft maintains for communicating service health: the Service Health Dashboard, the Service Status page, and the Microsoft 365 Status Twitter feed. Finally, you learned about opening and managing support requests from the Microsoft 365 admin center.

It is important to understand the support levels for release categories and the incident response matrix, both for the exam and day-to-day operational requests.

In the next chapter, we'll cover the Microsoft 365 service's life cycle.

Questions

Answer the following questions to test your knowledge of this chapter. You can find the answers in *Chapter 18, Assessments*:

1. Which of these is *not* a way to view service status updates for Microsoft 365?

    A.   Twitter

    B.   Service Health Dashboard

    C.   Security & Compliance Center

    D.   Service Status page

2. The general SLA for Microsoft 365 availability is expressed as which of the following?

    A.   99%

    B.   99.9%

    C.   99.99%

    D.   99.999%

3. When opening a service ticket, which severity level is used to indicate a significant loss or degradation of services that requires immediate attention?

   A. Severity A

   B. Severity B

   C. Severity C

   D. Severity 1

   E. Severity 2

   F. Severity 3

4. Which severity level indicates business hours-only support?

   A. Severity A

   B. Severity B

   C. Severity C

   D. Severity D

5. What is the name of the paid support service that Microsoft provides?

   A. Priority Support

   B. Priority Access

   C. Prestige

   D. Premier

16
Service Life Cycle in Microsoft 365

Microsoft 365 is an evergreen product, meaning it's continuously under development and being updated. New features are constantly being developed, tested, and released. As such, Microsoft 365 has a different life cycle than traditional software.

In a standard on-premises software life cycle, products typically go through pre-release stages where they're made available internally or to select customers for testing and then are eventually **Released To Manufacturing (RTM)**. After a product's release, it goes through a succession of product updates (typically, for 3 years) that can address features or security improvements. Each stage of a product's life cycle has defined support phases (standard support, extended support, and end-of-life), and each of these development and release milestones comes with different support terms.

With cloud products such as Microsoft 365, there are also several phases to the development process. Microsoft often seeks feedback from partners and customers on how well the features work during the stages prior to deployment.

In this chapter, we'll look at the release and support cycles, including the following:

- Release stages
- Support policies
- Microsoft 365 Roadmap portal

Let's look at how the release stages of products and their support policies work together.

Release stages

In the Microsoft 365 and Azure clouds, Microsoft services generally go through the following stages of availability:

- Private preview
- Public preview
- General availability

Let's look at each availability stage in more detail.

Private preview

Private previews are the very earliest stage of availability, where the capability and stability of a product may be fluid and undergoing a lot of change. Private previews are typically handled as an invitation-only option, though sometimes you can register to be part of a private preview or, if you're an enterprise customer, you also may be nominated by your account team. Services that are in private preview should never be considered production ready. If you are participating in a private preview, you may have the ability to give developer feedback directly. Products in private preview may not be fully compliant or suitable for users in highly regulated industries, such as the financial or public sectors. It is important to verify what controls and protections are in place to ensure that your use of a service in private preview doesn't introduce unnecessary risk to your organization.

Public preview

Public preview is typically open to any customer with valid qualifying subscriptions. Depending on the product, you may need to sign up for or accept certain licensing terms. For example, Office 365 group-based licensing was in public preview for several months before it was moved to the next stage (general availability). However, customers who had a valid Azure Active Directory Premium subscription were able to use the service immediately without signing up for additional services or features.

Products and services in public preview typically have some documentation, though it may not be complete. Customers can frequently use products in public preview for little or no cost and will then be offered a chance to purchase the service at standard pricing once the product is fully released.

Products in public preview may or may not have regulatory compliance capabilities, such as eDiscovery or litigation hold. It is important to verify what controls, capabilities, and protections are available to enable your organization to comply with any necessary regulations. While services in public preview typically work without major issues, just like private previews, they should not be considered production ready.

Previews (both private and private) typically have their own terms of use and may be discontinued at any time without prior notification. Preview products, services, or features are not guaranteed to be brought forward into general availability. Previews are made available *as is* and *with all faults*, in line with Microsoft's supplemental terms. Unless explicitly stated otherwise, this means preview products have no guarantees or warranties. Additionally, products in public or private preview may be subject to reduced or different security capabilities, compliance, or privacy commitments.

Additional Preview Programs

Some services have a structured way of allowing organizations to have access to features in advance or through public preview programs for selected users or the entire organization. Among those services are the targeted release of Microsoft 365 (`https://docs.microsoft.com/en-us/microsoft-365/admin/manage/release-options-in-office-365`) and the public preview of Microsoft Teams (`https://docs.microsoft.com/en-us/MicrosoftTeams/public-preview-doc-updates`).

General availability

General availability (sometimes called **general release**), or simply **GA**, means that a product has matured to the point where it can be released for all customers to purchase. Products in general availability can be considered production ready. As with any new product, though, it's important to ensure the compliance and security controls available meet your organization's requirements.

Modern Lifecycle Policy

As per the Modern Lifecycle Policy, if a product is no longer to be supported, Microsoft will give a minimum prior notification of 12 months before the end of the service support.

You can review to learn more about configuring release options for general Microsoft 365 service features.

Next, we'll look at how the stage of the development and availability life cycle translates to support.

Support policies

Support policies govern how and when Microsoft will offer assistance for a particular product or service. From the support perspective, both public and private previews typically do not have to abide by the standard **Service-Level Agreement (SLA)** terms for the service. Public and private previews may have their own limited SLAs, may have no SLA defined, or may explicitly inform you that there is no expectation of any particular responsiveness or availability. And, as stated earlier, previews can be ended or discontinued at any time with no or limited warning.

Unless the preview's specific terms and conditions stipulate differently, preview products are excluded from all SLAs and warranty claims, and the unavailability of products in preview will not constitute an SLA breach that would result in service credit. An example set of preview terms is shown in the following screenshot:

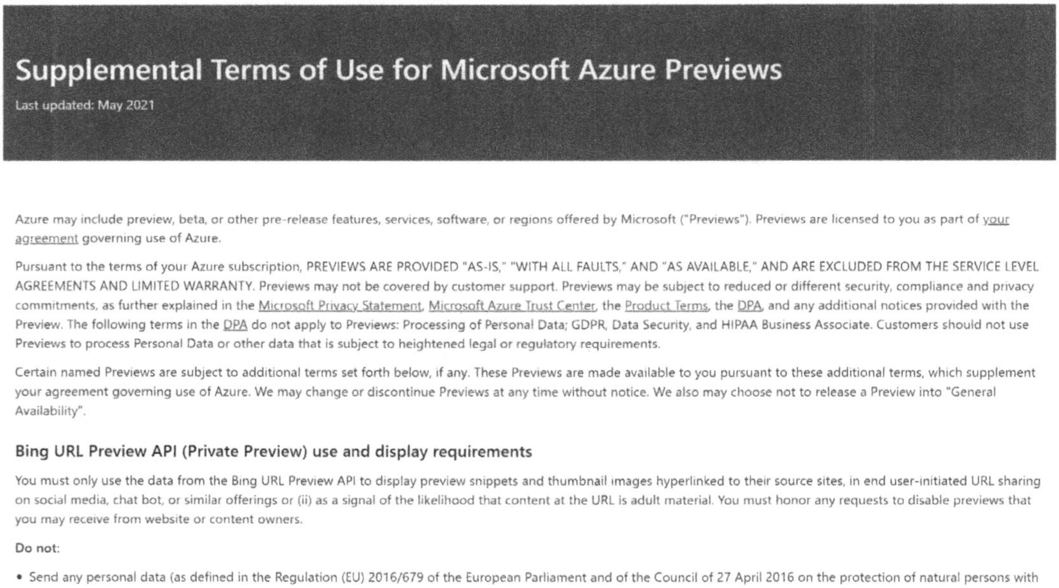

Supplemental Terms of Use for Microsoft Azure Previews
Last updated: May 2021

Azure may include preview, beta, or other pre-release features, services, software, or regions offered by Microsoft ("Previews"). Previews are licensed to you as part of your agreement governing use of Azure.

Pursuant to the terms of your Azure subscription, PREVIEWS ARE PROVIDED "AS-IS," "WITH ALL FAULTS," AND "AS AVAILABLE," AND ARE EXCLUDED FROM THE SERVICE LEVEL AGREEMENTS AND LIMITED WARRANTY. Previews may not be covered by customer support. Previews may be subject to reduced or different security, compliance and privacy commitments, as further explained in the Microsoft Privacy Statement, Microsoft Azure Trust Center, the Product Terms, the DPA, and any additional notices provided with the Preview. The following terms in the DPA do not apply to Previews: Processing of Personal Data; GDPR, Data Security, and HIPAA Business Associate. Customers should not use Previews to process Personal Data or other data that is subject to heightened legal or regulatory requirements.

Certain named Previews are subject to additional terms set forth below, if any. These Previews are made available to you pursuant to these additional terms, which supplement your agreement governing use of Azure. We may change or discontinue Previews at any time without notice. We also may choose not to release a Preview into "General Availability".

Bing URL Preview API (Private Preview) use and display requirements

You must only use the data from the Bing URL Preview API to display preview snippets and thumbnail images hyperlinked to their source sites, in end user-initiated URL sharing on social media, chat bot, or similar offerings or (ii) as a signal of the likelihood that content at the URL is adult material. You must honor any requests to disable previews that you may receive from website or content owners.

Do not:

• Send any personal data (as defined in the Regulation (EU) 2016/679 of the European Parliament and of the Council of 27 April 2016 on the protection of natural persons with

Figure 16.1 – Preview terms

Products in general availability are fully supported in line with the product's individual SLA. Support for products in general availability can be obtained through support tickets via the Microsoft 365 support portal, Microsoft phone support, or partners.

Microsoft 365 Roadmap portal

To provide clarity in terms of what's being worked on and expected to be released as part of product and service improvements, customers can access the Microsoft 365 Roadmap portal, where, for each of the available services, feature items, along with details, can be reviewed and can also be kept track of through RSS feeds. Features available in the Microsoft 365 Roadmap portal, from a stage perspective, can be in one of the following stages:

- **In development**: The engineering team is working through each of the release stages to bring a feature to general availability.

- **Rolling out**: The feature is typically already available in general availability and is being deployed in phases for each of the tenants and regions.

- **Launched**: The feature is expected to be available across all tenants in regions according to the scope of the feature.

In the Microsoft 365 Roadmap portal, customers can search for a specific feature or product or even filter by a service, as shown in the following screenshot:

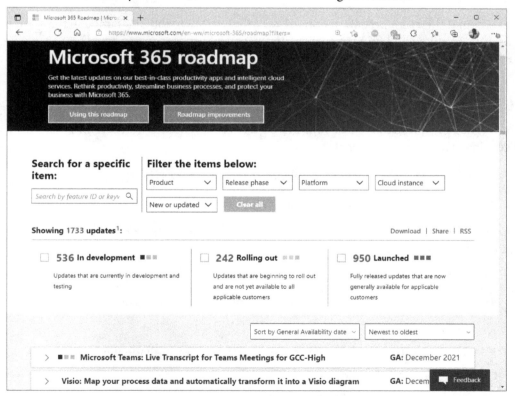

Figure 16.2 – Microsoft 365 Roadmap

In addition to the Roadmap, customers can also keep track of what's being delivered and to be released across services in the Message center, available in the Microsoft 365 admin center.

> **Microsoft 365 Roadmap Details**
>
> You can find more information about the Microsoft 365 Roadmap at `https://www.microsoft.com/en-us/microsoft-365/roadmap`.

Summary

In this chapter, we covered the different development and release stages of Microsoft 365 products, including both private and public previews as well as general availability. Preview products are subject to change or cancelation and have no SLAs associated with them, whereas generally available products are fully supported for all customers with valid subscriptions.

This concludes the exam preparation guide for MS-900: Microsoft 365 Fundamentals. In the final chapter, you will find the answers to the end-of-chapter assessments scattered throughout the book.

Questions

Use the following questions to test your knowledge of this chapter. You can find the answers in *Chapter 18, Assessments*:

1. Identify the SLA that generally applies to preview services:

    A. No SLA unless otherwise specified

    B. Standard Microsoft Online Services Agreement for individual products

    C. Azure Services Agreement

    D. Supplemental Online Services Agreement

2. Identify the SLA that generally applies to products in general availability:

    A. No SLA unless otherwise specified

    B. Standard Microsoft Online Services Agreement for individual products

    C. Azure Services Agreement

    D. Supplemental Online Services Agreement

3. Which release stage of a product is generally invitation-only?

   A. Private preview

   B. Public preview

   C. General availability

   D. Insider ring

4. At which release stage is a product fully documented and supported by a standard SLA?

   A. Private preview

   B. Public preview

   C. General availability

   D. Insider ring

5. The _____ provides details about upcoming service and feature releases for Microsoft 365.

   A. Admin guide

   B. Microsoft 365 Roadmap

   C. Microsoft Tech Community

   D. Cloud Solution Providers blog

Section 5: Practice Exams

This final section contains the questions and answers to help you prepare for the exam.

This section comprises the following chapters:

17
Mock Exam

The MS-900 exam varies in length from 32-43 questions, depending on your answers. The exam is timed at 60 minutes.

Exam questions

The following exam contains 40 questions. Set a timer for 60 minutes. The answers can be found at the end of the exam:

1. Exchange Online integrated with an on-premises Skype for Business Server 2015 deployment is an example of which of the following?

    A.   On-premises deployment

    B.   Cloud-only deployment

    C.   Mixed deployment

    D.   Hybrid cloud deployment

2. A custom Azure-based web and mobile application service is an example of which of the following?

    A.   **Platform as a Service (PaaS)**

    B.   **Infrastructure as a Service (IaaS)**

    C.   Hybrid cloud

    D.   Serverless

3. Identify which Microsoft platform provides hybrid capabilities for migrating from an on-premises deployment.

    A.   Microsoft Teams

    B.   Microsoft Exchange

    C.   Microsoft Yammer

    D.   Microsoft Excel Services

4. Lower costs, no hardware maintenance, near-unlimited scalability, and high reliability are all advantages of hosting a private cloud.

    A.   True

    B.   False

5. You need to deploy an application to Azure **IaaS**. Which three features are part of IaaS?

    A.   Business analytics

    B.   Real-time monitoring

    C.   Operating system

    D.   Servers and storage

    E.   Business applications

    F.   Firewall and network security

6. Microsoft Workplace Analytics supports weekly email digests.

    A.   True

    B.   False

7. A group of employees and users outside the company must collaborate using a meeting with a shared whiteboard. Which product should they use?

    A.   Microsoft Yammer

    B.   Microsoft Exchange

    C.   Office Graph

    D.   Microsoft Teams

8. You install Microsoft 365 Apps on five devices and sign in with the same licensed user account on those five devices. Later, you need to deactivate one of the licenses. Which task can you still perform on the device with a deactivated Microsoft 365 Apps license?

    A.   Edit an Excel spreadsheet.

    B.   Create a new Word document.

    C.   Co-author a presentation using PowerPoint.

    D.   View and print an existing Word document.

9. You need to ensure that the users in your organization's IT department receive the preview features of Office. Which two actions should you perform?

    A.   Instruct the IT department users to navigate to `https://insider.office.com` and sign up for Office Insider.

    B.   Instruct the IT department users to uninstall Microsoft Office 365 ProPlus and update to Microsoft 365 Apps.

    C.   Configure the tenant organizational profile update preference to **Targeted release for selected users**.

    D.   Configure the tenant organizational profile update preference to **Standard release**.

10. Your organization uses Windows Autopilot. You need to ensure that users can access data that is stored in OneDrive for Business. What should you do?

    A.   Enroll the devices in Microsoft Intune.

    B.   Enroll the users in multi-factor authentication.

    C.   Instruct the users to select **Keep me signed in** to the Office 365 portal.

    D.   Instruct the users to sign in to their devices using the Azure AD credentials.

11. Your company is evaluating the differences between deployments of Office 2016 and Microsoft 365 Apps. You need to determine the installation features of each deployment. Which feature is unique to Microsoft 365 Apps for Business?

    A.   Installation can be completed using System Center Configuration Manager.

    B.   Installation requires a license assignment from the Microsoft 365 admin center.

    C.   Installation is available for 32-bit and 64-bit versions.

    D.   Installation is performed on the user's local computer.

12. Your organization is deciding if it wants to use Microsoft 365 products that are in various development and release phases, including private preview, public preview, and **general availability (GA)**. You need to determine which development phases you can receive support through the Microsoft 365 admin center.

    A.   GA only

    B.   GA and public preview

    C.   GA and private preview

    D.   GA, public preview, and private preview

    E.   Public preview and private preview

13. Your organization is deciding which Microsoft 365 features and services to deploy. Business leaders have determined that they want the features of a chat-based workspace, as well as a private social network. Which two products, services, or features should you recommend?

    A.   Exchange Online

    B.   Yammer

    C.   Teams

    D.   Microsoft 365 Apps

    E.   SharePoint Online

14. Your organization has offices in multiple regions, as well as many users who work remotely. The organization is developing a new line-of-business app. You must meet the following requirements:

    • Minimize administrative costs.

    • Minimize employee interruption.

    • Track the devices that the app is installed on by using Microsoft cloud services.

    What should you do?

    A.   Copy the app to SharePoint Online. Instruct employees to download and install the app from SharePoint Online.

    B.   Copy the app to regional file servers. Instruct employees to connect to the corporate network via a **virtual private network (VPN)** to download and install the app.

    C.   Deploy the app to all devices using Group Policy.

    D.   Deploy the app to all devices using Microsoft Intune.

15. You plan to deploy Microsoft 365 services. You need to ensure that users can authenticate using smart cards. Which identity solution should you choose to implement?

    A.   Active Directory Federation Services

    B.   Azure Active Directory Connect with pass-through authentication

    C.   PingFederate

    D.   Azure Active Directory Connect with password hash synchronization

16. You need to ensure that the user authentication process confirms the identity of the user with an additional passcode, token, phone call, or app authentication. Which feature should you use?

    A.   **Data loss prevention (DLP)**

    B.   Microsoft Defender for Endpoint

    C.   Microsoft Defender for Office 365

    D.   **Mobile Application Management (MAM)**

    E.   **Multi-factor authentication (MFA)**

17. You are working with the security officer for your organization. The security officer instructs you to prevent employees from sharing documents with people outside of the organization. What are two steps can you take to achieve this requirement?

    A.   Configure **DomainKeys Identified Mail (DKIM)**.

    B.   Apply sensitivity labels to documents.

    C.   Configure a **data loss prevention (DLP)** policy.

    D.   Configure **Secure/Multipurpose Internet Mail Extensions (S/MIME)** settings for Outlook.

    E.   Instruct users to use a virtual private network.

18. Your organization stores sensitive information in the Microsoft 365 tenant. The security officer has requested that all users verify their identities when signing into Microsoft 365 by providing information in addition to their Azure AD password. Which two features, services, or tools should you select?

    A.   Customer Lockbox

    B.   Windows Hello for Business

    C.   Azure Security Center

    D.   Compliance Manager

    E.   Microsoft Authenticator

19. You need to ensure users receive a warning message if they select links in emails or documents that might be unsafe. What should you do?

    A.   Use Windows PowerShell to configure SharePoint Online updates.

    B.   Enable Microsoft Defender for Office 365.

    C.   Use the Microsoft Exchange admin center to configure a new spam filter policy.

    D.   Use the Microsoft Exchange admin center to create a transport rule.

20. Your organization must comply with a request to preserve the documents stored in SharePoint Online. Which tool should you use?

    A.   Compliance Manager

    B.   **Data loss prevention (DLP)**

    C.   eDiscovery case hold

    D.   Microsoft Power Apps

21. You need to configure a Microsoft Intune policy to enforce a PIN requirement on Outlook for mobile devices. Which type of policy should you use?

    A.   Device compliance

    B.   Device configuration

    C.   App protection

    D.   App configuration

22. You need to implement a data governance solution for your organization. The solution must meet the following requirements:

- Classify documents.

- Ensure classifications are enforced.

- Delete documents that are no longer used based on 7 years since their creation.

    Which two features, services, policies, or tools should you configure?

    A.   Configure auto-apply labels.

    B.   Configure the **data loss prevention (DLP)** policy.

    C.   Configure Outlook mail tips.

D.   Configure retention policies.

E.   Configure **MFA**.

F.   Configure eDiscovery cases.

G.   Define SharePoint permissions.

H.   Apply document permissions using Microsoft Graph.

23. You need to configure a solution that blocks users from accessing cloud apps from certain devices. What should you choose?

A.   Cloud Discovery dashboard

B.   Azure Security Center

C.   Conditional Access policy

D.   Azure Information Protection

24. Your organization has a business partner relationship with a regulated industry. The partner organization requires you to provide audit and attestation reports for data centers, including those hosting Microsoft 365 services. Where should you obtain this information?

A.   Service Trust Portal

B.   Compliance Manager

C.   Azure Security Center

D.   Microsoft 365 admin center

25. Your organization needs to protect documents and emails by automatically applying classifications and labels while minimizing costs. What should you recommend?

A.   Microsoft 365 E5

B.   Exchange Online P2

C.   Azure Information Protection P1

D.   Azure Information Protection P2

26. Your organization uses both System Center Configuration Manager and Microsoft Endpoint Manager. You need to manage the power settings for on-premises servers. Which tool should you choose?

A.   Configuration Manager

B.   Autopilot

C.   Intune

D.   Sentinel

27. Your organization is planning to deploy Microsoft 365 services. You need to protect the Windows 10 computers from malicious software. You also need to identify unauthorized cloud apps accessed by users. Which two applications, services, or features should you recommend?

A.   Microsoft Defender for Endpoint

B.   Microsoft Defender for Identity

C.   Microsoft Defender for Office 365

D.   Microsoft Cloud App Security

28. You are the security administrator for your organization. You need to identify the high-security risks, as well as the changes, that are recommended by Microsoft. Which tool should you choose?

A.   Microsoft Intune

B.   Azure Sentinel

C.   Azure Information Protection Scanner

D.   Advanced Threat Analytics

E.   Microsoft Secure Score

F.   Service Trust Portal

G.   Compliance Manager

29. After meeting with your organization's compliance officer, you need to configure policies to discover and act on malicious and inadvertent risk activities performed by employees. Which tool should you use?

A.   Compliance Manager

B.   Azure Sentinel

C.   Insider Risk Management

D.   Advanced Threat Protection

30. The security officer for your organization implements a policy to require additional verification when accessing a federated third-party application. However, this requirement also stipulates that users must not be prompted when they access Microsoft Outlook, SharePoint Online, or Microsoft Teams. What solution should you configure?

    A.   Conditional Access

    B.   MFA

    C.   Active Directory Federation Services

    D.   Passthrough authentication

31. Your organization wants to improve its compliance score based on Microsoft recommendations. You need to identify tasks that have the largest impact on the compliance score. What tasks should you choose?

    A.   Detective discretionary

    B.   Preventative mandatory

    C.   Corrective discretionary

    D.   Corrective mandatory

32. The security officer for your organization requires that all end user devices utilize full-disk encryption. Which solution should you choose?

    A.   Microsoft Intune

    B.   Azure Information Protection Scanner

    C.   Microsoft Cloud App Security

    D.   Azure Information Protection

33. Which of the following statements is false?

    A.   Microsoft Defender for Endpoint detects advanced attacks and automates investigation and remediation of security incidents.

    B.   Microsoft Cloud App Security provides a client **virtual private network (VPN)** for accessing Office 365 services.

    C.   Microsoft Defender for Office 365 helps protect against malicious attachments and links that are sent via email.

    D.   Microsoft Intune can be used to enforce restrictions on devices and applications.

34. An organization is purchasing a Microsoft 365 subscription and migrating its on-premises infrastructure and services to the cloud. What are three outcomes they can expect?

    A. Predictable Microsoft licensing costs

    B. Increased service scalability in the cloud

    C. Increased Exchange Server **Client Access License (CAL)** costs

    D. Increased Windows Server **Client Access License (CAL)** costs

    E. Decreased service scalability in the cloud

    F. Decreased on-premises infrastructure footprint

35. Your organization plans to deploy Microsoft 365 to all employees and contractors. Frontline employees need to be able to collaborate, but you must also minimize costs. Which subscription should you choose for the frontline users?

    A. Office 365 E3

    B. Microsoft 365 E3

    C. Microsoft 365 F3

    D. Microsoft 365 Personal

36. Licensing through a **Cloud Solution Provider** (CSP) allows you to receive subscription billing and additional support services in one bill from your provider.

    A. True

    B. False

37. The IT directory for your organization asks you if there is any upcoming maintenance that will affect your Microsoft 365 services. Where should you look?

    A. Azure Security Center

    B. Reports in the Microsoft 365 admin center

    C. Service Health in the Microsoft 365 admin center

    D. Message Center in the Microsoft 365 admin center

    E. Support in the Microsoft 365 admin center

38. You are a Microsoft 365 administrator for your organization. You need to assign roles to other individuals so that they can purchase licenses. Which two roles can purchase licenses?

    A.   Service administrator

    B.   Exchange administrator

    C.   Global administrator

    D.   Billing administrator

    E.   User management administrator

39. Your organization needs to implement Conditional Access to restrict administrative accounts when users authenticate from specific locations. You must minimize costs. Which license should you choose?

    A.   Microsoft EMS E3

    B.   Microsoft EMS E5

    C.   Azure Active Directory P1

    D.   Azure Active Directory P2

40. Your organization plans to deploy Microsoft 365. You have the following requirements:

    - Team 1 users need to use a web-based calendar and email.

    - Team 2 users need to use a desktop version of Outlook. They also need to be able to make and receive phone calls and host online meetings.

    - Team 3 users need to be able to access tools that provide task and shift management.

    You need to minimize costs. Which two licensing options meet these needs?

    A.   Team 1 and Team 3 should use Microsoft 365 F3.

    B.   Team 1 and Team 2 should use Microsoft 365 F3.

    C.   Team 2 and Team 3 should use Microsoft 365 E5.

    D.   Team 2 should use Microsoft 365 E5.

    E.   Team 2 should use Microsoft 365 E3.

    F.   Team 1 should use Microsoft 365 F3.

18
Assessments

In this chapter, you'll find the answers to the questions featured at the end of every chapter.

Chapter 1, Introduction to Cloud Computing

1. C: SaaS
2. A: Scalable; B: Current; D: Cost-effective
3. B: Desktop computer; D: Network cable
4. A: Microsoft 365 subscription; C: Storage maintenance fee
5. A: Capital expenditure
6. B: Ability to add or reduce service capacity on demand
7. A: Redundant hardware; B: Multiple network paths; C: Data backups
8. C: Infrastructure as a Service; F: Platform as a Service

Chapter 2, Cloud Deployment Models and Services

1. A: Private cloud; C: Hybrid cloud; E: Public cloud
2. C: Private cloud
3. A: Public cloud

4. A: IaaS; B: SaaS; C: Serverless

5. A: SaaS; B: PaaS; C: Serverless

6. D: Serverless computing

7. A: SaaS

8. D: IaaS

9. A: SaaS

10. B: Hybrid cloud

11. A: The cloud solution provider is responsible for managing application and software updates.; D: The customer only pays for what they use.

12. A: Disaster recovery; D: High-performance compute clusters

13. D: SaaS

14. B: Where will we place our resources?

15. B: What type of resources are we going to use?; C: How much infrastructure management control do we want?

16. B: PaaS

17. A: Flat, regardless of service usage

18. B: Billed on an hourly or monthly consumption model

19. C: Billed on a transaction level

20. B: Billed on an hourly or monthly consumption model

21. A: Serverless computing; C: Software as a Service

Chapter 3, Core Microsoft 365 Components

1. A: Enterprise Mobility + Security; B: Windows 10 Enterprise Edition; D: Office 365

2. B: Windows Hello for Business

3. C: Email and calendaring tasks

4. D: Compliance center

5. B: Hybrid cloud

6. E: Compliance center

7. C: Compliance center

8. C: Compliance center

9. A: Team site; C: Communication site

10. B: False
11. A: True
12. B: False
13. A: Android; B: iOS; D: Windows; E: macOS
14. C: Azure Information Protection
15. C: Cloud app security broker
16. B: Multi-factor authentication
17. C: Microsoft Forms
18. B: Power BI
19. A: Model-driven; B: Canvas; d: Portal
20. B: Portal; C: Model-driven
21. A: True
22. C: Microsoft Teams
23. D: 10,000

Chapter 4, Comparing Core Services in Microsoft 365

1. B: Cloud app security broker
2. C: Discover and manage the use of shadow IT.; D: Assess the compliance of cloud apps.
3. B: Conditional Access
4. B: Access reviews
5. C: Co-management
6. C: Allows cross-premises calendaring and free/busy.; D: Move mailboxes easily between on-premises and the cloud.
7. A: Migrating document library content
8. C: It doesn't replace any product.
9. A: Exchange Online license; C: SharePoint Online license; D: Microsoft Teams license
10. B: Factory reset; C: Remote control

Chapter 5, Understanding the Concepts of Modern Management

1. C: Deployment ring

2. A: Windows Insider; B: Semi-Annual Channel; C: Long-Term Servicing Channel

3. C: Global admin

4. A: Anything new such as improvements in a specific built-in application, visual refresh, or user experience.

5. B: Monthly release that contains both security and non-security maintenance fixes.

6. A: True

7. B: False

8. D: Purchase licenses

9. B: Access to data privacy messages in Message Center

10. D: Create and manage service requests.

11. C: Directory Synchronization Accounts

12. A: Teams Communication Support Engineer

Chapter 6, Deploying Microsoft 365 Apps

1. C: Semi-Annual Enterprise Channel; D: Semi-Annual Enterprise Channel (Preview)

2. B: Current Channel (Preview)

3. A: The user does not have a subscription for Microsoft 365 apps.; D: The Microsoft 365 apps activation service has been unable to connect to the internet for 30 days.

4. A: It is a subscription.; B: It is per-user based.

5. B: It is a perpetual license.; D: It is per-user or per-device based.

6. B: False

7. C: Click-to-Run

8. C: Office Customization Tool

9. C: `https://config.office.com`

10. A: Azure identity; B: Microsoft 365 apps subscription license

Chapter 7, Understanding Collaboration and Mobility with Microsoft 365

1. B: A business approach to enable users to accomplish their jobs from anywhere

2. B: Planner

3. C: Forms

4. A: Stream

5. B: False

6. A: True

7. A: Platform

8. C: Identity

9. B: Signing into the productivity applications using their Office 365 identity

10. D: Yammer

11. A: Microsoft **Mobile Device Management (MDM)**; c: Microsoft **Mobile Application Management (MAM)**

Chapter 8, Microsoft 365 Analytics

1. A: Microsoft 365 activity reports; d: Microsoft 365 usage a Analytics

2. B: MyAnalytics

3. A: Focus; C: Wellbeing; D: Network; E: Collaboration

4. A: Power BI; B: Power BI Desktop

5. B: Tenant ID

6. B: Microsoft 365 admin center

7. B: Anonymization

8. A: Viva

9. B: False

10. C: Opportunities

Chapter 9, Understanding Security and Compliance Concepts with Microsoft 365

1. A: Recommend security configurations for Microsoft 365 services.; C: Provide configuration steps for security recommendations or links to configuration controls.

2. A: Define application-based security policies.; C: Wipe the managed application profile.

3. B: Azure portal

4. C: Microsoft Endpoint Manager admin center

5. A: Microsoft 365 Groups; Bb: Security groups; C: Mail-enabled security groups; E: Distribution lists

6. B: Only cases that they created or are assigned to them

7. A: All cases

8. A: Identity; C: Data; F: Device; G: Apps

9. B: New and existing external users

10. A: They can have the same level of permissiveness as SharePoint sharing controls.; C: They can be less permissive than SharePoint sharing controls.

11. A: Two-stage recycle bin; C: Preservation Hold Library; D: Versioning

12. C: The on-premises Active Directory password control settings are synchronized to AAD.

13. C: AIP

14. A: At rest; D: In transit

15. B: Password writeback

16. A: True

17. B: Audit log search in the compliance center

18. D: Audit retention policies

19. C: Zero-trust

Chapter 10, Understanding Identity Protection and Management

1. B: Access reviews
2. C: Active Directory Federation Services
3. B: Pass-through Authentication; C: Active Directory Federation Services
4. A: Password hash synchronization; D: Cloud identity
5. A: SMS or text message; C: Phone call; D: One-time passcode
6. A: Something a user knows; B: Something a user has; C: Something a user is
7. D: Azure Active Directory Connect
8. E: Multi-factor authentication
9. D: Immutable ID
10. B: Cloud identity

Chapter 11, Endpoint and Security Management

1. A: AAD Premium P1
2. B: AAD Premium P2
3. A: True
4. D: Microsoft 365 E5
5. A: Privileged Identity Management
6. B. Access reviews
7. A: Azure Application Proxy
8. D: Identify shadow IT.
9. B: Custom banned password list
10. C: Self-service password reset
11. F: Mobile Application Management
12. C: Microsoft 365 Defender attack simulator
13. B: False
14. A: True

Chapter 12, Exploring the Service Trust Portal, Compliance Manager, and Microsoft 365 Security Center

1. C: Compliance Manager

2. A: BitLocker; D: **Internet Protocol Security (IPSec)**; E: **Transport Layer Security (TLS)**

3. B: Where is my data stored?

4. B: Separation of organizational data in a multi-tenant environment

5. A: At rest; B: In transit

6. A: True

7. B: General Data Protection Regulation

8. A: NIST 800-53; B: NIST CSF; D: GDPR

9. D: How is my data separated from other organizations?

10. B: Improvement action score; C: Control score; E: Assessment score

11. B: False

12. B: Insider risk management

13. A: Secure Score

14. B: Policies; C: Alerts; F: Triage; G: Investigate; J: Action

Chapter 13, Licensing in Microsoft 365

1. D: Microsoft 365 Business

2. B: False

3. B: Microsoft 365 **Government Community Cloud (GCC)**

4. A: Microsoft 365 Commercial

5. A: Plan for a baseline.; B: Define user profiles or personas.; C: Define service and feature requirements.

6. A: Productivity; D: Compliance

7. A: Security; B: Collaboration

8. C: Per-user

9. A: Public sector

10. B: IRS Publication 1075 Compliance; C: **Criminal Justice Information Services (CJIS)** Compliance; D: United States Data Residency

11. D: Compliance Manager

Chapter 14, Planning, Predicting, and Comparing Pricing

1. A: Cloud Solution Provider; C: Enterprise Agreement; E: Microsoft Open; F: Service Provider License Agreement

2. A: Improved security; C: Reduced TCO; E: Increased end user productivity; F: Improved availability

3. A: Employee savings with new or improved mobility scenarios; B: Improved compliance capability; D: Travel savings; E: Reduced downtime

4. A: Pays Microsoft directly

5. B: Pays a partner or VAR directly

6. D: Cloud Solution Provider

7. B: Enterprise Agreement

8. D: Cloud Solution Provider

Chapter 15, Support Offerings for Microsoft 365 Services

1. C: Security & Compliance Center

2. B: 99.9%

3. A: Severity A

4. C: Severity C

5. C: Premier

Chapter 16, Service Life Cycle in Microsoft 365

1. A: No SLA unless otherwise specified

2. B: Standard Microsoft Online Services Agreement for individual products

3. A: Private preview

4. C: General availability

5. B: Microsoft 365 Roadmap

Chapter 17, Mock Exam

1. D: Hybrid deployment

2. A: **Platform as a Service (PaaS)**

3. B: Microsoft Exchange

4. B: False

5. B: Real-time monitoring; D: Servers and storage; F: Firewall and network security

6. B: False

7. D: Microsoft Teams

8. D: View and print an existing Word document.

9. A: Instruct IT department users to navigate to `https://insider.office.com` and sign up for Office Insider.; C: Configure the tenant organizational profile update preference to **Targeted release for selected users**.

10. D: Instruct the users to sign in to their devices using the Azure AD credentials.

11. B: Installation requires a license assignment from the Microsoft 365 admin center.

12. B: GA and public preview

13. B: Yammer; C: Teams

14. D: Deploy the app to all devices using Microsoft Intune.

15. A: Active Directory Federation Services

16. E: **Multi-factor authentication (MFA)**

17. B: Apply sensitivity labels to documents.; C: Configure a **data loss prevention (DLP)** policy.

18. B: Windows Hello for Business; E: Microsoft Authenticator

19. B: Enable Microsoft Defender for Office 365.

20. C: eDiscovery case hold

21. C: App protection

22. A: Configure auto-apply labels.; D: Configure retention policies.

23. C: Conditional Access policy

24. A: Service Trust Portal

25. D: Azure Information Protection P2

26. A: Configuration Manager

27. A: Microsoft Defender for Endpoint; D: Microsoft Cloud App Security

28. E: Microsoft Secure Score

29. C: Insider risk management

30. A: Conditional Access

31. B. Preventative mandatory

32. A: Microsoft Intune

33. B: Microsoft Cloud App Security provides a client **virtual private network (VPN)** for accessing Office 365 services.

34. A: Predictable Microsoft licensing costs; B: Increased service scalability in the cloud; F: Decreased on-premises infrastructure footprint

35. C: Microsoft 365 F3

36. A: True

37. D: Message Center in the Microsoft 365 admin center

38. C: Global administration; D: Billing administrator

39. C: Azure Active Directory P1

40. A: Team 1 and Team 2 should use Microsoft 365 F3.; D: Team 2 should use Microsoft 365 E5.

Packt.com

Subscribe to our online digital library for full access to over 7,000 books and videos, as well as industry leading tools to help you plan your personal development and advance your career. For more information, please visit our website.

Why subscribe?

- Spend less time learning and more time coding with practical eBooks and Videos from over 4,000 industry professionals

- Improve your learning with Skill Plans built especially for you

- Get a free eBook or video every month

- Fully searchable for easy access to vital information

- Copy and paste, print, and bookmark content

Did you know that Packt offers eBook versions of every book published, with PDF and ePub files available? You can upgrade to the eBook version at packt.com and as a print book customer, you are entitled to a discount on the eBook copy. Get in touch with us at customercare@packtpub.com for more details.

At www.packt.com, you can also read a collection of free technical articles, sign up for a range of free newsletters, and receive exclusive discounts and offers on Packt books and eBooks.

Other Books You May Enjoy

If you enjoyed this book, you may be interested in these other books by Packt:

Mastering Microsoft Dynamics 365 Business Central

Stefano Demiliani, Duilio Tacconi

ISBN: 978-1-78995-125-7

- Create a sandbox environment with Dynamics 365 Business Central
- Handle source control management when developing solutions
- Explore extension testing, debugging, and deployment
- Create real-world business processes using Business Central and different Azure services
- Integrate Business Central with external applications
- Apply DevOps and CI/CD to development projects
- Move existing solutions to the new extension-based architecture

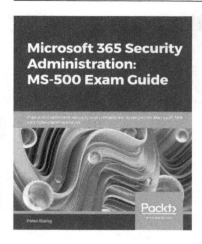

Microsoft 365 Security Administration: MS-500 Exam Guide

Peter Rising

ISBN: 978-1-83898-312-3

- Get up to speed with implementing and managing identity and access
- Understand how to employ and manage threat protection
- Get to grips with managing governance and compliance features in Microsoft 365
- Explore best practices for effective configuration and deployment
- Implement and manage information protection
- Prepare to pass the Microsoft exam and achieve certification with the help of self-assessment questions and a mock exam

Packt is searching for authors like you

If you're interested in becoming an author for Packt, please visit `authors.packtpub.com` and apply today. We have worked with thousands of developers and tech professionals, just like you, to help them share their insight with the global tech community. You can make a general application, apply for a specific hot topic that we are recruiting an author for, or submit your own idea.

Share Your Thoughts

Now you've finished *Microsoft 365 Certified Fundamentals MS-900 Exam Guide - Second Edition*, we'd love to hear your thoughts! Scan the QR code below to go straight to the Amazon review page for this book and share your feedback or leave a review on the site that you purchased it from.

`https://packt.link/r/1803231165`

Your review is important to us and the tech community and will help us make sure we're delivering excellent quality content.

Index

CPSIA information can be obtained
at www.ICGtesting.com
Printed in the USA
LVHW020719020222
709972LV00005B/337

9 781803 231167